IN TWO VOLUMES
VOLUME TWO

John L. Stephens

Incidents of Travel in Yucatan

127 ENGRAVINGS
by
FREDERICK CATHERWOOD

EDICIONES

INCIDENTS OF TRAVEL IN YUCATAN
John L. Stephens
(tomo II)

© Producción Editorial Dante, S.A.
   Calle 59 # 472
   Mérida, Yucatán, México

Queda hecho el depósito que marca la ley
I.S.B.N. 968-7232-37-4

Ilustraciones: Frederick Catherwood
Diseño de portada: Carlos Cámara

IMPRESO EN MEXICO
PRINTED IN MEXICO

IN TWO VOLUMES
VOLUME TWO

John L. Stephens

Incidents of Travel in Yucatan

127 ENGRAVINGS
by
FREDERICK CATHERWOOD

YUCATAN BEFORE AND AFTER
THE CONQUEST
Fray Diego de Landa

© Producción Editorial Dante, S.A.
  Calle 59 # 472
  Mérida, Yucatán, México.

Queda hecho el depósito que marca la ley
I.S.B.N. 968-7232-35-8

Traducción y notas: William Gates
Diseño de portada: Carlos Cámara

IMPRESO EN MEXICO
PRINTED IN MEXICO

CONTENTS

CHAPTER I

CHAPTER II

Contents

CHAPTER III

CHAPTER IV

CHAPTER V

Contents

CHAPTER VI

CHAPTER VII

CHAPTER VIII

Contents

CHAPTER XII

CHAPTER XIII

CHAPTER XIV

CHAPTER XV

Contents

Contents

Contents

CHAPTER XXII

CHAPTER XXIII

Contents

CHAPTER XXIV

CHAPTER XXV

APPENDIX

CHAPTER XXIV

CHAPTER XXV

APPENDIX

LIST OF ILLUSTRATIONS

15

List of Illustrations

CHAPTER I

On the twenty-fourth of January we left Noh-cacab. It was a great relief to bid farewell to this place, and the only regret attending our departure was the reflection that we should be obliged to return. The kindness and attentions of the padrecito and his brother, and, indeed, of all the villagers, had been unremitted, but the fatigue of riding twelve miles every day over the same ground, and the difficulty of procuring Indians to work, were a constant source of annoyance; besides which, we had a feeling that operated during the whole of our journey: wherever we were taken ill we became disgusted with the place, and were anxious to leave it.

We were setting out on a tour which, according to the plan laid out, embraced a circuit of ruins, and required us to revisit Nohcacab, although our return would be only to make it a point of departure in another direction.

In consequence of this plan we left behind all our heavy luggage, and carried with us only the Daguerreotype apparatus, hammocks, one large box containing our tin table service, a candlestick, bread, chocolate, coffee, and sugar, and a few changes of clothing in pestaquillas. Besides Albino and Bernaldo we had a puny lad of about fifteen, named Barnaby, a much smaller pattern than either of the others, and all three together were hardly equal in bulk to one fairly developed man.

We were all provided with good horses for the road. Mr. Catherwood had one on which he could make a sketch without dismounting; Dr. Cabot could shoot from the back of his. Mine could, on an emergency, be pushed into a hard day's journey for a preliminary visit. Albino rode a hard-mouthed, wilful beast, which shook him constantly like a fit of the fever and ague, and which we distinguished by the name of the trotter. Bernaldo asked for a horse, because Albino had one, but, instead of riding, he had to put a strap across his forehead and carry his own luggage on his back.

We were about entering a region little or not at all frequented by white men, and occupied entirely by Indians. Our road lay through the ruins of Kabah, a league beyond which we reached the rancho of Chack. This was a large habitation of Indians, under the jurisdiction of the village of Nohcacab. There was not a white man in the place, and as we rode through, the women snatched up their children, and ran from us like startled deer. I rode up to a hut into which I saw a woman enter, and, stopping at the fence, merely from curiosity, took out a cigar, and, making use of some of the few Maya words we had picked up, asked for a light, but the door remained shut. I dismounted, and before I had tied my horse the woman rushed out and disappeared among the bushes. In one part of the rancho was a casa real, being a long thatched hut with a large square before it, protected by an arbour of leaves, and on one side was a magnificent seybo tree, throwing its shade to a great distance round.

On leaving this rancho we saw at a distance on the left a high ruined building standing alone amid a great intervening growth of woods, and apparently inaccessible. Beyond, and at the distance of four leagues from Nohcacab, we reached the rancho of Schawill, which was our first stopping-place, on account of the ruins of Zayi in its immediate neighbourhood. This place also was inhabited exclusively by Indians, rancho being the name given to a settlement not of sufficient importance to constitute a village. The casa real, like that at Chack, was a large hut, with mud walls and a thatched roof. It had an open place in front about a hundred feet square, enclosed by a fence made of poles, and shaded by an arbour of palm leaves. Around the hut were large seybo trees. The casa real is erected in every rancho of

Indians expressly for the reception of the cura on his occasional or perhaps barely possible visits, but it is occupied also by small dealers from the villages, who sometimes find their way to these ranchos to buy up hogs, maize, and fowls. The hut, when swept out, and comparatively clear of fleas, made a large and comfortable apartment, and furnished ample swinging room for six hammocks, being the number requisite for our whole retinue.

This place was under the parochial charge of our friend the cura of Ticul, who, however, owing to the multiplicity of his other occupations, had visited it but once. The padrecito had sent notice of our coming, and had charged the people to be in readiness to receive us. Immediately on our arrival, therefore, Indians were at hand to procure ramon for the horses, but there was no water. The rancho had no well, and was entirely dependant on that of Chack, three miles distant. For two reals, however, the Indians undertook to procure us four cantaros, one for each horse, which would serve for the night. In the evening we had a formal visit from the alcalde and his alguazils, and half the village besides.

Although we had been some time in the country, we regarded this as really the beginning of our travels; and though the scenes we had met with already were not much like any we had ever encountered before, our first day's journey introduced us to some that were entirely new. The Indians assembled under the arbour, where they, with great formality, offered us seats, and the alcalde told us that the rancho was poor, but they would do all they could to serve us. Neither he nor any other in the place spoke a word of Spanish, and our communications were through Albino. We opened the interview by remonstrating against the charge of two reals for watering our horses, but the excuse was satisfactory enough. In the rainy season they had sources of supply in the neighbourhood, and these were perhaps as primitive as in any other section of the habitable world, being simply deposites of rain-water in the holes and hollows of rocks, which were called sartenejas. From the rocky nature of the country, these are very numerous; during the rainy season they are replenished as fast as they are exhausted, and at the time of our visit, owing to the long continuance of the rains, they furnished a sufficient supply for domestic use, but the people were not able to keep horses or cows, or cattle of any kind, the only animals they had being hogs. In the dry season this source of supply failed them; the holes in the rocks were dry, and they were obliged to send to the rancho of Chack, the well of which

19

they represented as being half a mile under ground, and so steep that it was reached only by descending nine different staircases.

This account saved them from all imputation of churlishness in not giving our horses water. It seemed strange that any community should be willing to live where this article of primary necessity was so difficult to be obtained, and we asked them why they did not break up their settlement and go elsewhere; but this idea seemed never to have occurred to them; they said their fathers had lived there before them, and the land around was good for milpas. In fact, they were a peculiar people, and I never before regretted so much my ignorance of the Maya language. They are under the civil jurisdiction of the village of Nohcacab, but the right of soil is their own by inheritance. They consider themselves better off than in the villages, where the people are subject to certain municipal regulations and duties, or than on the haciendas, where they would be under the control of masters.

Their community consists of a hundred labradores, or working men; their lands are held and wrought in common, and the products are shared by all. Their food is prepared at one hut, and every family sends for its portion, which explained a singular spectacle we had seen on our arrival; a procession of women and children, each carrying an earthen bowl containing a quantity of smoking hot broth, all coming down the same road, and dispersing among the different huts. Every member belonging to the community, down to the smallest pappoose, contributed in turn a hog. From our ignorance of the language, and the number of other and more pressing matters claiming our attention, we could not learn all the details of their internal economy, but it seemed to approximate that improved state of association which is sometimes heard of among us; and as theirs has existed for an unknown length of time, and can no longer be considered merely experimental, Owen or Fourier might perhaps take lessons from them with advantage.

They differ from professed reformers in one important particular—they seek no converts. No stranger is allowed, upon any consideration, to enter their community; every member must marry within the rancho, and no such thing as a marriage out of it had ever occurred. They said it was impossible; it could not happen. They were in the habit of going to the villages to attend the festivals; and when we suggested a supposable case of a young man or woman falling in love with some village Indian, they said it might happen; there was no law against it; but none

could *marry* out of the rancho. This was a thing so little apprehended that the punishment for it was not defined in their penal
code; but being questioned, after some consultation they said
that the offender, whether man or woman, would be expelled.
We remarked that in their small community constant intermar-
riages must make them all relatives, which they said was the case
since the reduction of their numbers by the cholera. They were,
in fact, all kinsfolk, but it was allowable for kinsfolk to marry
except in the relationship of brothers and sisters. They were very
strict in attendance upon the ceremonies of the Church, and
had just finished the celebration of the carnival two weeks in
advance of the regular time; but when we corrected their chronology, they said they could celebrate it over again.

Early in the morning we set out for the ruins of Zayi, or
Salli. At a short distance from the rancho we saw in an overgrown milpa on our left the ruins of a mound and building, so
far destroyed that they are not worth presenting.

After proceeding a mile and a half we saw at some distance
before us a great tree-covered mound, which astonished us by its
vast dimensions, and, but for our Indian assistants, would have
frightened us by the size of the trees growing upon it. The woods
commenced from the roadside. Our guides cut a path, and, clearing the branches overhead, we followed on horseback, dismounting at the foot of the Casa Grande. It was by this name that the
Indians called the immense pile of white stone buildings, which,
buried in the depths of a great forest, added new desolation to
the waste by which they were surrounded. We tied our horses,
and worked our way along the front. The trees were so close that
we could take in but a small portion of it at once. If we had encountered these woods at Kabah, where we had such difficulties
in procuring Indians, we should have despaired of being able to
accomplish anything, but, fortunately so far, where our labours
were great we had at hand the means of performing them.

We were at no loss what to do, our great object now being
to economize time. Without waiting to explore the rest of the
ground, we set the Indians at work, and in a few minutes the
stillness of ages was broken by the sharp ringing of the axe and
the crash of falling trees. With a strong force of Indians, we were
able, in the course of the day, to lay bare the whole of the front.

Dr. Cabot did not arrive on the ground till late in the day,
and, coming upon it suddenly from the woods, when there were
no trees to obstruct the view, and its three great ranges and im-

mense proportions were visible at once, considered it the grandest spectacle he had seen in the country.

Plate I represents the front of this building. The view was taken from a mound, at the distance of about five hundred feet, overgrown and having upon it a ruined edifice. In clearing away the trees and undergrowth to this mound we discovered a pila, or stone, hollowed out, and filled with rain-water, which was a great acquisition to us while working at these ruins.

The plate represents so much of the building as now remains and can be presented in a drawing. It has three stories or ranges, and in the centre is a grand staircase thirty-two feet wide, rising to the platform of the highest terrace. This staircase, however, is in a ruinous condition, and, in fact, a mere mound, and all that part of the building on the right had fallen, and was so dilapidated that no intelligible drawing could be made of it; we did not even clear away the trees. The engraving represents all that part which remains, being the half of the building on the left of the staircase.

The lowest of the three ranges is two hundred and sixty-five feet in front and one hundred and twenty in depth. It had sixteen doorways, opening into apartments of two chambers each. The whole front wall has fallen; the interiors are filled with fragments and rubbish, and the ground in front was so encumbered with the branches of fallen trees, even after they had been chopped into pieces and beaten down with poles, that, at the distance necessary for making a drawing, but a small portion of the interior could be seen. The two ends of this range have each six doorways, and the rear has ten, all opening into apartments, but in general they are in a ruinous condition.

The range of buildings on the second terrace was two hundred and twenty feet in length and sixty feet in depth, and had four doorways on each side of the grand staircase. Those on the left, which are all that remain, have two columns in each doorway, each column being six feet six inches high, roughly made, with square capitals, like Doric, but wanting the grandeur pertaining to all known remains of this ancient order. Filling up the spaces between the doorways are four small columns curiously ornamented, close together, and sunk in the wall. Between the first and second and third and fourth doorways a small staircase leads to the terrace of the third range. The platform of this terrace is thirty feet in front and twenty-five in the rear. The building is one hundred and fifty feet long by eighteen feet

Plate I

deep, and has seven doorways opening into as many apartments. The lintels over the doorways are of stone.

The exterior of the third and highest range was plain; that of the two other ranges had been elaborately ornamented; and, in order to give some idea of their character, I present in Plate II a portion of the façade of the second range. Among designs common in other places is the figure of a man supporting himself on his hands, with his legs expanded in a curious rather than delicate attitude, of which a small portion appears on the right of the engraving; and again we have the "large and very well constructed buildings of lime and stone" which Bernal Dias saw at Campeachy, "with figures of *serpents* and of idols painted on the walls."

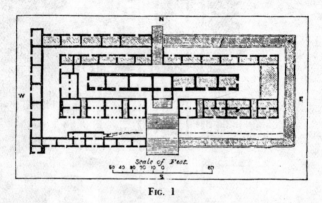

FIG. 1

Figure 1 represents the ground plan of the three ranges, and gives the dimensions of the terraces. The platforms are wider in front than in the rear; the apartments vary from twenty-three to ten feet, and the north side of the second range has a curious and unaccountable feature. It is called the Casa Cerrada, or closed house, having ten doorways, all of which are blocked up inside with stone and mortar. Like the well at Xcoch, it had a mysterious reputation in the village of Nohcacab, and all believed that it contained hidden treasure. Indeed, so strong was this belief, that the alcalde Segundo, who had never visited these ruins, resolved to take advantage of our presence; and, according to agreement in the village, came down with crowbars to assist us in breaking into the closed apartments and discovering the precious hoard. The first sight of these closed-up doorways gave us a strong desire to make the attempt; but on moving along we found that the Indians had been beforehand with us. In front of

Plate II

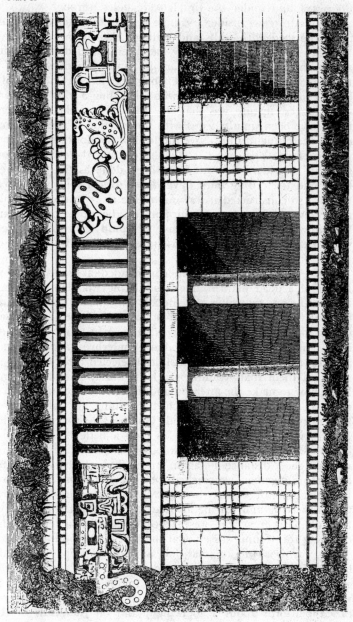

25

several were piles of stones, which they had worked out from the doorways, and under the lintels were holes, through which we were able to crawl inside; and here we found ourselves in apartments finished with walls and ceilings like all the others, but filled up (except so far as they had been emptied by the Indians) with solid masses of mortar and stone. There were ten of these apartments in all, 220 feet long and ten feet deep, which being thus filled up, made the whole building a solid mass; and the strangest feature was that the filling up of the apartments must have been simultaneous with the erection of the buildings, for, as the filling-in rose above the tops of the doorways, the men who performed it never could have entered to their work through the doors. It must have been done as the walls were built, and the ceiling must have closed over a solid mass. Why this was so constructed it was impossible to say, unless the solid mass was required for the support of the upper terrace and building; and if this was the case, it would seem to have been much easier to erect a solid structure at once, without any division into apartments.

The top of this building commanded a grand view, no longer of a dead plain, but of undulating woodlands. Toward the northwest, crowning the highest hill, was a lofty mound, covered with trees, which, to our now practised eyes, it was manifest shrouded a building, either existing or in ruins. The whole intervening space was thick wood and underbrush, and the Indians said the mound was inaccessible. I selected three of the best, and told them that we must reach it; but they really did not know how to make the attempt, and set out on a continuation of the road by which we had reached the ruins, and which led us rather from than to the mound. On the way we met another Indian, who turned back with us, and a little beyond, taking his range, he cut through the woods to another path, following which a short distance, he again struck through the woods, and, all cutting together, we reached the foot of a stony hill covered with the gigantic maguey, or Agave Americana, its long thorny points piercing and tearing all that touched them. Climbing up this hill with great toil, we reached the wall of a terrace, and, climbing this, found ourselves at the foot of the building.

It was in a ruinous condition, and did not repay us for the labour; but over the door was a sculptured head with a face of good expression and workmanship. In one of the apartments was a high projection running along the wall; in another a raised platform about a foot high; and on the walls of this apartment was the print of the red hand. The doorway commanded an extensive view of rolling woodland, which, with its livery of deep green, ought to have conveyed a sensation of gladness, but, perhaps from its desolation and stillness, it induced rather a feeling of melancholy. There was but one opening in the forest, being that made by us, disclosing the Casa Grande, with the figures of a few Indians still continuing their clearings on the top.

In front of the Casa Grande, at the distance of five hundred yards, and also visible from the top, is another structure, strikingly different from any we had seen, more strange and inexplicable, and having at a distance the appearance of a New-England factory.

FIG. 2

Figure 2 represents this building. It stands on a terrace, and may be considered as consisting of two separate structures, one above the other. The lower one, in its general features, resembled all the rest. It was forty feet front, low, and having a flat roof, and in the centre was an archway running through the building. The front is fallen, and the whole so ruined that nothing but the archway appears in the engraving. Along the middle of the roof, unsupported, and entirely independent of everything else, rises a perpendicular wall to the height of perhaps thirty feet. It is of stone, about two feet thick, and has oblong openings through it about four feet long and six inches wide, like small windows. It had been covered with stucco, which had fallen off, and left the face of rough stone and mortar; and on the other side were fragments of stuccoed figures and ornaments. An Indian appears before it in the act of killing a snake, with which all the woods of Yucatan abound. Since we began our exploration of American ruins we had not met with anything more inexplicable than this great perpendicular wall. It seemed built merely to puzzle posterity.

These were the only buildings in this immediate neighbourhood which had survived the wasting of the elements; but, inquiring among the Indians, one of them undertook to guide me to another, which he said was still in good preservation. Our direction was south-southwest from the Casa Grande; and at the distance of about a mile, the whole intermediate region being desolate and overgrown, we reached a terrace, the area of which far exceeded anything we had seen in the country. We crossed it from north to south, and in this direction it must have been fifteen hundred feet in length, and probably was quite as much in the other direction; but it was so rough, broken, and overgrown, that we did not attempt to measure it.

On this great platform was the building of which the Indian had told us; I had it cleared, and Mr. Catherwood drew it the next day, as it appears in Plate III. It measures one hundred and seventeen feet in front, and eighty-four feet deep, and contains sixteen apartments, of which those in front, five in number, are best preserved. That in the centre has three doorways. It is twenty-seven feet six inches long, by only seven feet six inches wide, and communicates by a single doorway with a back room eighteen feet long and five feet six inches wide. This room is raised two feet six inches above the one in front, and has steps to ascend. Along the bottom of the front room, as high as the sill of the door, is a row of small columns, thirty-eight in number, attached to the wall.

In several places the great platform is strewed with ruins, and probably other buildings lie buried in the woods, but without guides or any clew whatever, we did not attempt to look for them.

Plate III

ZAYI

Such, so far as we were able to discover them, are the ruins of Zayi, the name of which, to the time of our visit, had never been uttered among civilized men, and, but for the notoriety connected with our movements, would probably be unknown at this day in the capital of Yucatan. Our first accounts of them were from the cura Carillo, who, on the occasion of his only visit to this part of his curacy, passed a great portion of his time among them.

It was strange and almost incredible that, with these extraordinary monuments before their eyes, the Indians never bestowed upon them one passing thought. The question, who built them? never by any accident crossed their minds. The great name of Montezuma, which had gone beyond them to the Indians of Honduras, had never reached their ears, and to all our questions we received the same dull answer which first met us at Copan, "Quien sabe?" "Who knows?" They had the same superstitious feelings as the Indians of Uxmal; they believed that the ancient buildings were haunted, and, as in the remote region of Santa Cruz del Quiché, they said that on Good Friday of every year music was heard sounding among the ruins.

There was but one thing connected with the old city that interested them at all, and that was the subject of a well. They supposed that somewhere among these ruins, overgrown and lost, existed the fountain which had supplied the ancient inhabitants with water; and, believing that by the use of our instruments its site could be discovered, they offered to cut down all the trees throughout the whole region covered by the ruins.

CHAPTER II

The next morning, while Mr. Catherwood was engaged in drawing the building represented in the last engraving, Dr. Cabot and myself set out to visit the one which we had passed in coming from the rancho of Chack.

In the suburbs of the rancho we turned off to the right by a path, which we followed for some distance on horseback, when it changed its direction, and we dismounted. From this place our guides cut a path through the woods, and we came out upon a large field of táje, being long stems growing close together, eight or ten feet high, straight, and about half an inch thick, having a yellow flower on the top, which is a favourite food for horses. The stems, tied up in bundles three or four inches thick, are used for torches. On one side of this field we saw the high building before referred to, and on the other side was a second not visible before. A bird which the doctor wished to procure lighted on a tree growing upon the latter, and we went to it, but found nothing of particular interest, and struck across the field of táje for the former. This táje was as bad as the woods to walk through, for it grew so high as to exclude every breath of air, and was not high enough to be any protection against the sun.

The building stood on the top of a stony hill, on a terrace still firm and substantial. It consisted of two stories, the roof of the lower one forming the platform in front of the upper, and had a staircase, which was broken and ruined. The upper building had a large apartment in the centre, and a smaller one on each side, much encumbered with rubbish, from one of which we were driven by a hornet's nest, and in another a young vulture, with a hissing noise, flapped its plumeless wings and hopped out of the door.

The terrace commanded a picturesque view of wooded hills, and at a distance the Casa Grande, and the high wall before presented. They were perhaps three or four miles distant. All the intermediate space was overgrown. The Indians had traversed it in all directions in the dry season, when there was no foliage to hide the view, and they said that in all this space there were no vestiges of buildings. Close together as we had found the remains of ancient habitations, it seemed hardly possible that distinct and independent cities had existed with but such a little space between, and yet it was harder to imagine that one city had embraced within its limits these distant buildings, the extreme ones being four miles apart, and that the whole intermediate region of desolation had once swarmed with a teeming and active population.

Leaving this, we toiled back to our horses, and, returning to the road, passed through the rancho, about a mile beyond which we reached the pozo, or well, the accounts of which we had heard on our first arrival.

Near the mouth were some noble seybo trees, throwing their great branches far and wide, under which groups of Indians were arranging their calabashes and torches, preparing to descend; others, just out, were wiping their sweating bodies. At one moment an Indian disappeared, and at the next another rose up out of the earth. We noticed that there were no women, who, throughout Yucatan, are the drawers of water, and always seen around a well, but we were told that no woman ever enters the well of Chack; all the water for the rancho was procured by the men, which alone indicated that the well was of an extraordinary character. We had brought with us a ball of twine, and made immediate preparations to descend, reducing our dress as near as possible to that of the Indians.

Our first movement was down a hole by a perpendicular

ladder, at the foot of which we were fairly entered into a great cavern. Our guides preceded us with bundles of táje lighted for torches, and we came to a second descent almost perpendicular, which we achieved by a ladder laid flat against the rock. Beyond this we moved on a short distance, still following our guides, and still descending, when we saw their torches disappearing, and reached a wild hole, which also we descended by a long rough ladder. At the foot of this the rock was damp and slippery, and there was barely room enough to pass around it, and get upon another ladder down the same hole, now more contracted, and so small that, with the arms akimbo, the elbows almost touched on each side. At this time our Indians were out of sight; and in total darkness, feeling our way by the rounds of the ladder, we cried out to them, and were answered by distant voices directly underneath. Looking down, we saw their torches like moving balls of fire, apparently at an interminable distance below us.

At the foot of this ladder there was a rude platform as a resting-place, made to enable those ascending and descending to pass each other. A group of naked Indians, panting and sweating under the load of their calabashes, were waiting till we vacated the ladder above; and even in this wild hole, with loads on their backs, straps binding their foreheads, and panting from fatigue and heat, they held down their torches, and rendered obeisance to the blood of the white man. Descending the next ladder, both above and below us were torches gleaming in the darkness. We had still another ladder to descend, and the whole perpendicular depth of this hole was perhaps two hundred feet.

From the foot of this ladder there was an opening to the right, and from it we soon entered a low, narrow passage, through which we crawled on our hands and knees. With the toil and the smoke of the torches the heat was almost beyond endurance. The passage enlarged and again contracted, descending steeply, and so low that the shoulders almost touched the roof. This opened upon a great chasm at one side, and beyond we came to another perpendicular hole, which we descended by steps cut in the rock. From this there was another low, crawling passage, and, almost stifled with heat and smoke, we came out into a small opening, in which was a basin of water, being the well. The place was crowded with Indians filling their calabashes, and they started at the sight of our smoky white faces as if El Demonio had descended among them. It was, doubtless, the first time that the feet of a white man had ever reached this well.

On returning we measured the distance, Doctor Cabot going before with a line of about a hundred feet, in the wild and broken passages being soon out of sight, and sometimes out of hearing. I followed, with an Indian winding up the line, while I made notes. I had two Indians with long bundles of lighted sticks, who, whenever I stopped to write, either held them so far off as to be of no use, or else thrust them into my face, blinding the eyes with smoke and scorching the skin. I was dripping as if in a vapour-bath; my face and hands were black with smoke and incrusted with dirt; large drops of sweat fell upon my book, which, with the dirt from my hands, matted the leaves together, so that my notes are almost useless. They were, no doubt, imperfect, but I do not believe that, with the most accurate details, it is possible to convey a true idea of the character of this cave, with its deep holes and passages through a bed of solid rock, and the strange scene presented by the Indians, with torches and calabashes, unmurmuring and uncomplaining, at their daily task of seeking, deep in the bowels of the earth, one of the great elements of life.

The distance, as we traversed it, with its ladders, ascents and descents, winding and crawling passages, seemed a full half league, as represented by the Indians. By measurement it was not quite fifteen hundred feet, which is about equal to the length of the Park fronting on Broadway. The perpendicular depth to the water I am not able to give, but some idea may be formed of these passages from the fact that the Indians did not carry their calabashes on their shoulders, because, with the body bent, they would strike against the roof or roll over the head; but the straps across the forehead were let out so long that the calabashes rested below the hips, and in crawling on the hands and feet their loads did not rise above the line of the back.

And this well was not, as at Xcoch, the occasional resort of a straggling Indian, nor the mere traditional watering-place of an ancient city. It was the regular and only supply of a living population. The whole rancho of Chack was entirely dependant upon it, and in the dry season the rancho of Schawill, three miles distant.

The patient industry of such a people may well be supposed to have reared the immense mounds and the great stone structures scattered all over the country. We consumed a calabash of water in washing and quenching our thirst, and as we rode back to the rancho of Schawill, came to the conclusion that an admission into the community of this exclusive people was no great privilege, when it would entail upon the applicant, for six months in the year, a daily descent into this subterraneous well.

We arrived at the rancho in good season. Mr. Catherwood had finished his drawing, and Bernaldo was ready with his dinner. We had nothing to detain us, ordered carriers forthwith for our luggage, and at half past two we were in the saddle again in search of ruined cities.

The reader has some idea of the caminos reales of this country, and they were all like English turnpikes compared with that upon which we entered on leaving this rancho. In fact, it was a mere path through the woods, the branches of the trees being trimmed away to a height barely sufficient to admit of an Indian passing under with a load of maize on his back. We were advised that it would be very difficult to get through on horseback, and were obliged to keep dodging the head and bending the body to avoid the branches, and at times we were brought to a stand by some overhanging arm of a tree, and obliged to dismount.

At the distance of two leagues we reached the rancho of Sannacté, the Indians of which were the wildest people in appearance we had yet seen. As we rode through, the women ran away and hid themselves, and the men crouched on the ground bareheaded, with long black hair hanging over their eyes, gazing at us in stupid astonishment. The same scarcity of water still continued. The rancho was entirely destitute; it had no pozo or well of any kind, either ancient or modern, and the inhabitants procured their whole supply from the village of Sabachshé, two leagues, or six miles, distant! This supply, too, was brought daily on the backs of Indians; but again in this arid and destitute region was still another evidence of ancient population— another desolate and ruined city.

Beyond the outskirts of the rancho was a large clearing for a milpa, within which, naked and exposed to full view, were two ancient buildings. The milpa was enclosed by a fence, and was overgrown with táje. We tied our horses to the stems of the táje, and, leaving them eating the flowers, followed a path which led between the two buildings. Figure 3 represents the one on the left. It stands on a terrace, still strong and substantial, and, fortunately, clear of trees, though many were growing on the top. It has five apartments; the façade above the cornice is fallen, and between the doorways are fragments of small columns

FIG. 3

set in the wall. On the other side of the milpa was another edifice, holding aloft a high wall, like that we had seen at Zayi, extraordinary in its appearance and incomprehensible in its uses and purposes. From the tact and facility we had now acquired, a short time sufficed for our examination of this place, and, with one more added to our list of ruined cities, we mounted, and resumed our journey.

At half past five we reached the rancho of Sabachshé, lying on the camino real from Ticul to Bolonchen, and inhabited entirely by Indians. The casa real stood on an elevation in an open place; it was thatched with palm leaves, had mud walls, and an arbour before it, and a table and benches within. Altogether, it was better in appearance and furniture than the others we had encountered, which, as we afterward learned, was owing to the circumstance that, besides its regular uses, it was intended for the residence of the mistress on her annual visits to the rancho. But much more interesting and important was the fact, that this rancho was distinguished by a well, the sight of which was more grateful to us than that of the best hotel to the traveller in a civilized country. We were scratched with thorns, and smarting with garrapata bites, and looked forward to the refreshment of a bath. Very soon our horses had the benefit of it, the bath being in that country, where the currycomb and brush are entirely unknown, the only external refreshment these animals ever get. The well was built by the present owner, and formerly the inhabitants were dependant entirely upon the well at Tabi, six miles distant! Besides its real value, it presented a curious and lively spectacle. A group of Indian women was around it. It had no rope or fixtures of any kind for raising water, but across the mouth was a round beam laid upon two posts, over which the women were letting down and hoisting up little bark buckets. Every woman brought with her and carried away her own bucket and rope, the latter coiled up and laid on the top of her head, with the end hanging down behind, and the coil forming a sort of headdress.

Near the well was the hut of the alcalde, enclosed by a rude fence, and within were dogs, hogs, turkeys, and fowls, which all barked, grunted, gobbled, and cackled together as we entered. The yard was shaded by orange-trees loaded with ripe and unusually large fruit. Under one of them was a row of twenty or thirty wild boars' jaws and tusks, trophies of the chase, and memorials attesting the usefulness of the barking dogs. The noise brought the alcalde to the door, a heavy and infirm old man, apparently rich, and suffering from the high living indicated by his hogs and poultry; but he received us with meekness and humility. We negotiated forthwith for the purchase of some oranges, and bought thirty for a medio, stipulating that they should all be the largest and best on the trees; after which, supporting himself by his cane, he hobbled on to the casa real, had it swept out, and assigned Indians to attend upon us. If he wanted alacrity himself, he infused it into his people, and made up for all deficiencies by unqualified personal deference and respect. It was a fine evening, and we spread our supper-table under the arbour. The old alcalde remained with us, and a group of Indians sat on the steps, not like the proud and independent race of Schawill, but acknowledging themselves criados, or servants, bound to obey the orders of their mistress. La señora was, in their eyes, a miniature print of Queen Victoria, but skill in the use of figures may arrive at the value of at least this part of her possessions. There were fifty-five labradores, or labouring men, under an obligation to plant and harvest ten micates of maize for her benefit. Each micate produces ten cargas, or loads, making in all five hundred and fifty, which, at three reals per carga, gives as the revenue this lady comes regularly to collect, about two hundred dollars per annum; but this gives more power than lands or money to any amount in our country could give; and the labradores being all free and independent electors, fifty-five votes could always be calculated upon in an emergency for the side of principle and la señora.

Having made our arrangements for the next day, we went into the hut and shut the door. Some time afterward the old alcalde sent in to ask permission to go home, as he was very sleepy, which we graciously granted, and, by his direction, three or four Indians swung their little hammocks under the arbour, to be at hand in case we should need anything. During the night we found it extremely cold, and, with the little covering we had brought, could hardly keep ourselves comfortable.

Early in the morning we found a large gathering round the house to escort us to the ruins. In the suburbs of the rancho we turned off to the left, and passed among the huts of the Indians, almost smothered by weeds, and having at the doors rude boxes of earth set up on posts, for vegetables to grow in out of the reach of the hogs.

Crossing the fence of the last hut, we entered a thick growth of trees. As if instinctively, every Indian drew his machete, and in a few minutes they cut a path to the foot of a small building, not rich in ornament, but tasteful, having some shades of difference from any we had seen, overgrown by trees, and beautifully picturesque. On one corner of the roof a vulture had built her nest, and, scared away at our approach, hovered over our heads, looking down upon us as if amazed. We gave directions, all the Indians fell to work, and in a few minutes the small terrace in front was cleared. I had not expected so many Indians, and, not knowing what occasion I might have for their services, told them that I did not need so great a number, and should only pay those whom I had engaged. All stopped, and when the purport of my words was explained to them, said that made no difference; they immediately set to work again, and the machetes fell with a rapidity unparalleled in our experience. In half an hour space enough was cleared for Mr. Catherwood to set up his camera lucida. The same alertness was shown in preparing a place for him to stand in, and half a dozen stood ready to hold an umbrella for his protection against the sun.

Plate IV represents the front of the building. Its design is tasteful and even elegant, and when perfect it must have pre-

Plate IV

SABACHTSCHE

sented a fine appearance. It has a single doorway, opening into a chamber twenty-five feet long by ten wide. Above the door is a portion of plain masonry, and over this a cornice supporting twelve small pilasters, having between them the diamond ornament, then a massive cornice, with pilasters and diamond work, surmounted by another cornice, making in all four cornices; an arrangement we had not previously met with.

While Mr. Catherwood was making his drawing, the Indians stood around under the shade of the trees, looking at him quietly and respectfully, and making observations to each other. They were a fine-looking race. Some of them, one tall old man particularly, had noble Roman faces, and they seemed to have more respectability of appearance and character than was consistent with the condition of men not wearing pantaloons. All at once an enormous iguana, or lizard, doubled the corner of the building, ran along the front, and plunged into a crevice over the door, burying his whole body, but leaving the long tail out. Among these unsophisticated people this reptile is a table delicacy, and here was a supper provided for some of them. Machetes flew out, and, cutting down a sapling with a crotch in it, they rested it against the wall, and, standing in the crotch, pulled upon the tail; but the animal held on with his feet as if a part of the building. All the Indians, one after the other, had a pull at the tail, but could not make him budge. At length two of them contrived to get hold together, and, while pulling with all their strength, the tail came off by the roots, a foot and half long in their hands. The animal was now more out of their reach than before, his whole body being hidden in the wall; but he could not escape. The Indians picked away the mortar with their machetes, and enlarged the hole until they got his hind legs clear, when, griping the body above the legs, they again hauled; but, though he had only the fore legs to hold on with, they could not tear him out. They the untied the ropes of their sandals, and, fastening them above the hind legs, and pulling till the long body seemed parting like the tail, they at length dragged him out. They secured him by a gripe under the fore part of the body, cracked his spine, and broke the bones of his fore legs so that he could not run; pried his jaws open, fastened them apart with a sharp stick so that he could not bite, and then put him away in the shade. This refined cruelty was to avoid the necessity of killing him immediately, for if killed, in that hot climate he would soon be unfit for food; but, mutilated and mangled as he was, he could be kept alive till night.

This over, we moved on in a body, carrying the iguana, to the next building, which was situated in a different direction, about a quarter of a mile distant, and completely buried in woods. It was seventy-five feet long, and had three doorways, leading to the same number of apartments. A great part of the front had fallen; Plate V represents that which remains. With some slight difference in the detail of ornament, the character is the same as in all the other buildings, and the general effect pleasing. Growing on the roof are two maguey plants, Agave Americana, in our latitude called the century plant, but under the hot sun of the tropics blooming every four or five years. There are four species of this plant in Yucatan: the maguey, from which is produced the pulqué, a beverage common in all the Mexican provinces, which, taken in excess, produces intoxication; the henneken, which produces the article known in our markets as Sisal hemp; the sabila, with which the Indian women wean children, covering the breast with the leaf, which is very bitter to the taste; and the peta, having leaves twice as large as the last, from which a very fine white hemp is made. These plants, in some or all of their varieties, were found in the neighbourhood of all the ruins, forming around them a pointed and thorny wall, which we were obliged to cut through to reach the buildings.

While Mr. C. was engaged in drawing this structure, the Indians told us of two others half a league distant. I selected two of them for guides, and, with the same alacrity which they had shown in everything else, nine volunteered to accompany me. We had a good path nearly all the way, until the Indians pointed out a white object seen indistinctly through the trees, again uttering, with strong gutturals, the familiar sound of "Xlappahk," or old walls. In a few minutes they cut a path to it. The building was larger than the last, having the front ornamented in the same way, much fallen, though still presenting an interesting spectacle. As it was not much overgrown, we set to work and cleared it, and left it for another, in regard to which I formed some curious expectations, for the Indians described it as *very new*. It lay on the same path, to the left in returning to the rancho, and separated from us by a great field of táje, through which we were obliged to cut a path for several hundred yards to the foot of the terrace. The walls were entire and very massive; but climbing up it, I found only a small building, consisting of but two apartments, the front much fallen, and the doors filled up, but no sign or token distinguishing it as *newer*

Plate V

F. Catherwood.   S.H. Gimber

SABACHTSCHE

or more modern; and I now learned, what I might have done before by a little asking, that all they meant by their description of it was, that it was the *newest* known to them, having been discovered but twelve years before, accidentally, on clearing the ground for a milpa, until which time it was as much unknown to them as to the rest of the world. This intelligence gave great weight to the consideration which had often suggested itself before, that cities may exist equal to any now known, buried in the woods, overgrown and lost, which will perhaps never be discovered.

On the walls of this desolate edifice were prints of the "mano colorado," or red hand. Often as I saw this print, it never failed to interest me. It was the stamp of the living hand; it always brought me nearer to the builders of these cities, and at times, amid stillness, desolation, and ruin, it seemed as if from behind the curtain that concealed them from view was extended the hand of greeting. These prints were larger than any I had seen. In several places I measured them with my own, opening the fingers to correspond with those on the wall. The Indians said it was the hand of the master of the building.

The mysterious interest which, in my eyes, always attached to this red hand, has assumed a more definite shape. I have been advised that in Mr. Catlin's collection of Indian curiosities, made during a long residence among our North American tribes, was a tent presented to him by the chief of the powerful but now extinct race of Mandans, which exhibits, among other marks, two prints of the red hand; and I have been farther advised that the red hand is seen constantly upon the buffalo robes and skins of wild animals brought in by the hunters on the Rocky Mountains, and, in fact, that it is a symbol recognised and in common use by the North American Indians of the present day. I do not mention these as facts within my own knowledge, but with the hope of attracting the attention of those who have opportunities and facilities for investigation; and I suggest the interesting consideration that, if true, the red hand on the tent and the buffalo robes points back from the wandering tribes in our country to the comparatively polished people who erected the great cities at the south; and if true that it is at this day used as a sign or symbol by our North American Indians, its meaning can be ascertained from living witnesses, and through ages of intervening darkness a ray of light may be thrown back upon the now mysterious and incomprehensible characters which perplex the stranger on the walls of the desolate southern buildings.

On my return to the rancho I learned the cause of the extraordinary attention shown us, which, though we had received it as a matter of course, and no more than what, for some unknown reasons, was justly due to us, had, nevertheless, somewhat surprised us. Our movements in that neighbourhood were matters of some notoriety. Albino's preliminary visit and our intentions had reached the ears of the señora, and the evening before our arrival orders from her had arrived at the rancho for all the Indians to put themselves at our command; and this delicate manner of doing us a service is one of the many acts of kindness I have to acknowledge to the citizens of Yucatan. The old alcalde again waited till he became sleepy, when he asked permission to go to his hut, and four or five Indians again hung up their hammocks under the arbour.

CHAPTER III

The next morning we set out for the ruins of Labnà. Our road lay southeast, among hills, and was more picturesque than any we had seen in the country. At the distance of a mile and a half we reached a field of ruins, which, after all we had seen, created in us new feelings of astonishment. It was one of the circumstances attending our exploration of ruins in this country, that until we arrived on the ground we had no idea of what we were to meet with. The accounts of the Indians were never reliable. When they gave us reason to expect much we found but little, and, on the other hand, when we expected but little a great field presented itself. Of this place even our friend the cura Carillo had never heard. Our first intelligence of ruins in this region was from the brother of the padrecito at Nohcacab, who, however, had never seen them himself. Since our arrival in the country we had not met with anything that excited us more strongly, and now we had mingled feelings of pain and pleasure; of pain, that they had not been discovered before the sentence of irretrievable ruin had gone forth against them; at the same time it was matter of deep congratulation that, before the doom was accomplished, we were permitted to see these decaying, but still proud memorials of a mysterious

45

people. In a few years, even these will be gone; and as it has been denied that such things ever were, doubts may again arise whether they have indeed existed. So strong was this impression that we determined to fortify in every possible way our proofs. If anything could have added to the interest of discovering such a new field of research, it was the satisfaction of having at our command such an effective force of Indians. No time was lost, and they began work with a spirit corresponding to their numbers. Many of them had hachas, or small axes, and the crash of falling trees was like the stirring noise of felling in one of our own forests.

Plate VI represents a pyramidal mound, holding aloft the most curious and extraordinary structure we had seen in the country. It put us on the alert the moment we saw it. We passed an entire day before it, and, in looking back upon our journey among ruined cities, no subject of greater interest presents itself to my mind. The mound is forty-five feet high. The steps had fallen; trees were growing out of the place where they stood, and we reached the top by clinging to the branches; when these were cleared away, it was extremely difficult to ascend and descend. The maguey plants cut down in making the clearing appear fallen on the steps.

A narrow platform forms the top of the mound. The building faces the south, and when entire measured forty-three feet in front and twenty feet in depth. It had three doorways, of which one, with eight feet of the whole structure, has fallen, and is now in ruins. The centre doorway opens into two chambers, each twenty feet long and six feet wide.

Above the cornice of the building rises a gigantic perpendicular wall to the height of thirty feet, once ornamented from top to bottom, and from one side to the other, with colossal figures and other designs in stucco, now broken and in fragments, but still presenting a curious and extraordinary appearance, such as the art of no other people ever produced. Along the top, standing out on the wall, was a row of death's heads; underneath were two lines of human figures in alto relievo (of which scattered arms and legs alone remain), the grouping of which, so far as it could be made out, showed considerable proficiency in that most difficult department of the art of design. Over the centre doorway, constituting the principal ornament of the wall, was a colossal figure seated, of which only a large tippet and girdle, and some other detached portions, have been preserved. Conspicuous over the head of this principal figure is

Plate VI

LABNAH

a large ball, with a human figure standing up beside it, touching it with his hands, and another below it with one knee on the ground, and one hand thrown up as if in the effort to support the ball, or in the apprehension of its falling upon him. In all our labours in that country we never studied so diligently to make out from the fragments the combinations and significance of these figures and ornaments. Standing in the same position, and looking at them all together, we could not agree.

Mr. Catherwood made two drawings at different hours and under a different position of the sun, and Dr. Cabot and myself worked upon it the whole day with the Daguerreotype. With the full blaźe of a vertical sun upon it, the white stone glared with an intensity dazzling and painful to the eyes, and almost realizing the account by Bernal Dias in the expedition to Mexico, of the arrival of the Spaniards at Cempoal. "Our advanced guard having gone to the great square, the buildings of which had been lately whitewashed and plastered, in which art these people are very expert, one of our horsemen was so struck with the splendour of their appearance in the sun, that he came back at full speed to Cortez, to tell him that the walls of the houses were of silver."

Our best view was obtained in the afternoon, when the edifice was in shade, but so broken and confused were the ornaments that a distinct representation could not be made even with the Daguerreotype, and the only way to make out all the details was near approach by means of a ladder; we had all the woods to make one of, but it was difficult for the Indians to make one of the length required; and when made it would have been too heavy and cumbersome to manage on the narrow platform in front. Besides, the wall was tottering and ready to fall. One portion was already gone in a perpendicular line from top to bottom, and the reader will see in the engraving that on a line with the right of the centre doorway the wall is cracked, and above is gaping, and stands apart more than a foot all the way to the top. In a few years it must fall. Its doom is sealed. Human power cannot save it; but in its ruins it gave a grand idea of the scenes of barbaric magnificence which this country must have presented when all her cities were entire. The figures and ornaments on this wall were painted; the remains of bright colours are still visible, defying the action of the elements. If a solitary traveller from the Old World could by some strange accident have visited this aboriginal city when it was yet perfect, his account would have seemed more fanciful than any in Eastern

Plate VII

GATEWAY at LABNA

J. N. Gimbrede.

49

story, and been considered a subject for the Arabian Nights' Entertainments.

At the distance of a few hundred feet from this structure, in sight at the same time as we approached it, is an arched gateway, remarkable for its beauty of proportions and grace of ornament. Plate VII represents this gateway. On the right, running off at an angle of thirty degrees, is a long building much fallen, which could not be comprehended in the view. On the left it forms an angle with another building, and on the return of the wall there is a doorway, not shown in the engraving, of good proportions, and more richly ornamented than any other portion of the structure. The effect of the whole combination was curious and striking, and, familiar as we were with ruins, the first view, with the great wall towering in front, created an impression that is not easily described.

The gateway is ten feet wide, passing through which we entered a thick forest, growing so close upon the building that we were unable to make out even its shape; but, on clearing away the trees, we discovered that this had been the principal front, and that these trees were growing in what had once been the area, or courtyard. The doors of the apartments on both sides of the gateway, each twelve feet by eight, opened upon this area. Over each doorway was a square recess, in which were the remains of a rich ornament in stucco, with marks of paint still visible, apparently intended to represent the face of the sun surrounded by its rays, probably once objects of adoration and worship, but now wilfully destroyed. Plate VIII represents this front. The buildings around the area formed a great irregular pile, measuring in all two hundred feet in length. The plan was different from that of any we had seen, but, having so many subjects to present, I have not had it engraved.

Northeast from the mound on which the great wall stands, and about one hundred and fifty yards distant, is a large building, erected on a terrace, and hidden among the trees growing thereupon, with its front much ruined, and having but few remains of sculptured ornaments. Still farther in the same direction, going through the woods, we reach the grand, and, without extravagance, the really magnificent building represented in the frontispiece to this volume. It stands on a gigantic terrace, four hundred feet long and one hundred and fifty feet deep. The whole terrace is covered with buildings. The front represented measures two hundred and eighty-two feet in length. It consisted of three distinct parts, differing in style, and perhaps

Plate VIII

INTERIOR OF GATEWAY AT LABNA.

erected at different times. At a distance, as seen indistinctly through the trees, we had no idea of its extent. We came upon it at the corner which appears on the right in the engraving. Our guide cut a path along the front wall, and stopping, as we did, to look at the ornaments, and entering the apartments as we went along, the building seemed immense.

The whole long façade was ornamented with sculptured stone, of which, large as the engraving is, the details cannot appear; but, to give some idea of their character, a detached portion is represented in Plate IX, and, I ought at the same time to remark, is perhaps the most curious and interesting of any. It is at the left end of the principal building, and in the angle of the corner are the huge open jaws of an alligator, or some other hideous animal, enclosing a human head.

The reader will form some idea of the overgrown and shrouded condition of this building from the fact that I had been at work nearly the whole day upon the terrace, without knowing that there was another building on the top. In order to take in the whole front at one view, it was necessary to carry the clearing back some distance into the plain, and in doing this I discovered the upper structure. The growth of trees before it was almost equal to that on the terrace, or in any part of the forest. The whole had to be cleared, the trees thrown down upon the terrace, and thence dragged away to the plain. This building consists of single narrow corridors, and the façade is of plain stone, without any ornaments.

The platform in front is the roof of the building underneath, and in this platform was a circular hole, like those we had seen at Uxmal and other places, leading to subterraneous chambers. This hole was well known to the Indians, and had a marvellous reputation; and yet they never mentioned it until I climbed up to examine the upper building. They said it was the abode of el dueño de la casa, or the owner of the building. I immediately proposed to descend, but the old Indian begged me not to do so, and said apprehensively to the others, "Who knows but that he will meet with the owner?" I immediately sent for rope, lantern, and matches; and, absurd as it may seem, as I looked upon the wild figures of the Indians standing round the hole, and their earnest faces, it was really exciting to hear them talk of the owner. As there was a difficulty in procuring rope, I had a sapling cut and let down the hole, by means of which I descended with a lantern. The news of my intention and of the preparations going on had spread among the Indians, and all

Plate IX

LABNAH.

53

left off work and hurried to the spot. The hole was about four feet deep, and, just as my head sunk below the surface, I was startled by an extraordinary scratching and scampering, and a huge iguana ran along the wall, and escaped through the orifice by which I had entered.

The chamber was entirely different in shape from those I had seen before. The latter were circular, and had dome-shaped ceilings. This had parallel walls and the triangular-arched ceiling; in fact, it was in shape exactly like the apartments above ground. It was eleven feet long, seven wide, and ten high to the centre of the arch. The walls and ceiling were plastered, and the floor was of cement, all hard and in a good state of preservation. A centipede was the only tenant after the evasion of the iguana.

While I was making these measurements, the Indians kept up a low conversation around the hole. A mystery hung around it, transmitted to them by their fathers, and connected with an indefinable sense of apprehension. This mystery might have been solved at any time in five minutes, but none of them had ever thought of doing it, and the old man begged me to come out, saying that if I died they would have to answer for it. Their simplicity and credulity seem hardly credible. They had all sense enough to take their hands out of the fire without being told, but probably to this day they believe that in that hole is the owner of the building. When I came out they looked at me with admiration. They told me that there were other places of the same kind, but they would not show them to me, lest some accident should happen; and as my attempt drew them all from work, and I could not promise myself any satisfactory result, I refrained from insisting.

This chamber was formed in the roof of the lower building. That building contained two corridors, and we had always supposed that the great interval between the arches of the parallel corridors was a solid mass of masonry. The discovery of this chamber brought to light a new feature in the construction of these buildings. Whether the other roofs, or any of them, contained chambers, it is impossible to say. Not suspecting anything of the kind, we had made no search for them, and they may exist, but with the holes covered up and hidden by the growth and decay of vegetation. Heretofore I had inclined to the opinion that the subterraneous chambers I had met with were intended for cisterns or reservoirs of water. The position of this in the roof of a building seemed adverse to such an idea, as, in case of a breach, the water might find its way into the apartment below.

The Ramon Tree

At the foot of the terrace was a tree, hiding part of the building. Though holding trees in some degree of reverence, around these ruined cities it was a great satisfaction to hear them fall. This one was a noble ramon, which I had ordered to be cut down, and being engaged in another direction, I returned, and found that the Indians had not done so, and they said it was so hard that it would break their axes. These little axes seemed hardly capable of making any impression upon the trunk, and I gave them directions, perhaps still more barbarous, to cut away the branches and leave the trunk. They hesitated, and one of them said, in a deprecating tone, that this tree served as food for horses and cattle, and their mistress had always charged them not to cut down such. The poor fellow seemed perplexed between the standing orders of the rancho and the special instructions to do what I required.

The ramon tree was growing out of the mouth of a cave which the Indians said was an ancient well. I should perhaps not have observed it, but for the discussion about cutting down the tree. I had no great disposition for another subterraneous scramble, but descended the cavity or opening for the purpose of taking a bird's-eye view of the mouth. On one side was a great ledge of stone projecting as a roof, and under this was a passage in the rock, choked up by masses of fallen stone. It was impossible to continue if I had been so disposed, but there was every reason to believe that formerly there had been some wild passage through the rocks as at Xcoch and Chack, which led to a subterraneous deposite of water, and that this had been one of the sources from which the ancient inhabitants procured their supply.

From the number of Indians at our command, and their alacrity in working, we had been enabled to accomplish much in a very short time. In three days they finished all that I required of them. When I dismissed them, I gave a half dollar extra to be divided among seventeen, and as I was going away Bernabé exclaimed, "Ave Maria, que gracias dan a vd." "Ave Maria, what thanks they give you."

The evening closed with a general gathering of the Indians under the arbour in front of the casa real. Before setting out in the morning the alcalde asked me whether I wished them to assemble for the purpose of talking with them, and we had provided for their entertainment a sheep and a turkey, to which Bernaldo had devoted the day. At sundown all was ready. We insisted upon seating the old alcalde on a chair. Bernaldo served out meat and tortillas, and the alcalde presided over the agua ardiente, which, as it was purchased of himself, and to prove that it was not bad, he tasted before serving the rest, and took his share afterward. Supper over, we began our conversation, which consisted entirely of questions on our part and answers on theirs, a manner of discourse even in civilized life difficult to be kept up long. There was no unwillingness to give information, but there was a want of communicativeness which made all intercourse with them unprofitable and unsatisfactory. In fact, however, they had nothing to communicate; they had no stories or traditions; they knew nothing of the origin of the ruined buildings; these were standing when they were born; had existed in the time of their fathers; and the old men said that they had fallen much within their own memory. In one point, however, they differed from the Indians of Uxmal and Zayi. They had no superstitious feelings with regard to the ruins, were not afraid to go to them at night, or to sleep in them; and when we told them of the music that was heard sounding among the old buildings of Zayi, they said that if it were heard among these, they would all go and dance to it.

There were other vestiges and mounds, all, however, in a ruinous condition. The last day, while Mr. Catherwood was finishing at Labnà, I rode with Bernaldo to the hacienda of Tabi, two leagues distant, which, and those of Xcanchakan, already presented in these pages, and Vayalke, belonging to the Señora Joaquina Peon, where we stopped on our first visit to Uxmal, were distinguished as the three finest in Yucatan. Before the gate were some noble seybo trees, and near it a tiendicita, or small shop, supplied with articles adapted to the wants of the Indians appertaining to the hacienda. The great yard was lined with buildings, among which were the church and an enclosure for a bullfight, prepared for a festival which was to commence the next day. In the wall of the hacienda were sculptured ornaments from the ruins of ancient buildings. At the foot of the steps was a double-headed eagle, well carved, holding in his claws a sort of sceptre, and underneath were the figures of two tigers four feet high. In the back of the house was a projecting stone figure, with its mouth open, an uncomfortable expression of face, arms akimbo, and hands pressing the sides, as if in a qualmish state. It was used as a water-spout, and a stream was pouring out of the mouth. The buildings from which these stones were taken were near the hacienda, but were mere piles of ruins. They had furnished materials for the construction of the church, walls, and all the edifices on the hacienda.

Besides this there was a great cave, of which I had heard in Merida from the owner, who said he had never visited it, but wished me to do so, and he would read my description of it. The major domo was an intelligent Mestizo, who had been at the cave, and confirmed all the accounts I had heard of it, of sculptured figures of men and animals, pillars, and a chapel of rock under the earth. He furnished me with a vaquero as a guide and a relief horse, and, setting out, a short distance from the hacienda we turned into a tree-encumbered path, so difficult to pass through that, before we had gone far, it seemed quite reasonable in the owner to content himself with reading our description of the cave, without taking the trouble to see it for himself. The vaquero was encased in the equipments with which that class ride into the woods after cattle. His dress was a small, hard, heavy straw hat, cotton shirt, drawers, and sandals; over his body a thick jacket, or overall, made of tanned cowhide, with the sleeves reaching below his hands, and standing out as if made of wood; his saddle had large leather flaps, which folded back and protected his naked legs, and leather stirrup flaps to protect his feet. Where he dashed through the bushes and briers unharmed, my thin blues got caught and torn; but he knew what garrapatas were, and said with emphasis, "Estos chicos son muy Demonios." "Those little ones are the very d—l."

At the distance of a league we reached the cave, and, tying our horses, descended by a great chasm to the depth of perhaps two hundred feet, when we found ourselves under a great shelf of overhanging rock, the cavern being dark as we advanced, but all at once lighted up from beyond by a perpendicular orifice, and exhibiting in the background magnificent stalactites, picturesque blocks and fragments of rock, which, in the shadows of the background, assumed all manner of fantastic shapes, and, from their fancied resemblance, had been called the figures of men and animals, pillars and chapels. I saw at once that there was another disappointment for me; there were no monuments of art, and had never been anything artificial; but the cave itself, being large and open, and lighted in several places by orifices above, was so magnificent that, notwithstanding the labour and disappointment, I did not regret my visit. I passed two hours in wandering through it, returned to the hacienda to dine, and it was after dark when I reached the rancho, and for the last time had the benefit of its well in the shape of a warm bath. Throughout Yucatan, every Indian, however poor, has, as part of the furniture of his hut, a baño, or sort of bathing-tub; and, next to making tortillas, the great use of a wife is to have warm water ready for him when he returns from his work. We had not the latter convenience, but at this place, for a medio, we had the alcalde's baño every evening. It was a wooden dug-out, flat bottomed, about three feet long, eighteen inches wide, three or four inches deep, and bathing in it was somewhat like bathing in the salver of a tea-table, but, covered as we were constantly with garrapata bites, mere ablution was as grateful as a Turkish or Egyptian bath.

CHAPTER IV

The next morning we resumed our journey in search of ruined cities. Our next point of destination was the rancho of Kewick, three leagues distant. Mr. Catherwood set out with the servants and luggage, Dr. Cabot and myself following in about an hour. The Indians told us there was no difficulty in finding the road, and we set out alone. About a mile from the rancho we passed a ruined building on the left, surmounted by a high wall, with oblong apertures, like that mentioned at Zayi as resembling a New-England factory. The face of the country was rolling, and more open than any we had seen. We passed through two Indian ranchos, and a league beyond came to a dividing point, where we found ourselves at a loss. Both were mere Indian footpaths, seldom or never traversed by horsemen, and, having but one chance against us, we selected that most directly in line with the one by which we had come. In about an hour the direction changed so much that we turned back, and, after a toilsome ride, reached again the dividing point, and turned into the other path. This led us into a wild savanna surrounded by hills, and very soon we found tracks leading off in different directions, among which, in a short time, we became perfectly bewildered. The whole distance to Kewick was but three leagues; we had been riding hard six hours, and began to fear that we had made a mistake in turning back, and at every step were going more astray. In the midst of our perplexities we came upon an Indian leading a wild colt, who, without asking any questions, or waiting for any from us, waved us back, and, tying his colt to a bush, led us across the plain into another path, following which some distance, he again struck across, and put us into still another, where he left us, and started to return to his colt. We were loth to lose him, and urged him to continue as our guide; but he was impenetrable until we held

FIG. 4

up a medio, when he again moved on before us. The whole region was so wild that even yet we had doubts, and hardly believed that such a path could lead to a village or rancho; but, withal, there was one interesting circumstance. In our desolate and wandering path we had seen in different places, at a distance, and inaccessible, five high mounds, holding aloft the ruins of ancient buildings; and doubtless there were more buried in the woods. At three o'clock we entered a dense forest, and came suddenly upon the casa real of Kewick, standing alone, almost buried among trees, the only habitation of any kind in sight; and, to increase the wondering interest which attended every step of our journey in that country, it stood on the platform of an ancient terrace, strewed with the relics of a ruined edifice. The steps of the terrace had fallen and been newly laid, but the walls were entire, with all the stones in place. Conspicuous in view was Mr. Catherwood with our servants and luggage, and, as we rode up, it seemed a strange confusion of things past and present, of scenes consecrated by time and those of every-day life, though Mr. Catherwood dispelled the floating visions by his first greeting, which was an assurance that the casa real was full of fleas. We tied our horses at the foot of the terrace, and ascended the steps. The casa real had mud walls and a thatched roof, and in front was an arbour. Sitting down under the arbour, with our hotel on this ancient platform, we had seldom experienced higher satisfaction on reaching a new and unknown field of ruins, though perhaps this was owing somewhat to the circumstances of finding ourselves, after a hot and perplexing ride, safely arrived at our place of destination. We had still two hours of daylight; and, anxious to have a glimpse of the ruins before night, we had some fried eggs and tortillas got ready, and while making a hasty meal, the proprietor of the rancho, attended by a party of Indians, came to pay us a visit.

This proprietor was a full-blooded Indian, the first of this ancient but degraded race whom we had seen in the position of land-owner and master. He was about forty-five years old, and highly respectable in his appearance and manners. He had inherited the land from his fathers, did not know how long it had been transmitted, but believed that it had always been in his family. The Indians on the rancho were his servants, and we had not seen in any village or on any hacienda men of better appearance, or under more excellent discipline. This produced on my mind a strong impression that, indolent, ignorant, and debased as the race is under the dominion of strangers, the Indian even now is not incapable of fulfilling the obligations of a higher station than that in which his destiny has placed him. It is not true that he is fit only to labour with his hands; he has within him that which is capable of directing the labour of others; and as this Indian master sat on the terrace, with his dependants crouching round him, I could imagine him the descendant of a long line of caciques who once reigned in the city, the ruins of which were his inheritance. Involuntarily we treated him with a respect we had never shown to an Indian before; but perhaps we were not free from the influence of feelings which govern in civilized life, and our respect may have proceeded from the discovery that our new acquaintance was a man of property, possessed not merely of acres, and Indians, and unproductive real estate, but also of that great desideratum in these trying times, ready money; for we had given Albino a dollar to purchase eggs with, who objected to it as too large a coin to be available on the rancho, but on his return informed us, with an expression of surprise, that the master had changed it the moment it was offered to him.

Our hasty dinner over, we asked for Indians to guide us to the ruins, and were somewhat startled by the objections they all made on account of the garrapatas. Since we left Uxmal the greatest of our small hardships had been the annoyance of these insects; in fact, it was by no means a small hardship. Frequently we came in contact with a bush covered with them, from which thousands swarmed upon us, like moving grains of sand, and scattered till the body itself seemed crawling. Our horses suffered, perhaps, more than ourselves, and it became a habit, whenever we dismounted, to rasp their sides with a rough stick. During the dry season the little pests are killed off by the heat of the sun, and devoured by birds, but for which I verily believe they would make the country uninhabitable. All along we had been told that the dry season was at hand, and they would soon be over; but we began to despair of any dry season, and had no hopes of getting rid of them. Nevertheless, we were somewhat startled at the warning conveyed by the reluctance of the Indians; and when we insisted upon going, they gave us another alarming intimation by cutting twigs, with which, from the moment of starting, they whipped the bushes on each side, and swept the path before them.

Beyond the woods we came out into a comparatively open field, in which we saw on all sides through the trees the Xlappahk, or old walls, now grown so familiar, a collection of vast remains and of many buildings. We worked our way to all within sight. The façades were not so much ornamented as some we had seen, but the stones were more massive, and the style of architecture was simple, severe, and grand. Nearly every house had fallen, and one long ornamented front lay on the ground cracked and doubled up as if shaken off by the vibrations of an earthquake, and still struggling to retain its upright position, the whole presenting a most picturesque and imposing scene of

Plate X

J. N. Gambardella

KEWICK

T. Fisherwood

ruins, and conveying to the mind a strong image of the besom of destruction sweeping over a city. Night came upon us while gazing at a mysterious painting, and we returned to the casa real to sleep.

Early the next morning we were again on the ground, with our Indian proprietor and a large party of his criados; and as the reader is now somewhat familiar with the general character of these ruins, I select from that great mass around only such as have some peculiarity.

The first is that represented in Plate X. It had been the principal doorway, and was all that now remained of a long line of front, which lay in ruins on the ground. It is remarkable for its simplicity, and, in that style of architecture, for its grandeur of proportions.

The apartment into which this door opened had nothing to distinguish it from hundreds of others we had seen, but in the corner one was the mysterious painting at which we were gazing the evening before, when night overtook us. The end wall had fallen inward; the others remained. The ceiling, as in all the other buildings, was formed by two sides rising to meet each other, and covered within a foot of the point of junction by a flat layer of stones. In all the other arches, without a single exception, the layer was perfectly plain: but this had a single stone distinguished by a painting, which covered the whole surface presented to view. The painting itself was curious; the colours were bright, red and green predominating; the lines clear and distinct, and the whole was more perfect than any painting we had seen. But its position surprised us more than the painting itself; it was in the most out-of-the-way spot in the whole edifice, and but for the Indians we might not have noticed it at all. Why this layer of stones was so adorned, or why this particular stone was distinguished above all others in the same layer, we were unable to discover, but we considered that it was not done capriciously nor without cause; in fact, we had long been of opinion that every stone in those ancient buildings, and every design and ornament that decorated them, had some certain though now inscrutable meaning.

Figure 5 represents this painting. It exhibits a rude human figure, surrounded by hieroglyphics, which doubtless contain the whole of its story. It is 30 inches long by 18 inches wide, and the prevailing colour is red. From its position in the wall, it was impossible to draw it without getting it out and lowering it to the ground, which I was anxious to accom-

Fig. 5

plish, not only for the sake of the drawing, but for the purpose of carrying it away. I had apprehensions that the proprietor would make objections, for both he and the Indians had pointed it out as the most curious part of the ruins; but, fortunately, they had no feeling about it, and were all ready to assist in any way we directed. The only way of getting at it was by digging down through the roof; and, as usual, a friendly tree was at hand to assist us in the ascent. The roof was flat, made of stone and mortar cemented together, and several feet in thickness. The Indians had no crowbar, but loosening the mortar with their machetes, and prying apart the stones by means of hard wood saplings with the points sharpened, they excavated down to the layer on the top of the arch. The stone lapped over about a foot on each side, and was so heavy that it was impossible to hoist it out of the hole; our only way, therefore, was to lower it down into the apartment. The master sent some Indians to the rancho to search for ropes, and, as a measure of precaution, I had branches cut, and made a bed several feet thick under the stone. Some of the Indians still at work were preparing to let it fall, when Dr. Cabot, who was fortunately on the roof at the time, put a stop to their proceedings.

The Indians returned with the rope, and while lowering the stone one of the strands broke, and it came thundering down, but the bed of branches saved the painting from destruction.

The proprietor made no objections to my carrying it away, but it was too heavy for a mule-load, and the Indians would not undertake to carry it on their shoulders. The only way of removing it was to have it cut down to a portable size; and when we left, the proprietor accompanied me to the village to procure a stonecutter for that purpose, but there was none in the village, nor any chance of one within twenty-seven miles. Unable to do anything with the stone, I engaged the proprietor to place it in an apartment sheltered from rain; and, if I do not mistake the character of my Indian friend and inheritor of a ruined city, it now lies subject to my order; and I hereby authorize the next American traveller to bring it away at his own expense, and deposite it in the National Museum at Washington.

I shall present but one more view from the ruins of Kewick. It is part of the front of a long building, forming a right angle with the one last referred to. The terraces almost join, and though all was so overgrown that it was difficult to make out the plan and juxtaposition, the probability is that they formed two sides of a grand rectangular area. The whole building measures two hundred and thirty feet in length. In the centre is a wide ruined staircase leading to the top. Plate XI represents half of the building to the line of the staircase, the other half being exactly similar. The whole could not be drawn without carrying back the clearing to some distance, and consuming more time than we thought worth while to devote to it. Below the cornice the entire edifice is plain; and above it is ornamented the whole length with small circular shafts set in the wall.

The remaining ruins of Kewick we left as we found them. Fallen buildings and fragments of sculptured stone strew the ground in every direction; but it is impossible to give the reader an idea of the impress produced by wandering among them. For a brief space only we broke the stillness of the desolate city, and left it again to solitude and silence. We had reason to believe that no white man had ever seen it, and probably but few will ever do so, for every year is hurrying it on to more utter destruction.

Plate XI

CHUNHUHU

67

The same scarcity of water which we had found all over this region, except at Sabachshé, exists here also. The source which supplied the ancient city had engaged the attention of its Indian proprietor, and while Mr. Catherwood was drawing the last building, the Indians conducted us to a cave, called in their language Actum, which they supposed was an ancient well. The entrance was by a hole under an overhanging rock, passing through which by means of a tree, with branches or crotches to serve as steps, we descended to a large platform of rock. Overhead was an immense rocky roof, and at the brink of the platform was a great cavern, with precipitous sides, thirty or forty feet deep, from which the Indians supposed some passage opened that would lead to water. As we flared our torches over the chasm, it presented a scene of wildness and grandeur which, in an hour of idleness, might have tempted us to explore it; but we had more than enough to occupy our time.

Coming out from the cave, we went on to the aguada, which was nearly a league distant. It was a small, muddy pond, with trees growing on the sides and into the water, which, in any other country, would be considered an unfit watering-place for beasts. The proprietor and all the Indians told us that in the dry season the remains of stone embankments were still visible, made, as they supposed, by the ancient inhabitants. The bank was knee deep with mud; a few poles were laid out on supporters driven into the mud, and along these the Indians walked to dip up water. At the time our horses were brought down to drink; but they had to be watered out of the calabashes or drinking-cups of the Indians.

At two o'clock we returned to the casa real. We had "done up" another ruined city, and were ready to set out again; but we had one serious impediment in the way. I have mentioned that on our arrival at this place we gave Albino a dollar, but I omitted to say that it was our last. On setting out on this journey, we had reduced our personal luggage to hammocks and petaquillas, the latter being oblong straw baskets without fastenings, unsafe to carry money in, and silver, the only available coin, was too heavy to carry about the person. At Sabachshé we discovered that our expenses had overrun our estimates, and sent Albino back to Nohcacab with the keys of our money trunk, and directions to follow us in all haste to this place. The time calculated for his overtaking us had passed, and he did not come. We should have thought nothing of a little delay but for our pressing necessities. Some accident might have happened to him, or the temptation might have been too strong. Our affairs were approaching a crisis, and the barbarism of the people of the country in matters of finance was hurrying it on. If we wanted a fowl, food for horses, or an Indian to work, the money must be ready at the moment. Throughout our journey it was the same; every order for the purchase of an article was null unless the money accompanied it. Brought up under the wings of credit, this system was always odious to us. We could attempt nothing on a liberal and enlightened scale, were always obliged to calculate our means, and could incur no expense unless we had the money to defray it on the spot. This, of course, trammelled enterprise, and now, on a mere miscalculation, we were brought suddenly to a stand still. On counting the scattering medios of private stock, we found that we had enough to pay for transporting our luggage to the village of Xul, but if we tarried over the night and Albino did not come, both ourselves and our horses must go without rations in the morning, and then we should have no means of getting away our luggage. Which of the two to choose? Whether it was better to meet our fate at the rancho, or go on to the village and trust to fortune?

In this delicate posture of affairs, we sat down to one of Bernaldo's best miscellaneous preparations of fowls, rice, and frigoles, and finished the last meal that we were able to pay for. This over, we had recourse to a small paper of Havana cigars, three in number, containing the last of our stock, reserved for some extraordinary occasion. Satisfied that no occasion could offer when we should be more in need of extraneous support, we lighted them and sat down under the arbour, and, as the smoke rolled away, listened for the tread of the trotter. It was really perplexing to know what to do; but it was very certain that if we remained at the rancho, as soon as a medio was not forthcoming the moment it was wanted we were undone. Our chance would be better at the village, and we determined to break up and go on.

Leaving special charge for Albino to follow, at three o'clock we set out. The proprietor accompanied us, and at half past five we made a dashing entry into the village of Xul, with horses, and servants, and carriers, and just one solitary medio left.

The casa real was the poorest we had seen in the country, and, under any circumstances, it was not the place for us, for, immediately on dismounting, it would be necessary to order ramon and maize for the horses, and the money must follow the order. There was a crowd of gaping loungers around the door,

69

and if we stopped at this place we should be obliged to expose ourselves at once, without any opportunity of telling our story to advantage, or of making friends.

On the opposite side of the plaza was one of those buildings which had so often sheltered us in time of trouble, but now I hesitated to approach the convent. The fame of the cura of Xul had reached our ears; report said that he was rich, and a money-making man, and odd. Among his other possessions, he was lord of a ruined city which we proposed to visit, particularly interesting to us from the circumstance that, according to the accounts, it was then inhabited by Indians. We wished to procure from him facilities for exploring this city to advantage, and doubted whether it would be any recommendation to his favour as a rich man to begin our acquaintance by borrowing money of him.

But, although rich, he was a padre. Without dismounting, I rode over to the convent. The padre came out to meet me, and told me that he had been expecting us every day. I dismounted, and he took my horse by the bridle, led him across the corridor, through the sala, and out to the yard. He asked why my companions did not come over, and, at a signal, in a few minutes their horses followed mine through the sala.

Still we were not entirely at ease. In Yucatan, as in Central America, it is the custom for a traveller, whether he alights at the casa real, convent, or the hacienda of a friend, to buy ramon and maize for his horses; and it is no lack of hospitality in the host, after providing a place for the beasts, to pay no more attention to them. This might have brought on a premature explanation; but presently four Indians appeared, each with a great back-load of ramon. We ventured to give a hint about maize, and in a moment all anxiety about our horses was at an end, and we had the whole evening to manage for ourselves.

Don José Gulielmo Roderigues, the cura of Xul, was a Guachapino, or native of Old Spain, of which, like all the old Spaniards in the country, he was somewhat proud. He was educated a Franciscan friar; but thirty years before, on account of the revolutions and the persecution of his order, he fled from Spain, and took refuge in Yucatan. On the destruction of the Franciscan Convent in Merida, and the breaking up of the Franciscan monks, he secularized, and entered the regular church; had been cura of Ticul and Nohcacab; and about ten years before had been appointed to the district of Xul. His curacy was one of those called beneficiaries; *i.e.*, in consideration of building the church, keeping it in repair, and performing the duties and services of a priest, the capitation tax paid by the Indians, and the fees allowed for baptism, marriages, masses, salves, and funeral services, after deducting one seventh for the Church, belonged to himself personally. At the time of his appointment, the place now occupied by the village was a mere Indian rancho. The land comprehended in his district was, in general, good for maize, but, like all the rest of that region, it was destitute of water, or, at least, but badly supplied. His first object had been to remedy this deficiency, to which end he had dug a well two hundred feet deep, at an expense of fifteen hundred dollars. Besides this, he had large and substantial cisterns, equal to any we had seen in the country, for the reception of rain-water; and, by furnishing this necessary of life in abundance, he had drawn around him a population of seven thousand.

But to us there was something more interesting than this creation of a village and a population in the wilderness, for here, again, was the same strange mingling of old things with new. The village stands on the site of an aboriginal city. In the corner of the plaza now occupied by the cura's house, the yard of which contains the well and cisterns, once stood a pyramidal mound with a building upon it. The cura had himself pulled down this mound, and levelled it so that nothing was left to indicate even the place where it stood. With the materials he had built the house and cisterns, and portions of the ancient edifice now formed the walls of the new. With singular good taste, showing his practical turn of mind, and at the same time a vein of antiquarian feeling, he had fixed in conspicuous places, when they answered his purpose, many of the old carved stones. The convent and church occupied one side of the plaza; along the corridor of the former was a long seat of time-polished stones taken from the ruins of an ancient building, and in every quarter might be seen these memorials of the past, connecting links between the living and the dead, and serving to keep alive the memory of the fact, which, but for them, would in a few years be forgotten, that on this spot once stood an ancient Indian city.

But the work upon which the padre prided himself most, and which, perhaps, did him most credit, was the church. It was one of the few the erection of which had been undertaken of late years, when the time had gone by for devoting the labour of a whole village to such works; and it presents a combination of simplicity, convenience, and good taste, in better keeping with the spirit of the age than the gigantic but tottering structures in the other villages, while it is not less attractive in the eyes of the Indians. The cura employed an amanuensis to write out a description of the church, as he said, for me to publish in my work, which, however, I am obliged to omit, mentioning only that over the principal altar were sixteen columns from the ruins at the *rancho* of Nohcacab, which were the next we proposed to visit.

During the evening we had a levée of all the principal white inhabitants, to the number of about six or eight. Among them was the proprietor of the *rancho* and ruins of Nohcacab, to whom we were introduced by the cura, with a tribute to our antiquarian, scientific, and medical attainments, which showed an appreciation of merit it was seldom our good fortune to meet with. The proprietor could give us very little information about the ruins, but undertook to make all the necessary arrangements for our exploration of them, and to accompany us himself.

At that moment we stood upon a giddy height. To ask the loan of a few dollars might lower us materially. The evening was wearing away without any opportunity of entering upon this interesting subject, when, to our great satisfaction, we heard the clattering of horses' hoofs, and Albino made his appearance. The production of a bag of dollars fixed us in our high position, and we were able to order Indians for the rancho of Nohcacab the next day. We finished the evening with a warm bath in a hand-basin, under the personal direction of the cura, which relieved somewhat the burning of garrapata bites, and then retired to our hammocks.

CHAPTER V

Early the next morning we set out for the rancho of Nohcacab, three leagues distant. The proprietor had gone before daylight, to receive us on the ground. We had not gone far when Mr. C. complained of a slight headache, and wishing to ride moderately, Dr. Cabot and myself went on, leaving him to follow with the luggage. The morning air was fresh and invigorating, and the country rolling, hilly, and picturesque. At the distance of two leagues we reached what was called a hebe, or fountain. It was a large rocky basin, about ninety feet in circumference and ten feet deep, which served as a receptacle for rain-water. In that dry country it was a grateful spectacle, and beside it was a large seybo tree, that seemed inviting the traveller to repose under its branches. We watered our horses from the same waccal, or drinking cup, that we used ourselves, and felt strongly tempted to take a bath, but, with our experience of fever and ague, were afraid to run the risk. This fountain was a league from the rancho to which we were going, and was the only watering-place for its inhabitants.

At nine o'clock we reached the rancho, which showed the truth of the Spanish proverb, "La vista del amo engorda el caballo;" "The sight of the master fattens the horse." The first huts were enclosed by a well-built stone wall, along which appeared, in various places, sculptured fragments from the ruins. Beyond was another wall, enclosing the hut occupied by the master on his visits to the rancho, the entrance to which was by a gateway formed of two sculptured monuments of curious design and excellent workmanship, raising high our expectations in regard to the ruins on this rancho, and sustaining the accounts we had heard of them.

The proprietor was waiting to receive us, and, having taken possession of an empty hut, and disposed of our horses, we accompanied him to look over the rancho. What he regarded as most worth showing was his tobacco crop, lying in some empty huts to dry, which he contemplated with great satisfaction, and the well, which he looked at with as much sorrow. It was three hundred and fifty-four feet deep, and even at this great depth it was dry.

While we were thus engaged, our baggage carriers arrived with intelligence that Mr. Catherwood was taken ill, and they had left him lying in the road. I immediately applied to the proprietor for a coché and Indians, and he, with great alacrity, undertook to get them ready; in the mean time I saddled my horse and hastened back to Mr. Catherwood, whom I found lying on the ground, with Albino by his side, under the shade of the tree by the fountain, with an ague upon him, wrapped up in all the coverings he could muster, even to the saddlecloths of the horses. While he was in this state, two men came along, bestriding the same horse, and bringing sheets and ponchas to make a covering for the coché; then came a straggling line of Indians, each with a long poie, and withes to lash them together; and it was more than an hour before the coché was ready. The path was narrow, and lined on each side with thorn bushes, the spikes of which stuck in the naked flesh of the Indians as they carried the coché, and they were obliged to stop frequently and disentangle themselves. On reaching the rancho I found Doctor Cabot down with a fever. From the excitement and anxiety of following Mr. Catherwood under the hot sun, and now finding Doctor Cabot down, a cold shivering crept over me, and in a few minutes we were all three in our hammocks. A few hours had made a great change in our condition; and we came near bringing our host down with us. He had been employed in preparing breakfast upon a large scale, and seemed mortified that there was no one to do it justice. Out of pure good feeling toward him, I had it brought to the side of my hammock. My effort made him happy, and I began to think my prostration was merely the reaction from over-excitement; and by degrees what I began to please our host I continued for my own satisfaction. The troubles of my companions no longer disturbed me. My equanimity was perfectly restored, and, breakfast over, I set out to look at the ruins.

Ever since our arrival in Yucatan we had received courtesies and civilities, but none more thorough than those bestowed by our host of Nohcacab. He had come out with the intention of passing a week with us, and the Indians and the whole rancho were at our service as long as we chose to remain.

Passing through one of the huts, we soon came to a hill covered with 'trees and very steep, up which the proprietor had cut, not a mere Indian path, but a road two or three yards wide, leading to a building standing upon a terrace on the brow of the hill. The façade above the cornice had fallen, and below it was of plain stone. The interior was entire, but without any distinguishing features. Following the brow of this hill, we came to three other buildings, all standing on the same range, and without any important variations in the details, except that in one the arch had no overlapping stone, but the two sides of the ceiling ran up to a point, and formed a complete angle. These, the Indians told us, were the only buildings that remained. That from which the pillars in the church at Xul were taken was a mere mass of ruins. I was extremely disappointed. From the accounts which had induced us to visit this place, we had made larger calculations. It was the first time I had been thoroughly disappointed. There were no subjects for the pencil, and, except the deep and abiding impression of moving among the deserted structures of another ruined and desolate city, there was nothing to carry away. The proprietor seemed mortified that he had not better ruins to show us, but I gave him to understand that it was not his fault, and that he was in nowise to blame. Nevertheless, it was really vexatious, with such good-will on his part, and such a troop of Indians at command, that there was nothing for us to do. The Indians sympathized in the mortification of their master, and, to indemnify me, told me of two other ruined cities, one of which was but two leagues from the village of Xul.

I returned and made my report, and Mr. Catherwood immediately proposed a return to the village. Albino had given him an alarming account of the unhealthiness of the rancho, and he considered it advisable to avoid sleeping there a single night. Doctor Cabot was sitting up in his hammock, dissecting a bird. A recurrence of fever might detain us some time, and we determined on returning immediately to Xul. Our decision was carried into execution as promptly as it was made, and, leaving our luggage to the care of Albino, in half an hour, to the astonishment of the Indians and the mortification of the proprietor, we were on our way to the village.

It was late in the evening when we arrived, but the cura received us as kindly as before. During the evening I made inquiries for the place of which the Indians at the rancho had told me. It was but two leagues distant, but of all who happened to drop in, not one was aware of its existence. The cura, however, sent for a young man who had a rancho in that direction, and who promised to accompany me.

At six o'clock the next morning we started, neither Mr. Catherwood nor Doctor Cabot being able to accompany me. At the distance of about two leagues we reached an Indian rancho, where we learned from an old woman that we had passed the path leading to the ruins. We could not prevail on her to go back and show us the way, but she gave us a direction to another rancho, where she said we could procure a guide. This rancho was situated in a small clearing in the midst of the woods, enclosed by a bush fence, and before the door was an arbour covered with palm leaves, with little hammocks swinging under it, and all together the picture of Indian comfort.

My companion went in, and I dismounted, thinking that this promised a good stopping-place, when, looking down, I saw my pantaloons brown with garrapatas. I laid hold of a twig, intending to switch them off, and hundreds fell upon my hand and arm. Getting rid of those in sight as well as I could, and mounting immediately, I rode off, hoping most earnestly not to find any ruins, nor any necessity of taking up our abode in this comfortable-seeming rancho.

We were fortunate in finding at this place an Indian, who, for reasons known to himself and the wife of the master, was making a visit during the absence of the latter at his milpa; but for which we should not have been able to procure a guide. Retracing our steps, and crossing the camino real, we entered the woods on the other side, and tying our horses, the Indian cut a path up the side of a hill, on the top of which were the ruins of a building. The outer wall had fallen, leaving exposed to view the inner half of the arch, by which, as we approached it, my attention was strongly attracted. This arch was plastered and covered with painted figures in profile, much mutilated, but in one place a row of legs remained, which seemed to have belonged to a procession, and at the first glance brought to my mind the funeral processions on the walls of the tombs at Thebes. In the triangular wall forming the end of the room were three compartments, in which were figures, some having their heads adorned with plumes, others with a sort of steeple cap, and carrying on their heads something like a basket; and two were standing on their hands with their heels in the air. These figures were about a foot high, and painted red. The drawing was good, the attitudes were spirited and life-like, and altogether, even in their mutilated state, they were by far the most interesting paintings we had seen in the country.

Another apartment had been plastered and covered with paintings, the colours of which were in some places still bright and vivid. In this apartment we cornered and killed a snake five feet long, and as I threw it out at the door a strong picture rose up before me of the terrific scenes which must have been enacted in this region; the cries of wo that must have ascended to Heaven when these sculptured and painted edifices were abandoned, to become the dwelling-place of vultures and serpents.

There was one other building, and these two, my guide said, were all, but probably others lie buried in the woods. Returning to our horses, he led me to another extraordinary subterraneous well, which probably furnished water to the ancient inhabitants. I looked into the mouth, and saw that the first descent was by a steep ladder, but had no disposition to explore it.

In a few minutes we mounted to return to the village. Ruins were increasing upon us, to explore which thoroughly would be the work of years; we had but months, and were again arrested by illness. For some days, at least, Mr. Catherwood would not be able to resume work. I was really distressed by the magnitude of what was before us, but, for the present, we could do nothing, and I determined at once to change the scene. The festival of Ticul was at hand, and that night it was to open with el báyle de las Mestizas, or the Mestiza ball. Ticul lay in our return route, nine leagues from the village of Xul, but I determined to reach it that evening. My companion did not sympathize in my humour; his vaquero saddle hurt him, and he could not ride faster than a walk. I had need to economize all my strength; but I took his hard-trotting horse and uneasy saddle, and gave him mine. Pushing on, at eleven o'clock we reached Xul, where I had my horse unsaddled and washed, ordered him a good mess of corn, and two boiled eggs for myself. In the mean time, Mr. Catherwood had a recurrence of fever and ague, and my horse was led away; but the attack proved slight, and I had him brought out again. At two o'clock I resumed my journey, with a sheet, a hammock, and Albino. The heat was scorching, and Albino would have grumbled at setting out at this hour, but he, too, was ripe for the fiesta of Ticul.

In an hour we saw in the woods on our right large mounds, indicating that here, too, had once stood an ancient city. I rode in to look at them, but the buildings which had crowned them were all fallen and ruined, and I only gained an addition to the stock of garrapatas already on hand. We had not heard of these ruins at the village, and, on inquiring afterward, I could find no name for them.

At the distance of three leagues we commenced ascending the sierra, and for two hours the road lay over an immense ledge of solid rock. Next to the Mico Mountain, it was the worst range I ever crossed, but of entirely different character; instead of gullies, and holes, and walls of mud, it consisted of naked, broken rock, the reflection of the sun upon which was intense and extremely painful to the eyes. In some places it was slippery as glass. I had crossed the sierra in two different places before, but they were comparatively like the passage of the Simplon with that of San Bernard or San Gothard across the Alps. My horse's hoofs clattered and rang at every step, and, though strong and sure-footed, he stumbled and slid in a way that was painful and dangerous to both horse and rider; indeed, it would have been an agreeable change to be occasionally stuck in the mud. It was impossible to go faster than a walk, and, afraid that night would overtake us, in which case, as there was no moon, we might lose our way, I dismounted and hurried on, leading my horse.

It was nearly dark when we reached the top of the last range. The view was the grandest I had seen in the country. On the very brink stood the church of La Hermita, below the village of Oxcutzcab, and beyond a boundless wooded plain, dotted in three places with villages. We descended by a steep and stony path, and, winding along the front of La Hermita, came upon a broad pavement of stones from the ruined buildings of an aboriginal town. We passed under an imposing gateway, and, entering the village, stopped at the first house for a draught of water, where, looking back, we saw the shades of night gathering over the sierra, a token of our narrow escape. There were ruined mounds in the neighbourhood, which I intended to look at in passing, but we had still four leagues to make, and pushed on. The road was straight and level, but stony, and very soon it became so dark that we could see nothing. My horse had done a hard day's work, and stumbled so that I could scarcely keep him from falling. We roused the barking dogs of two villages, of which, however, I could distinguish nothing but the outline of their gigantic churches, and at nine o'clock rode into the plaza of Ticul. It was crowded with Indians, blazing with lights, and occupied by a great circular scaffold for a bull-ring, and a long, enclosed arbour, from the latter of which strains of music gave notice that the báyle de las Mestizas had already begun.

Once more I received a cordial welcome from the cura Carillo; but the music from the arbour reminded me that the moments of pleasure were fleeting. Our trunks had been ordered over from Nohcacab, and, making a hurried toilet, I hastened to the ball-room, accompanied by the padre Brizeña; the crowd outside opened a way, Don Philippe Peon beckoned to me as I entered, and in a moment more I was seated in one of the best places at the báyle de las Mestizas. After a month in Indian ranchos, that day toiling among ruins, almost driven to distraction by garrapatas, clambering over a frightful sierra, and making a journey worse than any sixty miles in our country, all at once I settled down at a fancy ball, amid music, lights, and pretty women, in the full enjoyment of an armchair and a cigar. For a moment a shade of regret came over me as I thought of my invalid friends, but I soon forgot them.

The enramada, or enclosure for the ball-room, was an arbour about one hundred and fifty feet long and fifty feet wide, surrounded by a railing of rude lattice-work, covered with costal, or hemp bagging, as a protection against the night air and sun, and lighted by lamps with large glass shades. The floor was of hard cement; along the railing was a row of chairs, all occupied by ladies; gentlemen, boys, and girls, children and nurses, were sitting promiscuously on the floor, and Don Philippe Peon, when he gave me his chair, took a place among them. El báyle de las Mestizas was what might be called a fancy ball, in which the señoritas of the village appeared as las Mestizas, or in the costume of Mestiza women: loose white frock, with red worked border round the neck and skirt, a man's black hat, a blue scarf over the shoulder, gold nekclace and bracelets. The young men figured as vaqueros, or major domos, in shirt and pantaloons of pink striped muslin, yellow buckskin shoes, and low, round-crowned, hard-platted straw hat, with narrow brim rolled up at the sides, and trimmed with gold cord and tassels. Both costumes were fanciful and pretty, but at first the black hat was repulsive.

I had heard of the sombreros negros as part of the Mestiza costume, and had imagined some neat and graceful fabric of straw; but the faces of the girls were so soft and mild that even a man's hat could not divest them of their feminine charm. Altogether the scene was somewhat different from what I expected, more refined, fanciful, and picturesque.

To sustain the fancy character, the only dance was that of the toros. A vaquero stood up, and each Mestiza was called out in order. This dance, as we had seen it among the Indians, was extremely uninteresting, and required a movement of the body, a fling of the arms, and a snapping of the fingers, which were at least inelegant; but with las Mestizas of Ticul it was all graceful and pleasing, and there was something particularly winning in the snapping of the fingers. There were no dashing beauties, and not one who seemed to have any idea of being a belle; but all exhibited a mildness, softness, and amiability of expression that created a feeling of promiscuous tenderness. Sitting at ease in an arm-chair, after my sojourn in Indian ranchos, I was particularly alive to these influences. And there was such a charm about that Mestiza dress. It was so clean, simple, and loose, leaving

> "Every beauty free
> To sink or swell as Nature pleases."

The ball broke up too soon, when I was but beginning to reap the fruit of my hard day's work. There was an irruption of servants to carry home the chairs, and in half an hour, except along a line of tables in front of the audiencia, the village was still. For a little while, in my quiet chamber at the convent, the gentle figures of las Mestizas still haunted me, but, worn down by the fatigues of the day, I very soon forgot them.

At daylight the next morning the ringing of bells and firing of rockets announced the continuance of the fiesta; high mass was performed in the church, and at eight o'clock there was a grand exhibition of lassoing cattle in the plaza by amateur vaqueros. These were now mounted, had large vaquero saddles, spurs to match, and each was provided with a coil of rope in hand; bulls of two years old were let loose in the plaza, with the bull-ring to double round, and every street in the village open to them. The amateurs rode after them like mad, to the great peril of old people, women, and children, who scampered out of the way as well as they could, but all as much pleased with the sport as the bull or the vaqueros. One horse fell and hurt his rider, but there were no necks broken.

This over, all dispersed to prepare for the báyle de dia, or ball by daylight. I sat for an hour in the corridor of the convent, looking out upon the plaza. The sun was beaming with intense heat, and the village was as still as if some great calamity had suddenly overtaken it. At length a group was seen crossing the plaza: a vaquero escorting a Mestiza to the ball, holding over her head a red silk umbrella to protect her from the scorching rays of the sun; then an old lady and gentleman, children, and servants, a complete family group, the females all in white, with bright-coloured scarfs and shawls. Other groups appeared crossing in other directions, forming picturesque and pleasing spectacles in the plaza. I walked over to the arbour. Although in broad daylight, under the glare of a midday sun, and shaded only on one side by hemp bagging, as the Mestizas took their seats they seemed prettier than the night before. No adjustment of curtain light was necessary for the morning after the ball, for the ladies had retired at an early hour. The black hat had lost its repugnant character, and on some it seemed most becoming. The costumes of the vaqueros, too, bore well the light of day. The place was open to all who chose to enter, and the floor was covered with Indian women and children, and real Mestizoes in cotton shirts, drawers, and sandals; the barrier, too, was lined with a dense mass of Indians and Mestizoes, looking on good-humouredly at this personification of themselves and their ways. The whole gathering was more informal and gayer, and seemed more what it was intended to be, a fiesta of the village.

The báyle de dia was intended to give a picture of life at a hacienda, and there were two prominent personages, who did not appear the evening before, called fiscales, being the officers attendant upon the ancient caciques, and representing them in their authority over the Indians. These wore long, loose, dirty camisas hanging off one shoulder, and with the sleeves below the hands; calzoncillos, or drawers, to match, held up by a long cotton sash, the ends of which dangled below the knees; sandals, slouching straw hats, with brims ten or twelve inches wide, and long locks of horse hair hanging behind their ears. One of them wore awry over his shoulder a mantle of faded blue cotton cloth, said to be an heirloom descended from an ancient cacique, and each flourished a leather whip with eight or ten lashes. These were the managers and masters of ceremonies, with absolute and unlimited authority over the whole company, and, as they boasted, they had a right to whip the Mestizas if they pleased.

As each Mestiza arrived they quietly put aside the gentleman escorting her, and conducted the lady to her seat. If the gentleman did not give way readily, they took him by the shoulders, and walked him to the other end of the floor. A crowd followed wherever they moved, and all the time the company was assembling they threw everything into laughter and confusion by their whimsical efforts to preserve order.

At length they undertook to clear a space for dancing, backing the company in a summary way as far as they could go, and then taking the men and boys by the shoulder, and jamming them down upon the floor. While they were thus engaged, a stout gentleman, of respectable appearance, holding some high office in the village, appeared in the doorway, quietly lighting another straw cigar, and as soon as they saw him they desisted from the work they had in hand, and, in the capricious and wanton exercise of their arbitrary power, rushed across, seized him, dragged him to the centre of the floor, hoisted him upon the shoulders of a vaquero, and, pulling apart the skirts of his coat, belaboured him with a mock vigour and earnestness that convulsed the whole company with laughter. The sides of the elevated dignitary shook, the vaquero shook under him, and they were near coming down together.

This over, the rogues came directly upon me. El Ingles had not long escaped their eye. I had with difficulty avoided a scene, and my time seemed now to have come. The one with the cacique's mantle led the way with long strides, lash raised in the air, a loud voice, and his eyes, sparkling with frolic and mischief, fastened upon mine. The crowd followed, and I was a little afraid of an attempt to hoist me too on the shoulders of a vaquero; but all at once he stopped short, and, unexpectedly changing his language, opened upon me with a loud harangue in Maya. All knew that I did not understand a word he said, and the laugh was strong against me. I was a little annoyed at being made such a mark, but, recollecting the achievement of our vernacular at Nohcacab, I answered him with an English oration. The effect was instantaneous. He had never before heard a language that he could not understand, bent his ear earnestly, as if by close attention he could catch the meaning, and looked up with an air of real perplexity that turned the laugh completely against him. He began again, and I answered with a stanza of Greek poetry, which had hung by me in some unaccountable way; this, again, completely silenced him, and he dropped the title Ingles, put his arms around my neck, called me."amigo," and made a covenant not to speak in any language but Castilian.

This over, he ordered the music to commence, planted a vaquero on the floor, and led out a Mestiza to dance, again threw all the bystanders into confusion, and sat down quietly on the floor at my feet. All the Mestizas were again called out in order, presenting the same pretty spectacle I had seen the evening before. And there was one whom I had noticed then, not more than fifteen, delicate and fragile, with eyes so soft and dovelike that it was impossible to look upon them without a feeling of tenderness. She seemed sent into the world to be cherished and cared for, and closeted like the finest china, the very emblem of purity, innocence, and loveliness; and, as I had learned, she was the child of shame, being the crianza, or natural daughter, of a gentleman of the village; perhaps it was that she seemed so ill fitted to buffet with contumely and reproach that gave such an indescribable interest to her appearance; but, fortunately, brought up in her father's house, she may go through life without meeting an averted face, or feeling that a stain rests upon her name.

As may be supposed, the presence of this señorita on the floor did not escape the keen eyes of the mercurial fiscal. All at once he became excited and restless, and, starting to his feet, gazed at her for a moment as if entranced by a vision, and then, as if carried away by his excitement, and utterly unconscious of what he was about, he pushed aside the vaquero who was dancing with her, and, flinging his sombrero on the ground, cried out in a tone of ecstacy, "Voy baylár con vd, mi corazon!" "I am going to dance with you, my heart!" As he danced, his excitement seemed to increase; forgetting everything around him, the expression of his face became rapt, fixed, intense; he tore off his cacique's mantle, and, dancing toward her, spread it at the lady's feet. This seemed only to excite him more; and, as if forgetful of everything else, he seized the collar of his camisa, and, dancing violently all the time, with a nervous grasp, tugged as if he meant to pull it over his head, and throw all that he was worth at her feet. Failing in this, for a moment he seemed to give up in despair, but all at once he thrust his hands under the long garment, seized the sash around his waist, and, still dancing with all his might, unwound it, and, moving up to her with mingled grace, gallantry, and desperation, dropped it at her feet, and danced back to his place. By this time his calzoncillos, kept up by the sash, were giving way. Grasping them furiously, and holding them up with both hands, as if by a great effort, he went on dancing with a desperate expression of face that was irresistibly ludicrous.

During all this time the company was convulsed with laughter, and I could not help remarking the extreme modesty and propriety of the young lady, who never even smiled or looked at him, but, when the dance was ended, bowed and returned to her seat. The poor fiscal stood gazing at the vacant place where she had stood, as if the sun of his existence had set. At length he turned his head and called out "amigo," asked if there were any such Mestizas in my country; if I would like to take her home with me; then said that he could not spare this one, but I might take my choice of the others; insisting loudly upon my making a selection, and promising to deliver any one I liked to me at the convent.

At first I supposed that these fiscales were, like the vaqueros, the principal young men of the village, who, for that day, gave themselves up to frolic and fun, but I learned that these were not willing to assume such a character, but employed others known to them for wit and humour, and, at the same time, for propriety and respectability of behaviour. This was a *matador de cochinos*, or pig butcher, of excellent character, and *muy vivo*, by which may be understood "a fellow of infinite wit and humour." The people of the village seemed to think that the power given him to whip the Mestizas was the extremity of license, but they did consider that, even for the day, they put him on equal terms with those who, in his daily walks, were to him as beings of another sphere; for the time he might pour out his tribute of feeling to beauty and attraction, but it was all to be regarded as a piece of extravagance, to be forgotten by all who heard it, and particularly by her to whom it was addressed. Alas, poor matador de cochinos!

According to the rules, the mantle and sash which he had thrown at the feet of the lady belonged to her, and he was obliged to appeal to the charity of the spectators for money to redeem them. In the mean time the dance continued. The fiscales, having once taken ground as dancers, were continually ordering the vaqueros to step aside, and taking their places. At times, too, under the direction of the fiscales, the idle vaqueros seated themselves on the ground at the head of the arbour, and all joined in the hacienda song of the vaqueria, in alternate lines of Maya and Castilian. The chorus was led by the fiscales, with a noise that drowned every other sound; and while this boisterous merriment was going on, the light figures of the Mestizas were moving in the dance.

At twelve o'clock preparations were made for a déjeûner à la fourchette, dispensing, however, with knives and forks. The centre of the floor was cleared, and an enormous earthen jar, equal in capacity to a barrel, was brought in, containing frigoles, or black beans fried. Another vessel of the same size had a preparation of eggs and meat, and near them was a small mountain of tortillas, with all which it was the business of the Mestizas to serve the company. The fiscal did not neglect his amigo, but led to me one of whom I had expressed my opinion to him in confidence, and who brought in the palm of her hand a layer of tortillas, with frigoles in the centre, and turned up at the sides by means of the fingers, so as to prevent the frigoles from escaping. An attempt to acknowledge the civility was repressed by the fiscal, who crowded my hat over my eyes, saying that they passed no compliments on the haciendas, and we were all Indians together. The tortillas, with the frigoles in them, were not easy to hold without endangering my only pair of white pantaloons. I relieved myself by passing them over the railing, where any number of Indians stood ready to receive them; but I had hardly got rid of this when another Mestiza brought another portion, and while this engaged my one hand a third placed tortillas with eggs in the other, and left me afraid to move; but I contrived to pass both handfuls over the railing. Breakfast over, the dancing was resumed with new spirit. The fiscales were more amusing than ever; all agreed that the ball was muy allégre, or very gay, and I could not but notice that, amid all this motley company and extraordinary license, there was less noise than in a private drawing-room at home. At two o'clock, to my great regret, the ball of las Mestizas broke up. It was something entirely new, and remains engraven on my mind as the best of village balls.

CHAPTER VI

In the afternoon commenced the first bullfight. The bull-fights of Ticul had a great reputation throughout the country. At the last, a toreador was killed, which gave a promise of something exciting. The young men of the village still appeared in character as vaqueros, and before the fight they had a horse-race, which consisted in riding across the ring, one at a time, in at one door and out at the other, and then racing in the same way through the other two doors. It was a fine opportunity for exhibiting horses and horsemanship, and was a sort of pony scamper.

After these came the toreadores, or bull-fighters, who, to do them justice, were by far the worst-looking men I saw in the country, or anywhere else, except, perhaps, the libellous representatives of the twelve apostles in the feet-washing scene, at which I was once a spectator in Jerusalem. They were of a mixed blood, which makes, perhaps, the worst race known, viz., the cross of the Indian and African, and called Pardos. Their complexion is a black tinge laid upon copper, and, not satisfied with the bountiful share of ugliness which nature had given them, these worthies had done something for themselves in the way of costume, which was a vile caricature of the common European dress, with some touches of their own elegant fancy. Altogether, I could imagine that they had fitted themselves out with the unclaimed wardrobe of deceased hospital patients. Their horses, being borrowed by the committee of arrangements, with the understanding that if killed they were to be paid for, were spavined, foundered, one-eyed, wretched beasts. They had saddles covered with scarlet cloths, enormous spurs, with rowels six inches long, and murderous spears, discoloured with old stains of blood. The combination of colours, particularly the scarlet, was intended to frighten the bull, and all together they were almost enough to frighten el demonio.

The races over, the amateur vaqueros led in the first bull, having two real vaqueros at hand for cases of emergency. The toreadores charged upon him with spears brandished, and presenting a vivid picture of the infernals let loose; after which they dismounted and attacked him on foot. The bull was brought to bay directly under our box, and twice I saw the iron pass between his horns, enter the back of his neck with a dull, grating sound, and come out bloody, leaving a ghastly wound. At the third blow the bull staggered, struggled to sustain himself on his feet, but fell back on his haunches, and, with a feeble bellow, rolled over on his side; blood streamed from his mouth, his tongue hung out on the ground covered with dust, and in a few moments he was dead. The amateurs tied his hind legs, ropes were fastened to the saddles of two horsemen, others took hold, and as the carcase was dragged across the ring, a fair and gentle-voiced neighbour said, in a tone of surprise, "Dos caballos y seis Christianos!" "Two horses and six Christians!"

I omit the rest. From the bull-fight we again went to the ball, which, in the evening, was the báyle del etiquette, no gentleman being admitted without pantaloons. Society in Yucatan stands upon an aristocratic footing. It is divided into two great classes: those who wear pantaloons, and those who do not; the latter, and by far the most numerous body, going in calzoncillos, or drawers. The high-handed regulation of the ball of etiquette was aimed at them, and excluded many of our friends of the morning; but it did not seem to give any offence, the excluded quietly taking their places at the outside of the railing. El matador de cochinos, or the pig butcher, was admitted in drawers, but as assistant to the servants, handing refreshments to the ladies he had danced with in the morning. The whole aspect of things was changed; the vaqueros were in dress suits, or such undress as was not unbecoming at a village ball. The señoritas had thrown aside their simple Mestiza dresses, and appeared in tunicas, or frocks, made to fit the figure, or, rather, to cut the

figure in two. The Indian dances had disappeared, and qua-
drilles and contradances, waltzes and gallopades, supplied their
place. It wanted the piquancy of the báyle de las Mestizas; the
young ladies were not so pretty in their more fashionable costume. Still there was the same gentleness of expression, the
dances were slow, the music low and soft, and, in the quiet and
decorum of all, it was difficult to recognise the gay and tumul-
tuous party of the morning, and yet more difficult to believe
that these gentle and, in some cases, lovely faces, had been but a
few hours before lighted up with the barbarous excitement of
the bull-ring.

At ten the next day there was another bull-fight; then a
horse-race from the plaza down the principal street to the house
of Don Philippe Peon; and in the afternoon yet another bull-
fight, which opened for me under pleasant circumstances. I did
not intend to go, had not secured a seat, and took my place in
a box so full that I was obliged to stand up by the door. In
front was one of the prettiest of the Mestizas of the ball; on her
right was a vacant seat, and next to this sat a padre, who had
just arrived at the village. I was curious to know who could be
the proprietor of the vacant seat, when the gentleman himself
(an acquaintance) entered, and asked me to take it. I did not
require much urging, and, in taking it, turned first to the padre
to acknowledge my good fortune in obtaining it, which communication I thought he did not receive quite as graciously as
he might have done. The corrida opened bravely; bulls were
speared, blood flowed, and men were tumbled over. I had never
taken so much pleasure in the opening scenes; but a storm was
gathering; the heavens put on black; clouds whirled through the
air; the men stood up, seeming anxious and vexed, and the
ladies were uneasy about their mantillas and headdresses. Darkness increased, but man and beast went on fighting in the ring,
and it had a wild and strange effect, with the black clouds scud-
ding above us, to look from the fierce struggle up to the sea of
anxious faces on the other side of the scaffold, and beyond, over
the top, to the brilliant arch of a rainbow illuminating with a
single line the blackness of the sky. I pointed out the rainbow to
the lady as an indication that there would be no rain; but the
sign disappeared, a furious gust of wind swept over the frail
scaffold, the scalloped papers fluttered, shawls and handkerchiefs
flew, a few drops of rain fell, and in three minutes the Plaza de
Toros was empty. I had no umbrella to offer the lady; some ill-
natured person carried her off; and the matador de cochinos ex-

tended his poncha over my head, and escorted me to a house, where I made a great discovery, which everybody in the village knew except myself. The lady, whom I had supposed to be a señorita, was a *comprometida*, or compromised, or, to speak precisely, she was the *compagnera* of the padre who sat on the other side of me.

I have omitted to mention that a great change, or, as it is sometimes called in the country, a new reformation, is now going on in Yucatan, not like the reformations got up by disorganizing laymen, which have, at times, convulsed the whole Christian world, but peculiar and local, and touching only the domestic relations of the padres. It may be known to many of my readers that in the early ages of the Catholic Church priests were not forbidden to marry. In process of time the pope, to wean them from worldly ties, enjoined celibacy, and separation where marriage had already taken place. The priests resisted, and the struggle threatened to undermine the whole fabric of church government; but the pope prevailed, and for eight centuries, throughout those countries in which the spiritual domination of Rome is acknowledged, no priest has been allowed to marry. But in Yucatan this burden was found too heavy to be borne. Very early, from the necessity growing out of local position, some special indulgences had been granted to the people of this country, among which was a dispensation for eating meat on fast days; and, under the liberal spirit of this bull, or of some other that I am not aware of, the good padres have relaxed considerably the tightness of the cord that binds them to celibacy.

I am about making a delicate and curious communication. It may be considered an ill-natured attack upon the Catholic Church; but as I feel innocent of any such intention, this does not trouble me. But another consideration does. I have a strong liking to padres. I have received from them nothing but kindness, and wherever I have met with them I have found friends. I mean barely to mention the subject and pass on, though I am afraid that by this preface I am only calling more particular attention to it. I would omit it altogether, but it forms so striking a feature in the state of society in that country, that no picture can be complete without it. Without farther preface, then, I mention, but only for the private ear of the reader, that, except at Merida and Campeachy, where they are more immediately under the eyes of the bishop, the padres throughout Yucatan, to relieve the tedium of convent life, have compagneras, or, as they are sometimes called, *hermanas politicas*, or sisters-in-law; or, to speak with the precision I particularly aim at, the proportion of those who have to those who have not is about as the proportion in a well-regulated community of married to unmarried men.

I have now told the worst; the greatest enemy of the padres cannot say more. I do not express any opinion of my own upon this matter, but I may remark that with the people of the country it is no impeachment of a padre's character, and does not impair his usefulness. Some look upon this arrangement as a little irregular, but in general it is regarded only as an amiable weakness, and I am safe in saying that it is considered a recommendation to a village padre, as it is supposed to give him settled habits, as marriage does with laymen, and, to give my own honest opinion, which I did not intend to do, it is less injurious to good morals than the by no means uncommon consequences of celibacy which are found in some other Catholic countries. The padre in Yucatan stands in the position of a married man, and performs all the duties pertaining to the head of a family. Persons of what is considered respectable standing in a village do not shun left-hand marriage with a padre. Still it was to us always a matter of regret to meet with individuals of worth, and whom we could not help esteeming, standing in what could not but be considered a false position. To return to the case with which I set out: the padre in question was universally spoken of as a man of good conduct, a sort of pattern padre for correct, steady habits; sedate, grave, and middle-aged, and apparently the last man to have had an eye for such a pretty compagnera. The only comment I ever heard made was upon his good fortune, and on that point he knows my opinion.

The next day Mr. Catherwood and Doctor Cabot arrived. Both had had a recurrence of fever, and were still very weak. In the evening was the carnival ball, but before the company had all arrived. We were again scattered by the rain. All the next day it was more abundant than we had seen it in the country, and completely destroyed all the proposed gayeties of the carnival.

We had one clear day, which we devoted to taking Daguerreotype likenesses of the cura and two of the Mestizas; and, besides the great business of balls, bull-fights, Daguerreotyping, and superintending the morals of the padres, I had some light reading in a manuscript entitled, "Antigua Chronologia Yucateca," "Ancient Chronology of Yucatan; or, a simple Exposition of the Method used by the Indians to compute Time." This essay was presented to me by the author, Don Pio Perez, whom I had the satisfaction of meeting at this place. I had been advised that this gentleman was the best Maya scholar in Yucatan, and that he was distinguished in the same degree for the investigation and study of all matters tending to elucidate the history of the ancient Indians. His attention was turned in this direction by the circumstance of holding an office in the department of state, in which old documents in the Maya language were constantly passing under his eyes. Fortunately for the interests of science and his own studious tastes, on account of some political disgust he withdrew from public life, and, during two years of retirement, devoted himself to the study of the ancient chronology of Yucatan. It is a work which no ordinary man would have ventured to undertake; and, if general reputation be any proof, there was no man in the country so competent, or who could bring to it so much learning and research. It adds to the merit of his labours that, in prosecuting them, Don Pio stood alone, had none to sympathize with him, knew that the attainment of the most important results would not be appreciated, and had not even that hope of honourable distinction which, in the absence of all other prospects of reward, cheers the student in the solitary labours of his closet.

The essay explains at large the principles imbodied in the calendar of the ancient Indians. It has been submitted for examination (with other interesting papers furnished me by Don Pio, which will be referred to hereafter) to a distinguished gentleman, known by his researches into Indian languages and antiquities, and I am authorized to say that it furnishes a basis for some interesting comparisons and deductions, and is regarded as a valuable contribution to the cause of science.

The essay of Don Pio contains calculations and details which would not be interesting to the general reader; to some, however, even these cannot fail to be so, and the whole is published in the Appendix.* I shall refer in this place only to the result. From the examination and analysis made by the distinguished gentleman before referred to, I am enabled to state the interesting fact, that the calendar of Yucatan, though differing in some particulars, was substantially the same with that of the Mexicans. It had a similar solar year of three hundred and sixty-five days, divided in the same manner, first, into eighteen months of twenty days each, with five supplementary days; and, secondly, into twenty-eight weeks of thirteen days each, with an additional day. It had the same method of distinguishing the

*See Appendix to vol. i.

days of the year by a combination of those two series, and the same cycle of fifty-two years, in which the years, as in Mexico, are distinguished by a combination of the same series of thirteen, with another of four names or hieroglyphics; but Don Pio acknowledges that in Yucatan there is no certain evidence of the intercalation (similar to our leap year, or to the Mexican secular addition of thirteen days) necessary to correct the error resulting from counting the year as equal to three hundred and sixty-five days only.

It will be seen, by reference to the essay, that, besides the cycle of fifty-two years common to the Yucatecans and Mexicans, and, as Don Pio Perez asserts (on the authority of Veytia), to the Indians of Chiapas, Oaxaca, and Soconusco, those of Yucatan had another age of two hundred and sixty, or of three hundred and twelve years, equal to five or six cycles of fifty-two years, each of which ages consisted of thirteen periods (called Ajau or Ajau Katun) of twenty years each, according to many authorities, but, in Don Pio's opinion, of twenty-four years.

The fact that though the inhabitants of Yucatan and Mexico speak different languages, their calendar is substantially the same, I regard as extremely interesting and important, for this is not like a similarity of habits, which may grow out of natural instincts or identity of position. A calendar is a work of science, founded upon calculations, arbitrary signs, and symbols, and the similarity shows that both nations acknowledged the same starting points, attached the same meaning to the same phenomena and objects, which meaning was sometimes arbitrary, and not such as would suggest itself to the untutored. It shows common sources of knowledge and processes of reasoning, similarity of worship and religious institutions, and, in short, it is a link in a chain of evidence tending to show a common origin in the aboriginal inhabitants of Yucatan and Mexico. For this discovery we are indebted to Don Pio Perez.

CHAPTER VII

On the fourteenth of February we returned to Nohcacab. We had sent Albino before to make all our necessary arrangements, and on the fifteenth we took our final leave of this village. We had no regret; on the contrary, it was pleasant to think that we should not return to it. Our luggage was again reduced to the smallest possible compass: hammocks, a few changes of clothes, and Daguerreotype apparatus, all the rest being forwarded to meet us at Peto. The chief of our Indian carriers was a sexton, who had served out his time, an old neighbour in the convent, whom we had never seen sober, and who was this morning particularly the reverse.

To understand our route it will be necessary for the reader to consult the map. On setting out our direction was again south, and again our road was over the sepulchres of cities. At the distance of two miles we saw "old walls" on an eminence at the right; a little farther three ruined buildings on the same side of the road; and beyond these we came to the ruins of Sacbey. These consist of three buildings, irregularly disposed, one of which is represented in Plate XII. It faces the south, measures fifty-three feet front by twelve feet six inches deep, and has

Plate XII

SACBEY

A.Hulbert.

94

three small doorways. Another, a little farther south, is about the size of the former, and has three apartments, with two columns in the centre doorway. The third is so ruined that its plan could not be made out.

Near as they were to the village, the padrecito had never seen them. They stand about a hundred feet from the path, but so completely buried among the trees, that, though I had visited them before under the guidance of an Indian, I passed now without observing them.

A short distance beyond is one of the most interesting monuments of antiquity in Yucatan. It is a broken platform or roadway of stone, about eight feet wide and eight or ten inches high, crossing the road, and running off into the woods on both sides. I have before referred to it as called by the Indians Sacbey, which means, in the Maya language, a paved way of pure white stone. The Indians say it traversed the country from Kabah to Uxmal; and that on it couriers travelled, bearing letters to and from the lords of those cities, written on leaves or the bark of trees. It was the only instance in which we had found among the Indians anything like a tradition, and the universality of this legend was illustrated by the circumstances attending our arrival. While we were standing upon the road, an old Indian came up from the other direction, bending under a load, who, in crossing it, stopped, and, striking his stick against the stones, uttered the words Sacbey, and Kabah, and Uxmal. At the same time our carriers came up, the old sexton at their head, who, depositing his burden upon the ancient road, repeated Sacbey, and then favoured us with an oration, in which we could only distinguish Kabah and Uxmal.

It had been my intention to explore thoroughly the route of this ancient road, and, if possible, trace it through the woods to the desolate cities which it once connected, and it was among the vexations of our residence at Nohcacab that we had not been able to do so. The difficulty of procuring Indians to work, and a general recurrence of sickness, rendered it impossible. We could not tell how much time might be required; the whole country was overgrown with trees; in some places the track was but faintly marked, and in others it might be lost altogether. It remains, therefore, an unbroken ground for the future explorer.

Again passing "old walls" on each side of the road, at the distance of two leagues we reached Xampon, where stand the remains of an edifice which, when entire, must have been grand and imposing, and now, but for the world of ruins around, might excite a stranger's wonder. Its form was rectangular, its four sides enclosing a hollow square. It measured from north to south eighty feet, and from east to west one hundred and five. Two angles only remain, one of which is represented in Plate XIII. It stood alone, and an Indian had planted a milpa around it. From this "old walls" were again visible, which the Indians called Kalupok.

Beyond we saw at a distance two other places, called Hiokowitz and Kuepak, ruined and difficult of access, and we did not attempt to reach them.

It added to the effect of the ruins scattered in this region, that they were not on a camino real, but on a little-frequented milpa path, in some places so overgrown that we found it difficult to force a passage. The heat was intense; we exhausted our waccals of water, and as there was no stream or fountain, our only chance of a supply was from a deposite of rain-water in the hollow of some friendly rock.

At two o'clock we reached a small clearing, in which stood an arbour of leaves, and under it a rude cross, facing the road; beyond, on the left, was an overgrown path, which, for the first time in many years, had been opened for me on a former occasion, to enable me to visit the ruins of Zekilna.

This place had been the object of one of my bootless visits from Nohcacab. The account I had heard was of an apartment containing an altar for buring copal, with traces of its use as left by the ancient inhabitants. When I had arrived where it was necessary to turn off, it was some time before the Indian could discover any signs of a path; and when found, he had to clear every step of the way. By that time my views on the subject of ruined cities had become practical, and, perceiving the discomfort and hardship that must attend an exploration in so desolate a place, I did most earnestly hope that the path would lead to nothing that might require a second visit. I dismounted, and leading my horse as the Indian cleared the way, we came to a broken, stony ascent, climbing up which I discovered that we were upon the top of an ancient terrace. A fine alamo tree was growing on the terrace, under which I tied my horse, and descending on the other side, we crossed a closely-wooded hollow, which, from the excessive heat, I supposed to be between two mounds. In a few moments I found myself ascending the side of a lofty stone structure, on the top of which were the remains of a large building, with its walls fallen, and the whole side of the mound strewed with sculptured stones, a scene of irrecoverable

Plate XIII

XAMPON

ruin. Descending on the other side of this structure, we reached a broad platform, in a good state of preservation, with trees growing upon it, without brush or underwood, but so teeming with insects and large black ants that it was necessary to step from stone to stone, and avoid touching the ground: Running off lengthwise from this terrace was a small building, which the Indian pointed out as containing the altar and copal. Passing the first door, he went on to the second, put his head in cautiously, and, without entering, drew back. Going in, I found an apartment differing in nothing from the most ordinary we had seen in the country. For some time I could not get the Indian to enter, and when he did, standing in the doorway, and looking around cautiously, he waved his finger horizontally, according to the manner of the Indians, to indicate that there was nothing. Fortunately, however, I learned that the road we had left led to the ruins of Chunhuhu; and it shows the difficulty I had in ascertaining the juxtaposition of places, that though this was one of the places which I intended to visit, until this man mentioned it I had not been able to learn that it lay in the same neighbourhood. I determined at once to continue on, and it was what I saw on that occasion that now put our whole body in motion in this direction.

To return. It was late in the afternoon when we reached the savanna of Chunhuhu, and rode up to the hut at which I had tied my horse on my former visit.

The hut was built of upright poles, had a steep projecting roof thatched with palm leaves, and the sides protected by the same material; as we stopped in front, we saw a woman within mashing maize for tortillas, which promised a speedy supper. She said her husband was away; but this made no difference to us, and, after a few more words, we all entered, the woman at the moment bolting for the door, and leaving us in exclusive possession. Very soon, however, a little boy, about eight years old, came down and demanded the maize, which we were loth to give up, but did not consider ourselves authorized to retain. Albino followed him, in hopes of persuading the woman to return; but as soon as she caught a glimpse of him she ran into the woods.

The hut of which we thus became the sudden and involuntary masters was furnished with three stones for a fireplace, a wooden horse for kneading maize upon, a comal for baking tortillas, an earthen olla, or pot, for cooking, three or four waccals, or gourds, for drinking-cups, and two small Indian hammocks, which also were demanded and given up. Besides these, there was

a circular dining-table about a foot and a half in diameter, supported by three pegs about eight inches high, and some blocks of
wood about the same height for seats. Overhead, suspended from
the rafters, were three large bundles of corn in the husk and two
of beans in the pod; and on each string, about a foot above these
eatables, was half a calabash or squash, with the rounded side
up, like the shade over a lamp, which, besides being ornamental,
filled the office of a rat-trap; for these vermin, in springing from
the rafters to reach the corn and beans, would strike upon the
calabash, and fall to the ground.

Being provided for ourselves, we next looked to our horses.
There was no difficulty about their food, for a supply of corn
had fallen into our hands, and the grass on the savanna was the
best pasture we had seen in the country; but we learned, to our
dismay, from the little boy, who was the only person we saw,
that there was no water. The place was worse supplied than any
we had yet visited. There was neither well, cueva, nor aguada,
and the inhabitants depended entirely upon the rain-water collected in the hollows of the rocks. As to a supply for four horses,
it was utterly out of the question. Any long stay at this place
was, of course, impossible; but immediate wants were pressing.
Our horses had not touched water since morning, and, after a
long, hot, and toilsome journey, we could not think of their
going without all night.

The little boy was hovering about the rancho in charge of
a naked sister some two years old, and commissioned, as he told
us himself, to watch that we did not take anything from the hut.
For a medio he undertook to show me the place where they
procured water, and, mounting his little sister upon his back, he
led the way up a steep and stony hill. I followed with the bridle
of my horse in my hand, and, without any little girl on my back,
found it difficult to keep up with him. On the top of the hill
were worn and naked rocks, with deep hollows in them, some
holding perhaps as much as one or two pails of water. I led my
horse to one of the largest. He was always an extraordinary water
drinker, and that evening was equal to a whole temperance
society. The little Indian looked on as if he had sold his birth-
right, and I felt strong compunctions; but, letting the morrow
take care of itself, I sent up the other horses, which consumed at
a single drinking what might, perhaps, have sufficed the family a
month.

In the mean time our own wants were not slight. We had
been on the road all day, and had eaten nothing. Unluckily, the

Plate XIV

F. Catherwood.

Jordan & Halpin.

CHUNHUHU.

old sexton had taken for his load the box containing our table furniture and provisions for the road, and we had not seen him since we left him at Sacbey. All the other carriers had arrived. I had hired them to remain with us and work at the ruins, and then carry the luggage to the next village. Part of my contract was to feed them, and, knowing the state of things, they scattered in search of supplies, returning, after a long absence, with some tortillas, eggs, and lard. We had the eggs fried, and would, perhaps, have been content but for our vexation with the sexton. While we were swinging in our hammocks, we heard his voice at a distance, and presently he entered in the best humour possible, and holding up his empty bottle in triumph.

The next morning at daylight we sent Albino with the Indians to begin clearing around the ruins, and after breakfast we followed. The path lay through a savanna covered with long grass, and at the distance of a mile we reached two buildings, which I had seen before, and were the inducement to this visit.

The first is that represented in Plate XIV. It stands on a substantial terrace, but lower than most of the others. The front is one hundred and twelve feet long, and when entire must have presented a grand appearance. The end on the left in the engraving has fallen, carrying with it one doorway, so that now only four appear. The doorway was the largest and most imposing we had seen in the country, but, unfortunately, the ornaments over it were broken and fallen. In the centre apartment the back corridor is raised, and the ascent to it is by three steps.

All the doorways were plain except the centre one (the second to the left in the engraving), which is represented in Plate XV. It is in a dilapidated condition, but still presents bold and striking ornaments. Even on this scale, however, the details of the sitting figures above the cornice do not appear.

While we were engaged in making a clearing in front of this building, two young men came down upon the terrace from the corner that was fallen, and apparently from the top of the building, with long guns, the locks covered with deer-skin, and all the accoutrements of caçadores, or hunters. They were tall, fine-looking fellows, fearless and frank in appearance and manner. Dr. Cabot's gun was the first object that attracted their attention, after which they laid down their guns, and, as if for the mere sport of swinging their machetes, were soon foremost in making the clearing. When this was finished, Mr. C. set up his camera lucida, and though at first all gathered round, in a few minutes he was left with only the two brothers, one of them

Plate XV

CHUNHUHU

F. Catherwood.

Jordan & Halpin.

102

holding over him an umbrella to protect him from the sun.

Except the little boy and the woman, these were the first persons we had seen within speaking distance. We were so pleased with their appearance that we proposed to one of them to accompany us in our search after ruins. The elder was quite taken with the idea of rambling, but soon said, with a rather disconsolate tone, that he had a wife and children. His herman-ito, or younger brother, however, had no such ties, and would go with us. We made an agreement on the spot; and nothing can show more plainly the sense which we entertained of the security of travelling in Yucatan. In Central America we never dared to take a man into our service without strong recommendations, for he might be a robber or an assassin. These men we had never heard of till they came upon us with their guns. Their manly bearing as hunters inspired confidence, and the only suspicious circumstance was that they were willing to take us without references; but we found afterward that they had both known us at Nohcacab. The one whom we engaged was named Dimas, and he continued with us until we left the country.

On the same line, and but a short distance removed, though on a lower terrace, is another building, measuring eighty-five feet in front, which is represented in Plate XVI. It had a fresh-ness about it that suggested the idea of something more modern than the others. The whole was covered with a coat of plaster but little broken, and it confirmed us in the opinion we had entertained before, that the fronts of all the buildings had been thus covered.

Our meeting with these young men was a fortunate circum-stance for us in exploring these ruins. From boyhood their father had had his rancho on the savanna, and with their guns they had ranged over the whole country for leagues around.

From the terrace of the first building we saw at a distance a high hill, almost a mountain, on the top of which rose a wooded elevation surrounding an ancient building. There was something extraordinary in its position, but the young men told us it was entirely ruined, and, although it was then but eleven o'clock, if we attempted to go to it, we could not return till after dark. They told us, also, of others at the distance of half a league, more extensive, and some of which, they said, were, in finish and preservation, equal to these.

At one o'clock Doctor Cabot and myself, under the guidance of Dimas, set out to look for them. It was desperately hot. We passed several huts, and at one of them asked for some water; but

Plate XVI

F. Catherwood.

J. N. Gimbrede.

CHUNHUHU.

it was so full of insects that we could barely taste it. Dimas led us to the hut of his mother, and gave us some from a vessel in which the insects had settled to the bottom.

Beyond this we ascended the spur of a high hill, and coming down into a thickly-wooded valley, after the longest half league we ever walked, we saw through the trees a large stone structure. On reaching it, and climbing over a broken terrace, we came to a large mound faced on all sides with stone, which we ascended, and crossing over the top, looked down upon an overgrown area, having on each side a range of ruined buildings, with their white façades peering through the trees; and beyond, at a distance, and seemingly inaccessible, was the high hill with the ruins on the top, which we had seen from the terrace of the first building. Hills rose around us on every side, and, for that country, the scene was picturesque, but all waste and silent. The stillness of the grave rested upon the ruins, and the notes of a little flycatcher were the only sounds we heard.

The ruins in sight were much more extensive than those we had first visited, but in a more ruinous condition. We descended the mound to the area in front, and, bearing down the bushes, passed in the centre an uncouth, upright, circular stone, like that frequently referred to before, called the picote, or whipping-post, and farther on we reached an edifice, which Mr. Catherwood afterward drew, and which is represented in Plate XVII. It is thirty-three feet in front, and has two apartments, each thirteen feet long by eight feet six inches deep, and conspicuous in the façade are representations of three uncouth human figures, in curious dresses, with their hands held up by the side of the head, supporting the cornice.

These ruins, Dimas told us, were called Schoolhoke, but. like the others, they stand on what is called the savanna of Chunhuhu; and the ruined building on the top of the hill, visible from both places, seems towering as a link to connect them together. What the extent of this place has been it is impossible to say. Returning, overtaken by night, and in apprehension of rain, we were an hour and a half, which would make the two, by the path we took, at least five miles apart, though much nearer in a straight line. Supposing the two piles of ruins to have formed part of the same city, there is reason to believe that it once covered as much ground and contained as many inhabitants as any that has yet been presented.

The first intelligence I received of the existence of these ruins was from Cocom, who, the reader may remember, was our

Plate XVII

S H Gimbro

F Catherwood.

CHUNJUJU.

guide at Nohpat; and this is all that I am able to communicate in regard to their history.

We returned to the rancho worn down with fatigue, just in time to escape a violent rain. This brought within, as an accompaniment to the fleas of the night before, our carriers and servants, and we had eleven hammocks, in close juxtaposition, and through the night a concert of nasal trombones, with Indian variations. The rain continued all the next day, and as no work could be done, Mr. Catherwood took advantage of the opportunity to have another attack of fever. We were glad of it on another account, for we had kept a man constantly employed in the woods searching for water; our horses had exhausted all the rocky cavities around, and we could not have held out another day. The rain replenished them, and relieved us from some compunctions.

In the afternoon the little boy came down with a message from his mother, desiring to know when we were going away. Perhaps the reader is curious to know the costume of boys at Chunhuhu. It consists of a straw hat and a pair of sandals. This one had, besides, some distinguishable spots of dirt, and Mr. Catherwood made a drawing of him as he stood. Soon afterward the poor woman herself was seen hovering about the house. She considered that it was really time to come. We had made a great inroad upon her provisions; given the corn to our horses, and cooked the frigoles; but the special cause of her coming was to return a medio, which she said was bad. She was mild, amiable, and simple as a child; complained that we said we were only going to remain one night, and now she did not know when we were going away. With great difficulty, we prevailed upon her to enter the hut, and told her she might return whenever she pleased. She laughed good-naturedly, and, after looking round carefully to see that nothing was missing, went away comforted by our promise to depart the next day.

CHAPTER VIII

At daylight the next morning the woman was
on the spot to remind us of our promise. We gave her a cup of
coffee, and with a small present, which amply satisfied her for
our forcible occupation of her hut, left her again in possession.

Our party this morning divided into three parcels. The carriers set out direct for Bolonchen; Mr. Catherwood went, under
the guidance of Dimas, to make a drawing of the last building,
and Doctor Cabot, myself, and Albino to visit another ruined
city, all to meet again at Bolonchen in the evening.

Doctor Cabot and myself were warned that the path we
proposed taking was not passable on horseback. For the first
league our arms and legs were continually scratched and torn
by briers, and only our hats saved us from the fate of Absalom.
In that hot climate, it was always uncomfortable to tie the
sombrero under the chin; and there were few things more annoying than to have it knocked off every five minutes, and be
obliged to dismount and pick it up. Our Indian guide moved

easily on foot, just clearing the branches on each side and over-head. We had one alternative, which was to dismount and lead our horses; but, unused to having favours shown them, they pulled back, so that the labour of dragging them on added greatly to the fatigue of walking.

Emerging from this tangled path, we came out upon a large hacienda, and stopped before an imposing gateway, under the shade of great seybo trees, within which were large and well-filled water-tanks. Our horses had drunk nothing since the after-noon before; we therefore dismounted, loosened the saddle girths, and, as a matter of form, sent Albino to ask permission to water them, who returned with the answer that we might for a real. At Chunhuhu it always cost us more than this in the labour of Indians; but the demand seemed so churlish at the gate of this large hacienda, that we refused to pay, and again mounted. Albino told us that we might save a slight circuit by passing through the cattle-yard; and we rode through, close beside the water-tanks and a group of men, at the head of whom was the master, and, coming out upon the camino real, shook from off our feet the dust of the inhospitable hacienda. Our poor horses bore the brunt of sustaining our dignity.

At one o'clock we came to a rancho of Indians, where we bought some tortillas and procured a guide. Leaving the camino real, we turned again into a milpa path, and in about an hour came in sight of another ruined city, known by the name of Ytsimpte. From the plain on which we approached we saw on the left, on the brow of a hill, a range of buildings, six or eight hundred feet in length, all laid bare to view, the trees having just been felled; and as we drew near we saw Indians engaged in continuing the clearing. On arriving at the foot of the buildings, Albino found that the clearing was made by order of the alcalde of Bolonchen, at the instance and under the direction of the padre, in expectation of our visit and for our benefit!

We had another subject of congratulation on account of our horses. There was an aguada in the neighbourhood, to which we immediately sent them, and, carrying our traps up to the terrace of the nearest building, we sat down before it to meditate and lunch.

This over, we commenced a survey of the ruins. The clearings made by our unknown friends enabled us to form at once a general idea of their character and extent, and to move from place to place with comparative facility. These ruins lie in the village of Bolonchen, and the first apartment we entered showed the effects of this vicinity. All the smooth stones of the inner wall had been picked out and carried away for building purposes, and the sides presented the cavities in the bed of mortar from which they had been taken. The edifice was about two hundred feet long. It had one apartment, perhaps sixty feet long, and a grand staircase twenty feet wide rose in the centre to the top. This staircase was in a ruinous condition, but the outer stones of the lower steps remained, richly ornamented with sculpture; and probably the whole casing on each side had once possessed the same rich decoration.

Beyond this was another large building, square and peculiar in its plan. At the extreme end the whole façade lay unbroken on the ground, held together by the great mass of mortar and stones, and presenting the entire line of pillars with which it had been decorated. In the doorway of an inner apartment was an ornamented pillar, and on the walls was the print of the mysterious red hand. Turn which way we would, ruin was before us. At right angles with the first building was a line of ruined walls, following which I passed, lying on the ground, the headless trunk of a sculptured body; the legs, too, were gone. At the end was an arch, which seemed, at a distance, to stand entire and alone, like that named the arch of triumph at Kabah; but it proved to be only the open and broken arch of a ruined building. From the extent of these remains, the masses of sculptured stones, and the execution of the carving, this must have been one of the first class of the aboriginal cities. In moral influence there was none more powerful. Ruin had been so complete that we could not profit by the kindness of our friends, and it was melancholy that when so much had been done for us, there was so little for us to do. It was but another witness to the desolation that had swept over the land.

A short ride brought us to the suburbs of the village of Bolonchen, and we entered a long street, with a line of straggling houses or huts on each side. It was late in the afternoon. Indian children were playing in the road, and Indians, returned from their work, were swinging in hammocks within the huts. As we advanced, we saw a vecino, with a few neighbours around him, sitting in the doorway thrumming a guitar. It was, perhaps, a scene of indolence, but it was one of quiet and contentment, of comfort and even thrift. Often, in entering the disturbed villages of Central America, among intoxicated Indians and swaggering white men, all armed, we felt a degree of uneasiness. The faces that looked upon us seemed scowling and suspicious; we always apprehended insult, and frequently were not disappointed. Here all looked at us with curiosity, but without distrust; every face bore a welcome, and, as we rode through, all gave us a friendly greeting. At the head of the street the plaza opened upon us on a slight elevation, with groups of Indian women in the centre drawing water from the well, and relieved against a background of green hills rising above the tops of the houses, which, under the reflection of the setting sun, gave a beauty and picturesqueness of aspect that no other village in the country had exhibited. On the left, on a raised platform, stood the church, and by its side the convent. In consideration of what the cura had already done for us, and that we had a large party—perceiving, also, that the casa real, a long stone building with a broad portico in front, was really inviting in its appearance, we resolved to spare the cura, and rode up to the casa real. Well-dressed Indians, with a portly, well-fed cacique, stood ready to take our horses. We dismounted and entered the principal apartment. On one side were the iron gratings of the prison, and on the other two long beams of wood with holes in them for stocks, and a caution to strangers arriving in the village to be on their good behaviour. Our carriers had arrived. We sent out to buy ramon and corn for the horses, had our hammocks swung, and sat down under the corridor.

We had hardly time to seat ourselves before the vecinos, in their clean afternoon clothes, and some with gold-headed canes, came over to "call upon us." All were profuse in offers of services; and as it was the hour for that refreshment, we had a perplexing number of invitations to go to their houses and take chocolate. Among our visitors was a young man with a fine black beard all over his face, well dressed, and the only one wearing a black hat, whom, as we knew they were about drilling companies in the villages to resist the apprehended invasion of Santa Ana, we supposed to belong to the army, but we afterward learned that he was a member of the church militant, being the ministro, or assistant, of the cura. The cura himself did not come, but one of our visiters, looking over to the convent, and seeing the doors and windows closed, said he was still taking his siesta.

We had time to look at the only objects of interest in the village, and these were the wells, which, after our straits at Chunhuhu, were a refreshing spectacle, and of which our horses had already enjoyed the benefit by a bath.

Bolonchen derives its name from two Maya words: *Bolon*, which signifies nine, and *chen*, wells, and it means the nine wells.

From time immemorial, nine wells formed at this place the centre of a population, and these nine wells are now in the plaza of the village. Their origin is as obscure and unknown as that of the ruined cities which strew the land, and as little thought of.

These wells were circular openings cut through a stratum of rock. The water was at that time ten or twelve feet from the surface, and in all it was at the same level. The source of this water is a mystery to the inhabitants, but there are some facts which seem to make the solution simple. The wells are mere perforations through an irregular stratum of rock, all communicate, and in the dry season a man may descend in one and come out by another at the extreme end of the plaza; it is manifest, therefore, that the water does not proceed from springs. Besides, the wells are all full during the rainy season; when this is over the water begins to disappear, and in the heat of the dry season it fails altogether; from which it would appear that under the surface there is a great rocky cavern, into which the floods of the rainy season find a way by crevices or other openings, which cannot be known without a survey of the country, and, having little or no escape, are retained, and furnish a supply so long as they are augmented by the rains.

The custody and preservation of these wells form a principal part of the business of the village authorities, but, with all their care, the supply lasts but seven or eight months in the year. This year, on account of the long continuance of the rainy season, it had lasted longer than usual, and was still abundant. The time was approaching, however, when these wells would fail, and the inhabitants be driven to an extraordinary cueva at half a league from the village.

At about dark Mr. Catherwood arrived, and we returned to the casa real. In a room fifty feet long, free from fleas, servants, and Indian carriers, and with a full swing for our hammocks, we had a happy change from the hut at Chunhuhu.

During the evening the cura came over to see us, but, finding we had retired, did not disturb us; early in the morning he was rapping at our door, and would not leave us till we promised to come over and take chocolate with him.

As we crossed the plaza he came out to meet us, in black gown and cape, bare-headed, with white hair streaming, and both arms extended; embraced us all, and, with the tone of a man who considered that he had not been treated well, reproached us for not coming directly to the convent; then led us in, showed us its comforts and conveniences, insisted upon sending for our luggage, and only consented to postpone doing so while we consulted on our plans.

These were, to leave Bolonchen in the afternoon for the ruins of San Antonio, four leagues distant. The cura had never heard of such ruins, and did not believe that any existed, but he knew the hacienda, and sent out to procure information. In the mean time it was arranged that we should employ the morning in a visit to the cueva, and return to dine with him. He reminded us that it was Friday, and, consequently, fast day; but, knowing the padres as we did, we had no apprehension.

There was one great difficulty in the way of our visiting the cueva at this time. Since the commencement of the rainy season

FIG. 6

it had not been used; and every year, before having recourse to it, there was a work of several days to be done in repairing the ladders. As this, however, was our only opportunity, we determined to make the attempt.

The cura undertook to make the arrangements, and after breakfast we set out, a large party, including both Indians and vecinos.

At the distance of half a league from the village, on the Campeachy road, we turned off by a well-beaten path, following which we fell into a winding lane, and, descending gradually, reached the foot of a rude, lofty, and abrupt opening, under a bold ledge of overhanging rock, seeming a magnificent entrance to a great temple for the worship of the God of Nature. Figure 6 represents this aperture, an Indian with a lighted torch being seen just entering.

We disencumbered ourselves of superfluous apparel, and, following the Indian, each with a torch in hand, entered a wild cavern, which, as we advanced, became darker. At the distance of sixty paces the descent was precipitous, and we went down by a ladder about twenty feet. Here all light from the mouth of the cavern was lost, but we soon reached the brink of a great perpendicular descent, to the very bottom of which a strong body of light was thrown from a hole in the surface, a perpendicular depth, as we afterward learned by measurement, of two hundred and ten feet. As we stood on the brink of this precipice, under the shelving of an immense mass of rock, seeming darker from the stream of light thrown down the hole, gigantic stalactites and huge blocks of stone assumed all manner of fantastic shapes, and seemed like monstrous animals or deities of a subterranean world.

From the brink on which we stood an enormous ladder, of the rudest possible construction, led to the bottom of the hole. It was between seventy and eighty feet long, and about twelve feet wide, made of the rough trunks of saplings lashed together lengthwise, and supported all the way down by horizontal trunks braced against the face of the precipitous rock. The ladder was double, having two sets or flights of rounds, divided by a middle partition, and the whole fabric was lashed together by withes. It was very steep, seemed precarious and insecure, and confirmed the worst accounts we had heard of the descent into this remarkable well.

Our Indians began the descent, but the foremost had scarcely got his head below the surface before one of the rounds

Plate XVIII

F. Catherwood.   S.H.Gimber.

BOLONCHEN

Cueva or Well.

115

slipped, and he only saved himself by clinging to another. The ladder having been made when the withes were green, these were now dry, cracked, and some of them broken. We attempted a descent with some little misgivings, but, by keeping each hand and foot on a different round, with an occasional crash and slide, we all reached the foot of the ladder; that is, our own party, our Indians, and some three or four of our escort, the rest having disappeared.

Plate XVIII represents the scene at the foot of this ladder. Looking up, the view of its broken sides, with the light thrown down from the orifice above, was the wildest that can be conceived. As yet the reader is only at the mouth of this well; but, to explain to him briefly its extraordinary character, I give its name, which is Xtacumbi Xunan. The Indians understand by this La Señora escondida, or the lady hidden away; and it is derived from a fanciful Indian story that a lady stolen from her mother was concealed by her lover in this cave.

Every year, when the wells in the plaza are about to fail, the ladders are put into a thorough state of repair. A day is appointed by the municipality for closing the wells in the plaza, and repairing to the cueva; and on that day a great village fête is held in the cavern at the foot of this ladder. On the side leading to the wells is a rugged chamber, with a lofty overhanging roof and a level platform; the walls of this rocky chamber are dressed with branches and hung with lights, and the whole village comes out with refreshments and music. The cura is with them, a leader of the mirth; and the day is passed in dancing in the cavern, and rejoicing that when one source of supply fails another is opened to their need.

Figure 7 will give some imperfect idea of a section of this cave from the entrance to the foot of the great ladder, with the orifice through which the light descends from above, and the wild path that leads deeper into the bowels of the rock and down to the water.

On one side of the cavern is an opening in the rock, as shown in the engraving, entering by which, we soon came to an abrupt descent, down which was another long and trying ladder. It was laid against the broken face of the rock, not so steep as the first, but in a much more rickety condition; the rounds were loose, and the upper ones gave way on the first attempt to descend. The cave was damp, and the rock and the ladder were wet and slippery. At this place the rest of our attendants left us, the ministro being the last deserter. It was evident that the

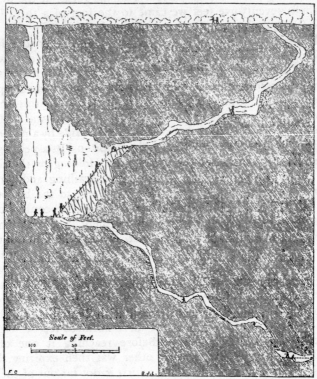

FIG. 7

labour of exploring this cave was to be greatly increased by the
state of the ladders, and there might be some danger attending
it, but, even after all that we had seen of caves, there was something so wild and grand in this that we could not bring ourselves
to give up the attempt. Fortunately, the cura had taken care to
provide us with rope, and, fastening one end round a large stone,
an Indian carried the other down to the foot of the ladder. We
followed, one at a time; holding the rope with one hand, and
with the other grasping the side of the ladder, it was impossible
to carry a torch, and we were obliged to feel our way in the dark,
or with only such light as could reach us from the torches above
and below. At the foot of this ladder was a large cavernous
chamber, from which irregular passages led off in different directions to deposits or sources of water. Doctor Cabot and myself,
attended by Albino, took one of the passages indicated by the
Indians, of which some imperfect idea is given in the section.

117

Moving on by a slight ascent over the rocks, at the distance of about seventy-five feet we came to the foot of a third ladder nine feet long, two or three steps beyond another five feet high, both which we had to go up, and six paces farther a fifth, descending, and eighteen feet in length. A little beyond we descended another ladder eleven feet long, and yet a little farther on we came to one—the seventh—the length and general appearance of which induced us to pause and consider. By this time Albino was the only attendant left. This long ladder was laid on a narrow, sloping face of rock, protected on one side by a perpendicular wall, but at the other open and precipitous. Its aspect was unpropitious, but we determined to go on. Holding by the side of the ladder next the rock, we descended, crashing and carrying down the loose rounds, so that when we got to the bottom we had cut off all communication with Albino; he could not descend, and, what was quite as inconvenient, we could not get back. It was now too late to reflect. We told Albino to throw down our torches, and go back for Indians and rope to haul us out. In the mean time we moved on by a broken, winding passage, and, at the distance of about two hundred feet, came to the top of a ladder eight feet long, at the foot of which we entered a low and stifling passage; and crawling along this on our hands and feet, at the distance of about three hundred feet we came to a rocky basin full of water. Before reaching it one of our torches had gone out, and the other was then expiring. From the best calculation I can make, which is not far out of the way, we were then fourteen hundred feet from the mouth of the cave, and at a perpendicular depth of four hundred and fifty feet. As may be supposed from what the reader already knows of these wells, we were black with smoke, grimed with dirt, and dripping with perspiration. Water was the most pleasant spectacle that could greet our eyes; but it did not satisfy us to drink it only, we wanted a more thorough benefit. Our expiring torch warned us to forbear, for in the dark we might never be able to find our way back to upper earth; but, trusting that if we did not reappear in the course of the week Mr. Catherwood would come to the rescue, we whipped off our scanty covering, and stepped into the pool. It was just large enough to prevent us from interfering with each other, and we achieved a bath which, perhaps, no white man ever before took at that depth under ground.

The Indians call this basin Chacka, which means agua colorada, or red water; but this we did not know at the time, and we did not discover it, for to economize our torch we avoided flaring it, and it lay on the rock like an expiring brand, admonishing us that it was better not to rely wholly upon our friends in the world above, and that it would be safer to look out for ourselves. Hurrying out, we made a rapid toilet, and, groping our way back, with our torch just bidding us farewell, we reached the foot of the broken ladder, and could go no farther. Albino returned with Indians and ropes. We hauled ourselves up, and got back to the open chamber from which the passages diverged; and here the Indians pointed out another, which we followed till it became lower than any we had yet explored; and, according to Doctor Cabot's measurement, at the distance of four hundred and one paces, by mine, three hundred and ninety-seven, we came to another basin of water. This, as we afterward learned, is called Puɔuelha, meaning that it ebbs and flows like the sea. The Indians say that it recedes with the south wind, and increases with the northwest; and they add that when they go to it silently they find water; but when they talk or make a noise the water disappears. Perhaps it is not so capricious with white men, for we found water, and did not approach it with sealed lips. The Indians say, besides, that forty women once fainted in this passage, and that now they do not allow the women to go to it alone. In returning we turned off twice by branching passages, and reached two other basins of water; and when we got back to the foot of the great staircase, exhausted and almost worn out, we had the satisfaction of learning, from friends who were waiting to hear our report, that there were seven in all, and we had missed three. All have names given them by the Indians, two of which I have already mentioned.

The third is called Sallab, which means a spring; the fourth Akahba, on account of its darkness; the fifth Chocohá, from the circumstance of its being always warm; the sixth Oɔiha, from being of a milky colour; and the seventh Chimaisha, because it has insects called ais.

It was a matter of some regret that we were not able to mark such peculiarities or differences as might exist in these waters, and particularly that we were not provided with barometer and thermometer to ascertain the relative heights and temperatures. If we had been at all advised beforehand, we should at least have carried the latter with us, but always in utter ignorance of what we were to encounter, our great object was to be as free as possible from all encumbrances; besides which, to tell the truth, we did some things in that country, among which was the exploring of these caves, for our own satisfaction, and without much regard to the claims of science. The surface of the country is of transition or mountain limestone; and though almost invariably the case in this formation, perhaps here to a greater extent than anywhere else, it abounds in fissures and caverns, in which springs burst forth suddenly, and streams pursue a subterranean course. But the sources of the water and the geological formation of the country were, at the moment, matters of secondary interest to us. The great point was the fact, that from the moment when the wells in the plaza fail, the whole village turns to this cave, and four or five months in the year derives from this source its only supply. It was not, as at Xcoch, the resort of a straggling Indian, nor, as at Chack, of a small and inconsiderable rancho. It was the sole and only watering place of one of the most thriving villages in Yucatan, containing a population of seven thousand souls; and perhaps even this was surpassed in wonder by the fact that, though for an unknown length of time, and through a great portion of the year, files of Indians, men and women, are going out every day with cantaros on their backs, and returning with water, and though the fame of the Cueva of Bolonchen extends throughout Yucatan, from the best information we could procure, not a white man in the village had ever explored it.

We returned to the casa real, made a lavation, which we much needed, and went over to the cura's to dine. If he had not reminded us beforehand that it was Friday and Lent, we should not have discovered it. In fact, we were not used to da ties, and perhaps the good cura thought we had never dined ɔefore. It was not in nature to think of moving that afternoon, and, besides, we were somewhat at a loss what to do. The cura had unsettled our plans. He had made inquiries, and been informed that there were no ruins at San Antonio, but only a cueva, and we had had enough of these to last us for some time; moreover, he advised us of other ruins, of which we had not heard before. These were on the rancho of Santa Ana, belonging to his friend Don Antonio Cerbera, the alcalde. Don Antonio had never seen them, but both he and the cura said they intended to visit them; and they spoke particularly of a casa cerrada, or closed house, which, as soon as the dry season came on, they intended to visit con bombas, to blow it up! The cura was so bent upon our visiting this place, that almost in spite of ourselves we were turned in that direction.

CHAPTER IX

Early the next morning we resumed our journey. On leaving the village we were soon again in the wilderness. Albino remained behind to breakfast; we had not gone far before we came to a fork of the road, and took one of the branches, by which we missed our way, and rode on over a great plain covered with bushes above our horses' heads, the path finally becoming so completely choked up that it was impossible to continue. We turned back and took another; and, keeping as near as possible, by the compass, what we understood to be the direction, came out upon a muddy aguada, covered with weeds, and beyond this a sugar rancho, the first we had seen in Yucatan, indicating that we were entering a different section of country. We had escaped the region of eternal stones, and the soil was rich and loamy. A league beyond this we reached the rancho of Santa Rosa. It was a very rare thing in this country to notice any place for its beauty of situation, but we were struck with this, though perhaps its beauty consisted merely in standing upon a slight elevation, and commanding a view of an open country.

The major domo was somewhat surprised at the object of our visit. The ruins were about two leagues distant, but he had never seen them, and had no great opinion of ruins generally. He immediately sent out, however, to notify the Indians to be on the ground in the morning, and during the evening he brought in one who was to be our guide. By way of getting some idea of the ruins, we showed him some of Mr. Catherwood's drawings, and asked him if his bore any resemblance to them. He looked at them all attentively, and pointed to the blanks left for the doorways as the points of resemblance; from his manner we got the impression that we should have to thank the cura for a bootless visit.

The night at this rancho was a memorable one. We were so scourged by fleas that sleep was impossible. Mr. Catherwood and Dr. Cabot resorted to the Central American practice of sewing up the sheets into a bag, and all night we were in a fever.

The next morning we started for the ruins of Labphak, taking care to carry our luggage with us, and not intending, under any circumstances, to return. The major domo accompanied us. It was luxurious to ride on a road free from stones. In an hour we entered a forest of fine trees, and a league beyond found a party of Indians, who pointed us to a narrow path just opened, wilder than anything we had yet travelled. After following this some distance, the Indians stopped, and made signs to us to dismount. Securing the horses, and again following the Indians, in a few minutes we saw peering through the trees the white front of a lofty building, which, in the imperfect view we had of it, seemed the grandest we had seen in the country. It had three stories, the uppermost consisting of a bare dead wall, without any doorways, being, the Indians told us, the casa cerrada, or closed house, which the cura and alcalde intended to open con bombas. The whole building, with all its terraces, was overgrown with gigantic trees. The Indians cutting a path along the front, we moved on from door to door, and wandered through its desolate chambers. For the first time in the country we found interior staircases, one of which was entire, every step being in its place. The stones were worn, and we almost expected to see the foot-prints of the former occupants. With hurried interest we moved on till we reached the top. This commanded an extensive view over a great wooded and desolate plain, to which the appearance of the heavens gave at the moment an air of additional dreariness. The sky was overcast, and portended the coming of another Norte. The wind swept over the ruined building, so that in places we were obliged to cling to the branches of the trees to save ourselves from falling. An eagle stayed his flight through the air and hovered over our heads. At a great height Doctor Cabot recognised it as one of a rare species, the first which he had seen in the country, and stood with his gun ready, hoping to carry it home with him as a memorial of the place; but the proud bird soared away.

It seemed almost sacrilege to disturb the repose in which this building lay, and to remove its burial shroud, but soon, amid the ringing of the axe and machete, and the crash of falling trees, this feeling wore away. We had thirty Indians, who, working under the direction of the major domo, were equal to forty or fifty in our hands, and there was the most glorious excitement I had experienced in walking along these terraces, with Albino and the major domo to convey my directions to the Indians. Indeed, I can hardly imagine a higher excitement than to go through that country with a strong force, time, and means at command, to lay bare the whole region in which so many ruined cities are now buried.

In the mean time Mr. Catherwood, still an invalid, and deprived of sleep the night before, had his hammock slung in an apartment at the top of the building. By afternoon the clearing was finished, and he made his drawing, which appears in Plate XIX.

The lowest range or story is one hundred and forty-five feet in length. The roof and a portion of the façade have fallen, and almost buried the centre doorways. The apartments containing the staircases are indicated hereinafter in Figure 8. Each staircase consists of two flights, with a platform at the head of the first, which forms the foot of the second, and they lead out upon the roof, under the projection which stands like a watch-tower in the wall of the second range, and from this range two interior staircases lead out in the same way to the platform of the third.

The reader will observe that in the second and third ranges there are no openings of any kind except those at the head of the staircases, but simply a plain, solid wall. At first sight of this wall we thought we had really at last found a casa cerrada, and almost wished for the cura with his bombas. The major domo, looking up at it, called it so; but it seemed strange that such a character had ever been ascribed to it; for, barely working our way round the platform of the terrace, we found ranges of doorways opening into apartments, and that this was merely what we had often seen before, a back wall without doors or windows. And we made another much more interesting and important discovery. The elevation which we came upon first, facing the west, and shown in the engraving, noble and majestic as it was,

Plate XIX

LABPHAK.

F. Catherwood

was acutally the rear of the building, and the front, facing the east, presented the tottering remains of the grandest structure that now rears its ruined head in the forests of Yucatan.

In front was a grand courtyard, with ranges of ruined buildings, forming a hollow square, and in the centre a gigantic staircase rose from the courtyard to the platform of the third story. On the platform of the second terrace, at each end, stood a high square building like a tower, with the remains of rich ornaments in stucco; and on the platform of the third, at the head of the grand staircase, one on each side of it, stood two oblong buildings, their façades adorned with colossal figures and ornaments in stucco, seemingly intended as a portal to the structure on the top. In ascending the grand staircase, cacique, priest, or stranger had before him this gorgeously ornamented portal, and passed through it to enter the centre apartment of the upper story.

This apartment, however, does not correspond with the grandeur of the approach, and, according to our understanding of proprieties, the view of it is attended with disappointment. It is twenty-three feet long, only five feet six inches wide, and perfectly plain, without painting or ornament of any kind. But in this lofty chamber were strange memorials, tokens of recent occupation, indicating, amid the desolation and solitude around, that within a few years this ruined edifice, from which the owners had perhaps fled in terror, or been driven by the sword, had been the refuge and abode of man. In the holes of the archway were poles for the support of hammocks, and at each end were swinging shelves made of twigs and rods. When the cholera swept like a scourge over this isolated country, the inhabitants of the villages and ranchos fled for safety to the mountains and the wilderness. This desolate building was repeopled, this lofty chamber was the abode of some scared and stricken family, and here, amid hardships and privations, they waited till the angel of death passed by.

Figure 8 represents the ground-plan of the lower range. It consists of ranges of narrow apartments on all four of the sides, opening outward, and the reader will see that it has fitness, and uniformity of design and proportion. The grand staircase, forty feet wide, is indicated in the engraving. The interior, represented in black, forms the foundation for the support of the two upper ranges. It is cut off and enclosed on all sides by the inner wall, has no communication with any of the apartments, and is apparently a solid mass. Whether it really is solid or contains apart-

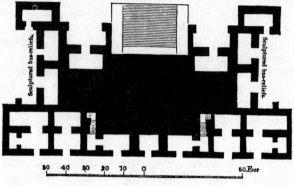

FIG. 8

ments, remains, as in other structures of the same kind, a question for the investigation of future explorers. Under the circumstances attending our visit, we were utterly unable to attempt anything of the kind.

The reader will notice in the plan two places marked "sculptured bas-reliefs." In these places are carved tablets set in the wall, as at Palenque, and, except at Palenque, this was the only place in all our wanderings in which we found bas-reliefs thus disposed. We were now moving in the direction of Palenque, though, of course, at a great distance from it; the face of the country was less stony, and the discovery of these bas-reliefs, and the increase and profusion of stuccoed ornaments, induced the impression that, in getting beyond the great limestone surface, the builders of these cities had adapted their style to the materials at hand, until, at Palenque, instead of putting up great façades of rudely-carved stone, they decorated the exterior with ornaments in stucco, and, having fewer carved ornaments, bestowed upon them more care and skill.

Plate XX represents the bas-reliefs referred to. Though resembling those at Palenque in general character and detail of ornament, they are greatly inferior in design and execution. Standing in the outer wall, they are much defaced and worn; the tablets on the south, both in the drawing and Daguerreotype view, presented a confused appearance. Both were composed of separate stones; but the subjects on the different pieces appeared, in some cases, to want adaptation to each other, and almost suggested the belief that they were fragments of other tablets, put together without much regard to design of any kind.

Night was almost upon us when Albino inquired in what

Plate XX

A. Jones sc.

L A B P H A K.
Bas relief on Stone.

F. Catherwood.

apartment he should hang up our hammocks. In the interest of our immediate occupations we had not thought of this; a buzzing in the woods gave ominous warning of moschetoes, and we inclined to the highest range; but it was unsafe to carry our things up, or to move about the broken terraces in the dark. We selected, as the most easy of access, the rooms indicated in the engraving by the second doorway on the left, which, as the reader may see, was partly encumbered in front by the ruins of the façade on the right. We secured the doorway against moschetoes with the black muslin used for the Daguerreotype tent. The kitchen was established in the corner room, and as soon as all was arranged we called in the servants, and associated them with us in an interesting and extraordinary sitting, as a committee of ways and means. The horses were well provided for in the way of green food, for many of the trees cut down were noble ramons, but there was neither corn nor water, and we were equally destitute ourselves. Except our staple stock of tea, coffee, chocolate, and a few rolls of Bolonchen bread (like all the bread of that country, sweetened, and only made to be used with chocolate), we had nothing. Morning would break upon us without materials for a breakfast. Summary measures were necessary, and I went out to consult with the major domo and the Indians. They had made a clearing near the horses, had their hammocks swung under the trees, and a large fire in the centre. All vacated their hammocks, and were docile as doves until I mentioned the necessity of sending immediately for provisions. Completely the creatures of habit, used to ending their labours with the sun, and then to gossip and repose, they could not bear to be disturbed. Money was no object to them; and but for the major domo I should not have been able to accomplish anything. He selected two, each of whom was intrusted with part of the commission, as one could not remember all the items, and a written memorandum would, of course, be of no use. There was one article, the procuring of which was doubtful, and that was an olla, or earthen pot, for cooking; no Indian had more than one in his hut, and that was always in use. Our messengers were instructed to buy, hire, or beg, or get in any other way their ingenuity might suggest, but not to come back without one.

Relieved in this important matter, the encampment under the trees, with the swarthy figures of the Indians lighted by the fire, presented a fine spectacle, and, but for the apprehension of moschetoes, I should have been tempted to hang up my hammock among them. As I returned, the moon was beaming magnificently over tne clearing, lighting up the darkness of the woods, and illuminating the great white building from its foundation to the summit.

We had some apprehensions for the night. My hammock was swung in the front apartment. Directly over my head, in the layer of flat stones along the arch, was the dim outline of a faded red painting like that first seen at Kewick. On the walls were the prints of the mysterious red hand, and around were the tokens of recent occupation before referred to, adding strength to the reflection always pressing upon our minds, what tales of fear and wonder these old walls, could they speak, might disclose. We had a large fire built in one corner of the apartment, but we heard no moschetoes, and there were no fleas. During the night we all woke up at the same moment, only to congratulate each other and enjoy the consciousness of feeling ourselves free from these little nuisances.

Our first business the next morning was to send our horses off to drink, and to procure water for ourselves, for the Indians had exhausted all that was found in the hollows of the rocks. At eleven o'clock our emissaries returned with fowls, eggs, tortillas, and an olla, the last of which they had hired for a medio, but for that day only.

Except a small ruined structure which we passed on the way to this building, as yet we had seen only this one with the ranges around the courtyard. It was clear that it did not stand alone; but we were so completely buried in the woods that it was utterly impossible to know which way to turn in search of others. In making our clearing we had stumbled upon two circular holes, like those found at Uxmal, which the Indians called chultunes, or cisterns, and which they said existed in all parts, and Doctor Cabot, in pursuit of a bird, had found a range of buildings at but a short distance, disconnected from each other, and having their façades ornmaented with stucco.

Going out to the path from which we had turned off to reach this edifice, and proceeding upon it a short distance, we saw through the trees the corner of a large building, which proved to be a great parallelogram, enclosing a hollow square. In the centre of the front range a grand but ruined staircase ascended from the ground to the top of the building, and, crossing the flat roof, we found a corresponding staircase leading down into the courtyard. The richest ornaments were on the side facing the courtyard, being of stucco, and on each side of the staircase were some of new and curious design, but, unfortunately, they were all in a ruinous condition. The whole court-yard was overgrown, so that the buildings facing it were but indistinctly visible, and in some places not at all.

In the afternoon the wind increased to a regular Norther, and at night all the Indians were driven in by the rain.

The next day the rain continued, and the major domo left us, taking with him nearly all the Indians. This put an end to the clearing, Mr. Catherwood had a recurrence of fever, and in the intervals of sunshine Dr. Cabot and myself worked with the Daguerreotype.

In the mean time, from the difficulty of procuring water and necessaries, we found our residence at these ruins uncomfortable. Our Indians, whom we had engaged to carry our luggage, complained of the detention, and, to crown our troubles, the owner of the olla came, and insisted upon having it returned. Mr. Catherwood, too, was unable to work, the woods were wet with the rain, and we considered it advisable to change the scene. There is no place which we visited that we were so reluctant to leave unfinished, and none that better deserved a month's exploration. It remains a rich and almost unbroken field for the future explorer, and, that he may have something to excite his imagination, and, at the same time, to show that the love of the marvellous is not confined to any one country, I may add that, upon the strength of a letter of mine to a friend in the interior, giving an account of the discovery of this place, and mentioning the vestiges of six buildings, we found, on our return to Merida, that these six had gone on accumulating, and had not been fairly brought to a stop till they had reached six hundred!

CHAPTER X

On Thursday, the twenty-fourth of February, we broke up and left the ruins. A narrow path brought us out into the camino real, along which we passed several small ranchos of sugar-cane. At eleven o'clock we reached the hacienda of Jalasac, the appearance of which, after a few days' burial in the woods, was most attractive and inviting; and here we ventured to ask for water for our horses. The master made us dismount, sent our horses to an aguada, and had some oranges picked from the tree, sliced, and sprinkled with sugar, for ourselves. He told us that his establishment was nothing compared with Señor Trego's, a league distant, whom, he said, we, of course, knew, and would doubtless stop with a few days. Not remembering ever to have heard of Señor Trego before, we had not formed unalterably any such intention, but it was manifest that all the world, and we in particular, ought to know Señor Trego; and we concluded that we would do him the honour of a visit as we passed through. This gentleman had forty criados, or servants, engaged in making sugar. And, on entering the sugar region, I may suggest that Yucatan seems to present some advantages for the cultivation of this necessary; not in the interior, on account of the expense of transportation, but along the coast, the whole line from Campeachy to Tobasco being good for that

131

purpose, and within reach of a foreign market. The advantages are, first, that slave labour is dispensed with, and, secondly and consequently, no outlay of capital is necessary for the purchase of slaves. In Cuba or Louisiana the planter must reckon among his expenses the interest upon the capital invested in the purchase of slaves, and the cost of maintaining them. In Yucatan he has to incur no outlay of capital; Indian labour is considered by those who have examined into the subject in Cuba, as about the same with that of the negroes; and by furnishing them constant employment, Indians can be procured in any numbers at a real per day, which is less than the interest upon the cost of a negro, and less than the expense of maintaining him if he cost nothing.

Resuming our journey, at the distance of a league we reached another rancho, which would have been creditable in any country for its neatness and arrangement. Our road ran through a plaza, or square, with large seybo trees in the centre, and neat white houses on all the sides; and before the door of one of them we saw a horse and cart! an evidence of civilization which we had not seen till that time in the country. This could be no other than Señor Trego's. We stopped in the shade, Señor Trego came out of the principal house, told the servants to take our chances for a dinner, we said nothing. Entering the house, were a little surprised, but, as we were very uncertain about our chances for a dinner, we said nothing. Entering the house, we fell into fine large hammocks; and Señor Trego told us that we were welcome on our own account, even without the recommendation of the padre Rodriguez of Xul. This gave us a key to the mystery. The padre Rodriguez had given us a letter to some one on this road, which we had accidentally left behind, and did not know the name of the person to whom it was addressed; but we now remembered that the cura, in speaking of him, had said deliberately, as if feeling the full import of his words, that he was rich and his friend; and we remembered, too, that the padre had frankly read to us the letter before giving it, in which, not to compromise himself with a rich friend, he had recommended us as worthy of Señor Trego's best offices upon our paying all costs and expenses; but we had reason to believe that the honest padre had reversed the custom of more polished lands, and that his private advices had given a liberal interpretation to his cautious open recommendation. At all events, Señor Trego made us feel at once that there was to be no reserve in his hospitality; and when he ordered some lemonade to be brought in immediately, we did not hesitate to suggest the addition of two fowls boiled, with a little rice thrown in.

While these were in preparation, Señor Trego conducted us round to look at his establishment. He had large sugar-works, and a distillery for the manufacture of habanera; and in the yard of the latter was a collection of enormous black hogs, taking a siesta in a great pool of mud, most of them with their snouts barely above water, a sublime spectacle for one interested in their lard and tallow, and Señor Trego told us that in the evening a hundred more, quite equal to these, would come in to scramble for their share of the bed. To us the principal objects of interest were in the square, being a well, covered over and dry, dug nearly to the depth of six hundred feet without reaching water, and the great seybo trees, which had been planted by Señor Trego himself; the oldest being of but twelve years' growth, and more extraordinary for its rapid luxuriance than that before referred to as existing at Ticul.

At four o'clock we resumed our journey, and toward dark, passing some miserable huts in the suburbs, we reached the new village of Iturbide, standing on the outposts of civilization, the great point to which the tide of emigration was rolling, the Chicago of Yucatan.

The reader may not consider the country through which we have been travelling as over-burdened with population, but in certain parts, particularly in the district of Nohcacab, the people did so consider it. Crowded and oppressed by the large landed proprietors, many of the enterprising yeomanry of this district determined to seek a new home in the wilderness. Bidding farewell to friends and relatives, after a journey of two days and a half they reached the fertile plains of Zibilnocac, from time immemorial an Indian rancho. Here the soil belonged to the government; every man could take up what land he pleased, full scope was offered to enterprise, and an opportunity for development not afforded by the over-peopled region of Nohcacab. Long before reaching it we had heard of this new pueblo and its rapid increase. In five years, from twenty-five inhabitants it had grown into a population of fifteen or sixteen hundred; and, familiar as we were with new countries and the magical springing up of cities in the wilderness, we looked forward to it as a new object of curiosity and interest.

The approach was by a long street, at the head of which, and in the entrance to the plaza, we saw a gathering, which in that country seemed a crowd, giving an indication of life and activity not usual in the older villages; but drawing nearer, we noticed that the crowd was stationary, and, on reaching it, we found that, according to an afternoon custom, all the principal inhabitants were gathered around a card-table, playing monte; rather a bad symptom, but these hardy pioneers exhibited one good trait of character in their close attention to the matter in hand. They gave us a passing glance and continued the game. Hanging on the outskirts of the crowd, however, were some who, not having the wherewithal to join in the stakes, bestowed themselves upon us. Among them was one who claimed us as acquaintances, and said that he had been anxiously looking for us. He had kept the "run" of us as far as Bolonchen, but had then lost us entirely, and was relieved when we accounted for ourselves by mentioning our disappearance in the woods of Labphak. This gentleman was about fifty, dressed in the light costume of the place, with straw hat and sandals, and it was no great recommendation to him when he told us that he had made our acquaintance at Nohcacab. He was an emigrant from that place, and on a visit when he saw us there. He claimed Dr. Cabot more particularly as his friend, and the latter remembered receiving from him some really friendly offices. He apologized for not being able to show us many attentions at that place; it was his pueblo, but he had no house there; this was his home, and here he could make amends. He told us that this was a new village, and had but few accommodations; the casa real had no doors, or they were not yet put on. He undertook to provide for us, however, and conducted us to a house adjoining that of his brother, and belonging to the latter, on the corner of the plaza. It had a thatched roof, and perhaps, by this time, the floor is cemented; but then it was covered with the lime and earth for making the cement, taking a good impression from every footstep, and throwing up some dust. It was, however, already in use as a store-room for the shop on the corner, and had demijohns, water-jars, and bundles of tobacco stowed along the wall; the middle was vacant, but there was no chair, bench, or table; but by an energetic appeal to the lookers-on these were obtained.

Our Nohcacab friend was most efficient in his attentions, and, in fact, constituted himself a committee to receive us; and after repeating frequently that at Nohcacab, though it was his village, he had no house, &c., he came to the point by inviting us forthwith to his house to take chocolate.

Tired of the crowd, and wanting to be alone, we declined, and unluckily assigned as a reason that we had ordered chocolate to be prepared. He went away with the rest, but very soon returned, and said that we had given him a bofetada, or rebuff, and had cheapened him in the estimation of his people. As he seemed really hurt, we directed our preparations to be discontinued, and went with him to his house, where we had a cup of very poor chocolate, which he followed up by telling us that we must eat at his house during the whole of our stay in the village, and that we must not spend a cent for la comida, or food. Our daily expenses at Nohcacab, he said, were enormous; and when we left he escorted us home, carrying with him a little earthen vessel containing castor oil with a wick in it, and said we must not spend any money for candles, and again came to the point by insisting upon our promising to dine at his house the next day.

In the mean time Albino had inquired him out, and we found that we had secured a valuable acquaintance. Don Juan was one of the oldest settlers, and one of the most influential inhabitants. He was not then in public office, but he was highly connected. One of his brothers was first alcalde, and another keeper of the gambling-table.

We considered his attentions for the evening at an end, but in a short time he entered abruptly, and with a crowd at his heels. This time he was really welcome, for he called us out to look at a lunar rainbow, which the people, looking at it in connexion with our visit and its strange objects, considered rather ominous, and Don Juan himself was not entirely at ease; but it did not disturb the gentlemen around the gambling-table, who had, in the mean time, to avoid the night air, moved under the shed of the proprietor, Don Juan's brother and our landlord.

The next morning a short time enabled us to see all the objects of interest in the new village of Iturbide. Five years before the plough had run over the ground now occupied by the plaza, or, more literally, as the plough is not known in Yucatan, the plaza is on the ground formerly occupied by an old milperia, or cornfield. In those ancient days it was probably enclosed by a bush fence; now, at one corner rises a thatched house, with an arbour before it, and a table under the arbour, at which, perhaps, at this moment the principal inhabitants are playing monte. Opposite, on the other corner, stood, and still stands if it has not fallen down, a casa de paja (thatched house) from which the thatching had been blown away, and in which were the undisposed-of remains of an ox for sale. Along the sides were whitewashed huts, and on one corner a large, neat house, belonging to our friend Señor Trego; then a small edifice with a cross in the roof, marking it as a church; and, finally, an open casa publica, very aptly so called, as it had no doors. Such are the edifices which in five years have sprung up in the new village of Iturbide; and attached to each house was a muddy yard, where large black pigs were wallowing in the mire, the special objects of their owner's care, soon to become large black hogs, and to bring ten or twelve dollars a piece in the Campeachy market. But, interesting as it is to watch the march of improvement, it was not for these we had come to Iturbide. Within the plaza were memorials of older and better times, indications of a more ingenious people than the civilized whites by whom it is now occupied. At one end was a mound of ruins, which had once supported an ancient building; and in the centre was an ancient well, unchanged from the time of its construction, and then, as for an unknown length of time before, supplying water to the inhabitants. There could be no question about the antiquity of this well; the people all said that it was a work of the antiguos, and paid respect to it and valued it highly on that account, for it had saved them the labour and expense of digging a new one for themselves.

It was about a yard and a quarter wide at the mouth, and seven or eight yards in depth, circular, and constructed of stones laid without plaster or cement of any kind. The stones were all firmly in their places, and had a polish which, with creases made by ropes in the platform at the top, indicated the great length of time that water had been drawn from it.

Besides these memorials, from a street communicating with the plaza we saw a range of great mounds, the ruins of the ancient city of Zibilnocac, which had brought us to Iturbide.

Don Juan was ready to accompany us to the ruins, and while he was waiting at our door, one person and another came along and joined him, until we had an assemblage of all the respectable citizens, apparently just risen from the gambling-table, of wan and miserable aspect, and, though they had ponchas wrapped about them, shivering with cold.

On the way to the ruins we passed another ancient well, of the same construction with that in the plaza, but filled up with rubbish, and useless. The Indians called it Stu-kum, from a subject familiar to them, and presenting not a bad idea of a useless well; the word meaning a calabash with the seeds dried up. A short walk brought us into an open country, and among the towering ruins of another ancient city. The field was in many places clear of trees, and covered only with plantations of to-bacco, and studding it all over were lofty ranges and mounds, enshrouded in woods, through which white masses of stone were glimmering, and rising in such quick succession, and so many at once, that Mr. Catherwood, in no good condition for work, said, almost despondingly, that the labours of Uxmal were to begin again.

Among them was one long edifice, having at each end what seemed a tower; and, attended by our numerous escort, we approached it first. It was difficult to imagine what could have procured us the honour of their company. They evidently took no interest in the ruins, could give us no information about them, nor even knew the paths that led to them; and we could not flatter ourselves that it was for the pleasure of our society. The building before us was more ruined than it seemed from a distance, but in some respects it differed from all the others we had seen. It required much clearing; and when this was signified to our attendants, we found that among them all there was not a single machete. Generally, on these occasions, there were some who were ready to work, and even on the look-out for a job; but among these thriving people there was not one who cared to labour in any capacity but that of a looker-on. A few, however, were picked out as by general consent the proper persons to work, upon whom all the rest fell and drove them to the village for their machetes. At the same time, many of those who remained took advantage of the opportunity to order their breakfast sent out, and all sat down to wait. Mr. Catherwood, already unwell, worried by their chattering, lay down in his poncha on the ground, and finally became so ill that he returned to the house. In the mean time I went to the foot of the building, where, after loitering more than an hour, I heard a movement overhead, and saw a little boy of about thirteen cutting among the branches of a tree. Half a dozen men placed themselves within his hearing, and gave him directions to such an extent that I was obliged to tell them I was competent to direct one such lad myself. In a little while another lad of about fifteen joined him, and for some time these boys were the only persons at work, while lazy beggars were crouching on every projecting stone, industriously engaged in looking at them. Finally, one man came along with his machete, and then others, until five were at work. They were occupied the greater part of the day, but to the last there were some trees, obstructing the view of particular parts, which I could not get cut down. All this time the spectators remained looking on as if in expectation of some grand finale; toward the last they began to show symptoms of anxiety, and during this time, through the unintentional instrumentality of Don Juan, I had made a discovery. The fame of the Daguerreotype, or la machina, had reached their ears, greatly exaggerated. They, of course, knew but little about it, but had come out with the expectation of seeing its miraculous powers exercised. If the reader be at all malicious, he will sympathize in my satisfaction, when all was cleared and ready to be drawn, in paying the men and walking back to the village, leaving them sitting on the stones.

The untoward circumstances of the morning threw Don Juan into a somewhat anxious state; he had incurred the expense of preparations, and was uncertain whether we intended to do him the honour of dining with him; apprehensive of another bofetada, he was afraid to mention the subject, but on reaching his house he sent to give notice that dinner was ready, and to inquire when he should send it to us. To make amends, and again conciliate, we answered that we would dine at his house, which he acknowledged through Albino as a much higher honour.

His house was on the principal street, but a short distance from the plaza, and one of the first erected, and the best in the place. He had been induced to settle in Iturbide on account of the facilities and privileges offered by the government, and the privilege which he seemed to value most was that of selling out. As he told us himself, when he came he was not worth a medio, and he seemed really to have held his own remarkably well. But appearances were deceitful, for he was a man of property. His house, including doors and a partition at one end, had cost him thirty dollars. The doors and partition his neighbours regarded as a piece of pretension, and he himself supposed that these might have been dispensed with, but he had no children, and did not mind the expense. At one end of the room was a rude frame, supporting the image of a tutelary saint. Near it was a stick thrust into the mud floor, with three prongs at the upper end, in which rested an earthen vessel containing castor oil, with a wick in it, to light up the mansion at night; a sort of bar with bottles containing agua ardiente flavoured with anise, for retailing to the Indians, which, with a small table and three hammocks, constituted the furniture of Don Juan's house. These last served for chairs, but as he had never anticipated the extraordinary event of dining three persons, they could not be brought into right juxtaposition to the table. Consequently, we sent for our two borrowed chairs, and, with the table in front of one of the hammocks, we were all seated except our host, who proposed to wait upon us. There was one aristocratic arrangement in Don Juan's household. His kitchen was on the other side of the street, a rickety old frame of poles, and Don Juan, after running across several times, bare-headed, to watch the progress of the dinner, returned and threw himself into a hammock a little within the doorway, crying out across the street, "Trae la comida, muchacha." "Bring the dinner, girl." The first course included a bowl of soup, a plate of rice, and three spoons; rather an alarming intimation, but at the same time rather grand, and much better than the alternative that sometimes happened, of three plates and one spoon, or none at all; and all apprehension was dissipated by the reappearance of the girl with another bowl and plate. Don Juan himself followed with each hand full, and we had a bowl, plate, and spoon apiece. The contents disposed of, another dish was served, which, by counting the wings and legs, we ascertained to be the substance of two fowls; and while attending to them, we were engaged in the friendly office, which guests but rarely do for their host, of calculating the expense he was incurring. We had too good an opinion of Don Juan's shrewdness to believe that he was making this lavish expenditure in mere wantonness, and wondered what he could expect to get out of us in return. We had hardly begun to speculate upon this when, as if knowing what was passing in our minds, he called in his wife, a respectable-looking elderly person, and disclosed another design upon the Daguerreotype. At Nohcacab he had heard of portraits being taken, and wanted one of his wife, and he was somewhat disappointed, and, perhaps, went over the calculation we had just made, when he learned that, as there were no subjects on which it could be used to advantage, we had determined not to open the apparatus.

But he did not let us off yet. His next attempt was upon Dr. Cabot, and this, too, was in favour of his old wife. Taking her by the hand, he led her before the doctor, and, with an earnestness that gave dignity to his scanty wearing apparel, and ought to have found its way to the depths of medical science, explained the nature of her maladies. It was really a delicate case, and made more so by the length of time that had elapsed since marriage. No such case had ever occurred in my practice, and even Doctor Cabot was at a loss.

While the matter was under discussion several men came in. No doubt they had all received a hint to drop in at that hour. One had an asthma, another a swelling, and there were so many of Don Juan's friends afflicted that we made an abrupt retreat.

In the evening Don Juan's brother, the alcalde, called upon Dr. Cabot for advice for a sick child, which the course he was pursuing would soon have put beyond the reach of medicine. Doctor Cabot made him desist, and in the morning it was so much better that all the people conceived a good opinion of his abilities, and determined to patronise him in earnest.

The condition of the whole country in regard to medical aid is deplorable. Except at Campeachy and Merida there are no regular physicians, nor even apothecaries' shops. In the villages where there are curas, the whole duty of attending the sick devolves upon them. They have, of course, no regular medical education, but practise upon some old treatise or manuscript recipes, and even in their small practice they are trammelled by want of medicines. But in villages where there are no curas, there is no one to prescribe for the sick. The rich go to Campeachy or Merida, and put themselves under the hands of a physician; the poor linger and die, the victims of ignorance and empiricism.

Dr. Cabot's fame as a curer of biscos had spread throughout the country, and whenever we reached a village there was a curiosity, which threw Mr. Catherwood and me into the shade, to see the medico. Frequently we overheard the people say, "Tan joven," "So young:" "Es muchacho," "He is a boy;" for they associated the idea of age with that of a great medico. He was often consulted upon cases for which he could not prescribe with any satisfaction. Treatment which might be proper at the moment might not answer a few days afterward, and the greatest annoyance was that, if our travelling chest could not furnish the medicine, the prescription had to wait an opportunity of beeing sent to Merida; but when the medicine arrived, the case might have altered so much that this medicine had become altogether improper for it. It is gratifying to know that, in general, his practice gave satisfaction, yet, at the same time, it must be admitted that there were complaints. The terms could not well have been made easier, but the ground of dissatisfaction was, that he did not always furnish medicine as well as advice. I do not mention this reproachfully, however; throughout the country he had a fair share of patronage, and the run reached its climax at Iturbide. Unluckily, the day on which the inhabitants resolved to take him up in earnest it rained, and we were kept nearly all the time within doors, and there were so many applications from men, women, and children, many of whom came with Don Juan's recommendation, that the doctor was seriously annoyed. Every latent disease was brought out, and he could even have found business in prescribing for cases that might possibly occur, as well as for those already existing.

The next morning Mr. Catherwood made an effort to visit the ruins. Our numerous escort of the former occasion were all missing, and, except an Indian who had a tobacco patch in the neighbourhood, we were entirely alone. This Indian held an umbrella over Mr. Catherwood's head to protect him from the sun, and, while making the drawing, several times he was obliged by weakness to lie down and rest. I was disheartened by the spectacle. Although, considering the extent of illness in our party, we had in reality not lost much time, we had been so much embarrassed, and it was so disagreeable to be moving along with this constant liability to fever and ague, that here I felt very much disposed to break up the expedition and go home, but Mr. Catherwood persisted.

Plate XXI represents the front of this building. It is one hundred and fifty-four feet in front and twenty feet seven inches in depth. It differed in form from any we had seen, and had square structures rising in the centre and at each end, as seen in ruins in the engraving; these were called towers, and at a distance had that appearance. The façades of the towers were all ornamented with sculptured stone. Several of the apartments had tobacco leaves spread out in them to dry. In the centre, one apartment was encumbered with rubbish, cutting off the light from the door, but in the obscurity we saw on one of the stones, along the layer in the arch, the dim outline of a painting like that at Kewick; in the adjoining apartment were the remains of paintings, the most interesting, except those near the village of Xul, that we had met with in the country, and, like those, in position and general effect reminding me of processions in Egyptian tombs. The colour of the flesh was red, as was always the case with the Egyptians in representing their own people. Unfortunately, they were too much mutilated to be drawn, and seemed surviving the general wreck only to show that these aboriginal builders had possessed more skill in the least enduring branch of the graphic art.

The first accounts we heard of these ruins date back to the

Plate XXI

ITURBIDE.

time of my first visit to Nohpat. Among the Indians there at work was one who, while we were lunching, sitting apart under a tree, mentioned these ruins in exaggerated terms, particularly a row of painted soldiers, as he called them, which, from his imperfect description, I supposed might bear some resemblance to the stuccoed figures on the fronts of the buildings at Palenque; but, on pushing my inquiries, he said these figures carried muskets, and was so pertinacious on this point that I concluded he was either talking entirely at random, or of the remains of old Spanish structures. I noted the place in my memorandum book, and having had it for a long time upon our minds, and received more different accounts of it than of any other, none proved more unlike what we expected to find. We looked for few remains, but these distinguished for their beauty and ornament, and high state of preservation, instead of which we found an immense field, grand, imposing, and interesting from its vastness, but all so ruined that, with the exception of this one building, little of the detail could be discovered.

Back of this building, or, rather, on the other front, was a thriving tobacco patch, the only thriving thing we saw at Iturbide; and on the border another ancient well, now, as in ages past, furnishing water, and from which the Indian attending the tobacco patch gave us to drink. Beyond were towering mounds and vestiges, indicating the existence of a greater city than any we had yet encountered. In wandering among them Dr. Cabot and myself counted thirty-three, all of which had once held buildings aloft. The field was so open that they were all comparatively easy of access, but the mounds themselves were overgrown. I clambered up them till the work became tiresome and unprofitable; they were all, as the Indians said, puras piedras, pure stones; no buildings were left; all had fallen; and though, perhaps, more than at any other place, happy that it was our fortune to wander among these crumbling memorials of a once powerful and mysterious people, we almost mourned that our lot had not been cast a century sooner, when, as we believed, all these edifices were entire.

CHAPTER XI

Our journey in this direction is now ended. We were on the frontier of the inhabited part of Yucatan, and within a few leagues of the last village. Beyond was a wilderness, stretching off to the Lake of Peten, and that region of Lacandones, or unbaptized Indians, in which, according to the suggestion made in my previous volumes, lay that mysterious city never reached by a white man, but still occupied by Indians precisely in the same state as before the discovery of America. During my sojourn in Yucatan, my account of this city was published in one of the Merida papers, and among intelligent persons there was a universal belief that beyond the Lake of Peten there was a region of unconverted Indians of whom nothing was known. We had been moving on in the track of ruined cities. A venerable ecclesiastic in Merida had furnished me with an itinerary of the journey through the wilderness to the Lake of Peten, and I had some hope of being led on from place to place until we should reach a point which might unravel all mystery, and establish a connecting link between the past and present; but this hope was accompanied by a fear, and, perhaps fortunately for us, we did not hear of ruins beyond. If we had, we should not have attempted to go in search of them, and it would have been painful to turn back. I am far from believing, however, that because we did not hear of them none exist. On the contrary, it may well be that wrecks of cities lie buried but a few leagues farther on, the existence of which is entirely unknown at the village of Iturbide, for at that place there was not a single individual who had ever heard of the ruins at Labphak, which we had visited just before, until they heard of them from us.

As yet, however, our face is still set toward the Lake of Peten. In this lake are numerous islands, one of which is called Peten Grande, Peten itself being a Maya word, signifying an island; and before turning back I wish to present this island for one moment to the reader. It now belongs to the government of Guatimala, and is under the ecclesiastical jurisdiction of the Bishop of Yucatan. Formerly it was the principal place of the province of Itza, which province, for one hundred and fifty years after the subjugation of Yucatan, maintained its fierce and native independence. In the year 1608, sixty-six years after the conquest, two Franciscan monks, alone, without arms, and in the spirit of peace, set out to conquer this province by converting the natives to Christianity. The limits of these pages will not permit me to accompany them in their toilsome and dangerous journey, but, according to the account of one of them as given by Cogolludo, at ten o'clock at night they landed on the island, were provided with a house by the king, and the next day preached to the Indians; but the latter told them that the time had not yet come for them to become Christians, and advised the monks to go away and return at some other day. Nevertheless, they carried them round to see the town, and in the middle of one of the temples they saw a great idol of the figure of a horse, made of lime and stone, seated on the ground on his haunches, with his hind legs bent, and raised on his fore feet, being intended as an image of the horse which Cortez left at that place on his great journey from Mexico to Honduras. On that occasion the Indians had seen the Spaniards fire their muskets from the backs of the horses, and supposing that the fire and noise were caused by the animals, they called this image Tzimin Chac, and adored it as the god of thunder and lightning. As the monks saw it, one of them, says the author of the account, seemed as if the Spirit of the Lord had descended upon him; and, carried away by zealous fervour, seized the foot of the horse with his hand, mounted upon the statue, and broke it in pieces. The Indians immediately cried out to kill them; but the king saved them, though they were obliged to leave the island.

In the beginning of October, 1619, the same two monks, undaunted by their previous ill success, again appeared on the island; but the people rose up against them. One of the padres remonstrated; an Indian seized him by the hair, twisted his neck, and hurled him to the ground, tearing out his hair by the roots, and throwing it away. He was picked up senseless, and, with his companion and the accompanying Indians, put on board a bad canoe, without anything to eat, and again sent away. With all their fanaticism and occasional cruelty, there is something soul-stirring in the devotion of these early monks to the business of converting the souls of the Indians.

In the year 1695, Don Martin Ursua obtained the government of Yucatan, and, in pursuance of a proposal previously submitted by him to the king, and approved by the council of the Indies, undertook the great work of opening a road across the whole continent from Campeachy to Guatimala. The opening of this road led to the conquest of Itza, and we have a full and detailed account of this conquest, written by the licenciado, or lawyer, Don Juan Villagutierres, a native of Yucatan. It is entitled, "A History of the Conquest of Itza, reduction and progress of that of Lacandon, and other barbarous Nations of Gentile Indians in the Mediacion of Yucatan and Guatimala." It was published at Madrid in the year 1701, and, what gives it great value, within four years after the events referred to took place.

The work of opening the road was begun in 1695. In prosecuting it, the Spaniards encountered vestiges of ancient buildings raised on terraces, deserted and overgrown, and apparently very ancient. These, it is true, may have been abandoned long before the conquest; but, as the Spaniards had now been in the country one hundred and fifty years, it is not unreasonable to suppose that the terror of their name may have made desolate many places which their arms never reached.

On the twenty-first of January, 1697, Don Martin de Ursua set out from Campeachy to take command of the expedition in person, with a vicar-general and assistant, already nominated by the bishop, for the province of Itza. On the last day of February he had timber cut on the borders of Peten for the construction of vessels which should convey them to the island. He sent before a proclamation, giving notice that the time had come when they should have one cup and one plate with the Spaniards. "If not," says the proclamation, "I will do what the king commands me, but which it is not necessary now to express." The thirteenth of March was appointed for the day of embarcation. Some of the

Spaniards, knowing the immense number of Indians on the island, and the difficulty of conquering it, represented to the general the rashness of his undertaking; but, says the historian, carried away by his zeal, faith, and courage, he answered that, having in view the service of God and the king, and the drawing of miserable souls from the darkness of heathenism, under the favour and protection of the Virgin Mary, whose image he carried on the royal standard, and engraven on his heart, he alone was sufficient for this conquest, even if it were much more difficult.

He embarked with one hundred and eight soldiers, leaving one hundred and twenty, with auxiliary Indians, and two pieces of artillery, as a garrison for the camp. The vicar blessed the vessel, and as the sun rose she got under way for the island, two leagues distant. The vicar offered up a prayer, and the Spaniards cried "Viva la ley de Dios!" Half way across he encountered fleets of canoes filled with warlike Indians; but taking no notice of them, and moving on toward the island, the Spaniards saw assembled immense numbers, prepared for war; Indians crowded the tops of the small islands around; the canoes followed them on the lake, and enclosed them in a half moon between themselves and the shore. As soon as within reach, the Indians, by land and water, poured upon them a shower of arrows. The general, Don Martin Ursua, cried out in a loud voice, "Silence! let no one begin fighting, for God is on our side, and there is nothing to fear." The Spaniards were enraged, but Don Martin still cried out, "Let no one fire, on pain of death!" The arrows from the shore were like thick rain. The Spaniards could scarcely be restrained, and one soldier, wounded in the arm, and enraged by the pain, fired his musket; the rest followed; the general could no longer control them, and, without waiting till they reached the shore, as soon as the oars stopped all threw themselves into the water, Don Martin de Ursua among them. The Indians were thick as if collected at the mouth of a cannon; but at the horrible noise and destruction of the fire-arms they broke and fled in terror. The vessel, with twenty soldiers, attacked the canoes, and those both in the canoes and on the land, from the king to the smallest creature, all leaped into the water, and from the island to the main nothing was to be seen but the heads of Indians, men, women, and children, swimming for life. The Spaniards entered the deserted town, and hoisted the royal standard on the highest point of Peten. With a loud voice they returned thanks to God for his mercies, and Don Martin Ursua took formal possession of the island and the territory of Itza in the name of the king. The vicar claimed it as belonging to the bishopric of Yucatan, and in stole and bonnet blessed the lake. This took place on the thirteenth of March, 1697, one hundred and fifty-five years after the foundation of Merida, and but one hundred and forty-five years ago.

We have, then, accounts of visits by the padres sixty years after the subjugation of Yucatan, and a detailed account of the conquest of Itza, one hundred and fifty-five years afterward; and what did they find on the island? The monks say that, when taken to look over the city, they went to the middle and highest part of the island to see the kues and adoratorios of the heathen idols, and that "there were twelve or more of the size of the largest churches in the villages of the Indians in the province of Yucatan, each one of which was capable of containing more than one thousand persons."

The Spanish soldiers, too, almost before they had time to sheath their blood-stained swords, were seized with holy horror at the number of adoratorios, temples, and houses of idolatry. The idols were so numerous, and of such various forms, that it was impossible to give any description of them, or even to count them; and in the private houses of these barbarous infidels, even on the benches on which they sat, were two or three small idols.

According to the historical account, there were twenty-one adoratorios, or temples. The principal one was that of the great false priest Quin-canek, first cousin of the king Canek. It was of square form, with handsome breastwork, and nine steps, all of wrought stone, and each front was about sixty feet, and very high. It is again mentioned as being in the form of a castillo, and this name, perhaps, makes a stronger impression on my mind from the fact that in the ruined cities of Chichen and Tuloom, which will be presented to the reader hereafter, there is an edifice bearing to this day the name of El Castillo, given to it by the Spaniards, doubtless, from the same resemblance to a castle which induced General Ursua to apply that name to the adoratorio in Peten. On the last step at the entrance was an idol in a squatting position, sitting close to the ground, in human form, but with a very unprepossessing countenance.

Another great adoratorio is described, of the same form and similar construction, and the rest are mentioned only with reference to the number and character of the idols they contained; but, probably, if there had been any material difference in form or construction, it would have been mentioned, and there is reason to believe that they were all alike. These descriptions are brief and general, but, in my opinion, they are sufficient to identify the adoratorios and temples on this island as being of the same general character with all the ruined buildings scattered over this country; and this presumption has great additional interest from another important consideration, for we have clear and authentic historical accounts, perhaps more reliable than any others relating to the aborigines of this country, of the very people by whom and the very time within which these kues, adoratorios, and temples were erected.

According to both Cogolludo and Villagutierres, who drew their conclusions from occurrences of such late date as to leave but little room for error, the Itzites, or people of Itza, were originally from the land of Maya, now Yucatan, and once formed part of that nation. At the time of the insurrection of the caciques of Maya, and the destruction of Mayapan, Canek, one of the rebellious caciques, got possession of the city of Chichen Itza. As it is sometimes said, on account of the foretelling of the arrival of the Spaniards by one of their prophets, but more probably on account of the insecurity of his possessions, he withdrew with his people from the province of Chichen Itza to the most hidden and impenetrable part of the mountains, and took possession of the Lake of Peten, establishing his residence on the large island which now bears that name. This emigration, according to the history, took place but about one hundred years before the arrival of the Spaniards. It follows, therefore, that all the adoratorios and temples which Don Martin Ursua found on the island must have been erected within that time. The conquest took place in March, 1697, and we have the interesting fact, that but about one hundred and forty-five years ago, within the period of two lives, a city existed occupied by unbaptized Indians, precisely in the same state as before the arrival of the Spaniards, having kues, adoratorios, and temples of the same general character with the great structures now scattered in ruins all over that country. This conclusion cannot be resisted except by denying entirely the credit of all the historical accounts existing on the subject.

And where are these kues, adoratorios, and temples now? In both my journeys into that country, it was always my intention to visit the island of Peten, and it has been a matter of deep regret that I was never able to do so; but as the result of my inquiries, particularly from the venerable cura who furnished me with the itinerary, and who lived many years on the island, I am induced to believe that there are no buildings left, but that there are feeble vestiges, not enough in themselves to attract the attention of mere curiosity, but which may possess immense antiquarian interest, as making manifest the hand of the builders of the American cities. But even if these twenty-one kues, adoratorios, or temples have entirely disappeared, not one stone being left upon another, this does not impeach the truth of the historical account that they once existed, for in the history of the Spaniards' first day on the island we have an indication of what the same ruthless spirit might accomplish in one hundred and forty-five years. General Ursua took possession of the island at half past eight o'clock in the morning, and, immediately after returning thanks to God for the victory, the first order he issued was for each captain and officer, with a party of soldiers, to proceed forthwith to different parts of the city to reconnoiter all the temples, and houses of idolaters and of individuals, and to hurl down and break the idols. The general himself set out, accompanied by the vicar and assistant, and we learn incidentally, and only as a means of conveying an idea of the multitude of idols and figures thrown down by the Spaniards, that the taking of the island having been at half past eight in the morning, they were occupied, with but little intermission, in throwing down, breaking, and burning idols and statues, from that hour until half past five in the evening, when the drum called them to eat, which, says the historian, was very necessary after so great labour; and if one day served for destroying the idols, one hundred and forty-five years, in which were erected a fort, churches, and other buildings that now exist, may well have effected the complete destruction of all the native edifices for idol worship.

I have asked where are the adoratorios and temples of Peten, and I am here tempted to ask one other question. Where are the Indians whose heads on that day of carnage and terror covered the water from the island to the main? Where are those unhappy fugitives, and the inhabitants of the other islands and of the territory of Itza? They fled before the terrible Spaniard, plunged deeper into the wilderness, and are dimly connected in my mind with that mysterious city before referred to; in fact, it is not difficult for me to believe that in the wild region beyond the Lake of Peten, never yet penetrated by a white man, Indians are now living as they did before the discovery of America; and it is almost a part of this belief that they are using and occupying adoratorios and temples like those now seen in ruins in the wilderness of Yucatan.

150

The reader will perhaps think that I have gone quite far enough, and that it is time to come back.

The next on our list were the ruins of Macoba, lying on the rancho of our friend the cura of Xul, and then in the actual occupation of Indians. We learned that the most direct road to this place was an Indian path, but the best way to reach it was to retrace our steps as far as the rancho of Señor Trego; at least, this was so near being the best that the opportunity of passing the night with him determined us to set out immediately by that route. We had our Indian carriers in attendance at the village; but, unluckily, while preparing to set out, Mr. Catherwood was taken with fever, and we were obliged to postpone our departure.

We had another subject of anxiety, but more moderate, in the conduct of Don Juan. He had not been near us all day, and we could not account for his neglect; but toward evening Albino learned that the night before he had lost sixteen dollars at the gaming-table, and had kept his hammock ever since.

The next day it rained. On Sunday the rain still continued. Early in the morning the ministro came over from the village of Hopochen to say mass, and, while lounging about to note the prospect in regard to the weather, I stopped under the shed where the gaming-table remained ready for use, to which, when mass was over, all the better classes came from the church in clean dresses, prepared for business.

It was a matter of some curiosity to me to know how these men lived; none of them worked. Their only regular business seemed to be that of gambling. On taking a seat among them, I learned the secret from themselves. Each man had several outstanding loans of four or five dollars made to Indians, or he had sold agua ardiente or some other trifling commodity, which created an indebtedness. This made the Indian a criado, or servant, and mortgaged his labour to the creditor or master, by the use of which, in milpas or tobacco plantations, the latter lived. By small occasional supplies of cocoa or spirit they keep alive the indebtedness; and as they keep the accounts themselves, the poor Indians, in their ignorance and simplicity, are ground to the earth to support lazy and profligate masters.

We had not formed any very exalted opinion of these people, and they did not rate themselves very high. Don Juan had told us that the Indians were all drunkards, and half the white people; and the other half had occasionally to take to the hammock; he said, too, that they were all gamblers, and the alcalde, as he shuffled the cards, confirmed it, and asked me to join them. He inquired if there was no gambling in my country, or what people did with their money if they did not gamble, and he allowed that to expend it in horses, carriages, dinners, furniture, dress, and other particulars suggested by some of them, was sensible enough; for, as he said very truly, when they died they could not carry it away with them. I mentioned that in my country gambling was forbidden by law, and that for gambling in the street, and on a Sunday, they would all be taken up and punished. This touched the alcalde in his office, and he started up with the cards in his hand, and looking indignantly at the people under his charge, said that there too it was forbidden by law; that any one who gambled, or who connived at it, or who permitted it in his house, was liable to be declared not a citizen; that they had laws, and very good ones; all knew them, but nobody minded them. Everybody gambled, particularly in that village; they had no money, but they gambled corn and tobacco, and he pointed to a man then crossing the plaza, who the night before had gambled away a hog. He admitted that sometimes it was a good way to make money, but he pointed to a miserable-looking young man, not more than two or three-and-twenty, whose father, he said, had ranchos, and Indians, and houses, and ready money, and was close-fisted, and had left all to that son, who was now looking for seven and sixpence to make up a dollar, and the young man himself, with a ghastly smile, confirmed the tale. The alcalde then continued with a running commentary upon the idleness and extravagance of the people in the village; they were all lazy, and having illustrations at hand, he pointed to an Indian just passing with three strings of beef, which, he said, had cost him a medio and a half, and would be consumed at a meal, and that Indian, he knew, had not a medio in the world to pay his capitation tax. One of the gentlemen present then suggested that the government had lately passed an iniquitous law that no Indian should be compelled to work unless he chose; if he refused, he could not be whipped or imprisoned, and what could be expected in such a state of things? Another gentleman interposed with great unction, declaring that the alcalde of a neighbouring village did not mind the law, but went on whipping the same as before. All this time a dozen Indians, by the constitution free and independent as themselves, sat on the ground without saying a word, merely staring from one to the other of the speakers.

After this the conversation turned upon our own party, and

finally settled upon Doctor Cabot. I regretted to find that, in a community which had patronised him so extensively, there was some diversity of opinion as to his qualifications. There was one dissenting voice, and the general discussion settled down into a warm argument between the two brothers of Don Juan, the alcalde and the keeper of the gambling-table, the latter of whom held up an ugly sandalled foot, with a great excrescence upon it, and said, rather depreciatingly, that the doctor did not cure his corns. The alcalde was stanch, and thrust forward his cured child, but his brother shook his head, still holding out his foot, and I am sorry to say that, so far as I could gather the sense of the community, Doctor Cabot's reputation as a medico received somewhat of a shock.

In the afternoon the rain ceased, and we bade farewell to the new village of Iturbide. As we passed, Don Juan left his place at the table to bid us goodby, and a little before dark we reached the rancho Noyaxche of Señor Trego, where we again received a cordial welcome, and in his intelligent society found a relief from the dulness of Iturbide.

CHAPTER XII

The next morning after breakfast we again set out. Señor Trego escorted us, and, following a broad wagon road made by him for the passage of the horse and cart, at the distance of a mile and a half we came to a large aguada, which is represented in Plate XXII. It was apparently a mere pond, picturesque, and shaded by trees, and having the surface covered with green water plants, called by the Indians Xicin-chah, which, instead of being regarded as a blot upon the picturesque, were prized as tending to preserve the water from evaporation. Indians were then filling their water-jars, and this aguada was the only watering-place of the rancho. These aguadas had become to us interesting objects of consideration. Ever since our arrival in the country, we had been told that they were artificial, and, like the ruined cities we were visiting, the works of the ancient inhabitants. At first we had considered these accounts unreliable, and so nearly approaching the marvellous that we put but little faith in them; but as we advanced they assumed a more definite character. We were now in a region where the people were entirely dependant upon the aguadas; all considered them the works of the antiguos; and we obtained at length what we had long sought for, certain, precise, and definite information, which would not admit of question or doubt.

Failing in his attempt to procure water from the well, before referred to, in the plaza, in 1835 Señor Trego turned his

Plate XXII

attention to this aguada. He believed that it had been used by the ancients as a reservoir, and took advantage of the dry season to make an examination, which satisfied him that his supposition was correct. For many years it had been abandoned, and it was then covered three or four feet deep with mud. At first he was afraid to undertake with much vigour the work of clearing it out, for the prejudices of the people were against it, and they feared that, by disturbing the aguada, the scanty supply then furnished might be cut off. In 1836 he procured a permission from the government, by great exertions secured the cooperation of all the ranchos and haciendas for leagues around, and at length fairly enlisting them all in the task, at one time he had at work fifteen hundred Indians, with eighty superintendents (major domos). On clearing out the mud, he found an artificial bottom of large flat stones. These were laid upon each other in this form , and the interstices were filled in with clay of red and brown colour, of a different character from any in the neighbourhood. The stones were many layers deep, and he did not go down to the bottom, lest by some accident the foundation should be injured, and the fault be imputed to him.

Near the centre, in places which he indicated as we rode along the bank, he discovered four ancient wells. These were five feet in diameter, faced with smooth stone not covered with cement, eight yards deep, and at the time of the discovery were also filled with mud. And, besides these, he found along the margin upward of four hundred casimbas, or pits, being holes into which the water filtered, and which, with the wells, were intended to furnish a supply when the aguada should be dry.

The whole bottom of the aguada, the wells, and pits, were cleared out; Señor Trego portioned off the pits among families, to be preserved and kept in order by them, and the dry basin was then given up to the floods of the rainy season. It so happened that the next year was one of unusual scarcity, and the whole country around was perfectly destitute of water. That year, Señor Trego said, more than a thousand horses and mules came to this aguada, some even from the rancho of Santa Rosa, eighteen miles distant, with barrels on their backs, and carried away water. Families established themselves along the banks; small shops for the sale of necessaries were opened, and the butcher had his shambles with meat; the aguada supplied them

156

all, and when this failed, the wells and the pits held out abundantly till the rainy season came on, and enabled them to return to their several homes.

Throughout our journey we had suffered from the long continuance of the rainy season, and at this place we considered it one of the greatest misfortunes that attended us, that we were unable to see the bottom of this aguada and these ancient wells. Señor Trego told us that usually, at this season, the aguada was dry, and the people were drawing from the wells and pits. This year, happily for them, but unluckily for us, water was still abundant. Still it was a thing of high interest to see this ancient reservoir recovered and restored to its original uses, and, as we rode along the bank, to have indicated to us the particular means and art used to render it available. Hundreds are perhaps now buried in the woods, which once furnished this element of life to the teeming population of Yucatan.

Leaving the aguada, our road lay over a level and wooded plain, then wet and muddy from the recent rains, and at the distance of a league we reached the sugar rancho of a gentleman from Oxcutzcab, who had been a co-worker with Señor Trego in clearing out the aguada, and confirmed all that the latter had told us. A league beyond we came to the rancho of 'Y-a-walthel, inhabited entirely by Indians, and beyond our road opened upon a fine savanna, in which were several aguadas. Beyond this we reached the rancho of Choop, and came into a good road, different from the usual milpa paths, and like a well-beaten camino real, made so by the constant travelling of beasts with water kegs to the aguadas.

In the afternoon we passed the campo santo of Macoba, and very soon, ascending a hill, we saw through the trees the "old walls" of the ancient inhabitants. It was one of the wildest places we had seen; the trees were grander, and we were somewhat excited on approaching it, for we had heard that the old city was repeopled, and that Indians were again living in the buildings. It was almost evening; the Indians had returned from their work; smoke was issuing from the ruins, and, as seen through the trees, the very tops seemed alive with people; but as we approached we almost turned away with sorrow. It was like the wretched Arabs of the Nile swarming around the ruined temples of Thebes, a mournful contrast of present misery and past magnificence. The doors were stopped with leaves and branches; the sculptured ornaments on the façades were blackened by smoke rolling from the doorways, and all around were the con-

157

fusion and filthiness of Indian housekeeping. As we rode up the Indians stared at us in astonishment, and the scared women snatched up their screaming children and ran away.

Among these ruins a rancho had been erected for the major domo, and as everything we had heretofore seen belonging to the cura of Xul was in fine order, we had no fears about our accommodations; but we found that nothing in this world must be taken for granted. The rancho was thatched, and had a dirty earthen floor, occupied by heaps of corn, beans, eggs, boxes, baskets, fowls, dogs, and pigs. There were two small, dirty hammocks, in one of which was swinging an Indian lad, and from the other had just been taken a dead man, whose new grave we had seen at the campo santo.

The major domo was a short, stupid, well-meaning old man, who apologized for the confusion on account of the death and burial that had just taken place. He was expecting us, had his master's orders to treat us with all due consideration, and we directed the rancho to be swept out. As night approached, we began to feel that our discomforts might be increased, for our carriers did not make their appearance. We had no apprehensions of robbery. Bernaldo was with them, and, knowing his propensities, we supposed that he had stopped at some rancho, where, in waiting to have some tortillas made, he had got belated, and was unable to find the road; but, whatever the cause, we missed the comforts of our travelling equipage. We were without candles, too, and sat in the miserable rancho in utter darkness, listening for the sound of the approaching carriers, until Albino procured a broken vessel of castor oil with a wick in it, which, by faintly illuminating one corner, disclosed more clearly the dreariness and discomfort of the scene.

But worse than all was the prospect of sleeping in the flea-infested hammocks, from one of which the body of a dead man had just been taken. We got the major domo to remove them and hire others, which, perhaps, were in reality not much better. Albino and Dimas had to lie down on the earthen floor, but they could not remain long. Dimas mounted lengthwise upon a log, and Albino doubled himself up in a baño, or bathing-tub, which kept him from the bare ground, but not above the jump of a flea. Fortunately, we suffered excessively from cold, which prevented us from being thrown into a fever, but it was one of the worst nights we had passed in the country.

Early in the morning Bernaldo made his appearance, he and the carriers having had a harder time than our own. They had been lost, and had wandered till ten o'clock, when they came to a rancho, where they learned their mistake, but were too much tired to carry their loads any farther, and, with an Indian from the rancho to guide them, had set out two hours before daylight.

The rancho of Macoba had been established but four years. It was situated in the midst of an immense forest; as yet it had been used only for the cultivation of maize, but the cura intended the ensuing year to commence a plantation of sugar. His inducement to establish a rancho at this place was the existence of the ruined buildings, which saved the expense of erecting huts for his criados; and he was influenced also by the wells and other remains of ancient watering-places. In the immediate vicinity of the buildings, without inquiring or seeking for them, we came across four wells, but all filled up with rubbish, and dry. Indeed, so many were known to exist, and the other means of supply were so abundant, that Señor Trego was about becoming a partner with the cura, under the expectation of clearing out and restoring these ancient reservoirs, furnishing an abundant supply of water, and calling around them a large Indian population.

In the mean time the cura had constructed two large tanks, or cisterns, one of which was twenty-two feet in diameter, and the same in depth, and the other eighteen. Both these were under a large circular roof, or top platform, covered with cement, and sloping toward the centre, which received the great body of rainwater that fell in the rainy season, and transmited it into the cisterns, and these furnished a supply during the whole of the dry season, as the major domo said, for fifty souls, besides fowls, hogs, and one horse.

The ruins at this place were not so extensive as we expected to find them. There were but two buildings occupied by the Indians, both in the immediate neighbourhood of our hut, and much ruined, one of which is represented in Plate XXIII. A noble alamo tree was growing by its side, and holding it up, which, while I was in another direction, the Indians had begun to cut down, but which, fortunately, I returned in time to save. The building is about 120 feet front, and had two stories, with a grand staircase on the other side, now ruined. The upper story was in a ruinous condition, but parts of it were occupied by Indians.

In the afternoon Doctor Cabot and myself set out for a ride to the aguada, induced somewhat by the forest character of the

Plate XXIII

MACOBA.

country, and the accounts the Indians gave us of rare birds, which they said were to be found in that direction. The road lay through a noble piece of woods, entirely different from the usual scrubby growth, with thorny and impenetrable underbrush, being the finest forest we had seen, and abounding in sapote and cedar trees. At the distance of half a league a path turned off to the right, overgrown, and hardly distinguishable, following which we reached the aguada. It was a mere hollow basin, overgrown with high grass. We rode down into it, and, dismounting, my first step from the side of my horse carried me into a hole, being a casimba, or pit, made by the Indians for the purpose of receiving the filtrations of water. We discovered others of the same kind, and to save our horses, backed them out to the edge of the aguada, and moved cautiously around it ourselves. These pits were no doubt of modern date, and we could not discover any indications of ancient wells; nevertheless, such may exist, for the aguada has been disused and neglected for an unknown length of time. Soil had accumulated, without removing which, the character and construction of the bottom could not be ascertained.

I returned from the aguada in time to assist Mr. Catherwood in taking the plan of the buildings. Our appearance in this wilderness had created astonishment among the Indians. All day, whenever we drew near to the buildings, the women and children ran inside, and now, when they found us entering their habitations, they all ran out of doors. The old major domo, unused to such a commotion among the women, followed us close, anxiously, but respectfully, and without uttering a word; and when we closed the book and told him we had finished, he raised both hands, and, with a relieved expression, exclaimed, "Gracias a Dios, la obra es acabada!" "Thank God, the work is done!"

I have nothing to say concerning the history of these ruins. They are the only memorials of a city which, but for them, would be utterly unknown, and I do not find among my notes any memoranda showing how or from whom we first received the intelligence of their existence.

March 2. Early in the morning we were again preparing to move, but, when on the eve of setting out, we learned that Bernaldo wanted to vary the monotony of travelling by getting married. He had met at the well an Indian girl of thirteen, he himself being sixteen. While assisting her to draw water, some tender passages had taken place between them, and he had disclosed to Albino his passion and his wishes; but he was trammelled by that impediment which all over the world keeps asunder those who are born for each other, viz., want of fortune. The girl made no objections on this score, nor did her father. On the contrary, the latter, being a prudent man, who looked to the future well-establishing of his daughter, considered Bernaldo, though not in the actual possession of fortune, a young man of good expectations, by reason of the wages that would be due to him from us; but the great difficulty was to get ready money to pay the padre. Bernaldo was afraid to ask for it, and the matter was not communicated to us until at the moment of setting out. It was entirely against hacienda law to marry off the estate; Don Simon would not like it; and, in the hurry and confusion of setting out, we had no time to deliberate; we therefore sent him on before us, and I am sorry to be obliged to say that this violence to his affections never made it necessary to change the appellation which we had given him very early after he came into our possession, namely, the fat boy.

We found among our carriers another youthful example of blighted affections, but recovering. He was a lad of about Bernaldo's age, to wit, sixteen, but had been married two years before, was a father, a widower, and about to be married again. The story was told us in his hearing, and, from his smiles at different parts of it, it was difficult to judge which he considered the most amusing; and we had still another interesting person, being a runaway Indian, who had been caught and brought back but a few days before, and upon whom the major domo charged all the others to keep a good look-out.

Our road lay through the same great forest in which the ruins stood. At the distance of a league we descended from the high ground, and reached a small aguada. From this place the road for some distance was hilly until we came out upon a great savanna covered with a growth of bushes, which rose above our heads so thick that they met across the path, excluding every breath of air, without shielding us from the sun, and exceedingly difficult and disagreeable to ride through. At one o'clock we reached the suburbs of the rancho of Puut. The settlement was a long line of straggling huts, which, as we rode through them under the blaze of a vertical sun, seemed to have no end. Mr. Catherwood stopped at one of them for a cup of water, and I rode on till I reached an open plain, forming a sort of square with thatched houses, and on one side a thatched church. I inquired of a woman peeping out of a door for the casa real, and was directed to a ruined hut on the same side, at the door, or, rather, at the doorway of which I dismounted, but had hardly crossed the threshold when I saw my white pantaloons speckled with little jumping black insects. I made a hasty retreat, and saw a man at the moment moving across the plaza, who asked me to his house, which was clean and comfortable, and when Mr. Catherwood came up the women of the house were engaged in preparing our dinner. Mr. Catherwood had just experienced the same kind of good feeling at an Indian hut. Water, in the Maya language, is expressed by the word *ha*, but, being that morning rather out of practice, Mr. Catherwood had asked for *ka*, which means fire, and the woman brought him a lighted brand. He motioned that away, but still continued asking for *ka*, fire. The woman went in, sat down, and made him a straw cigar, which she brought out to him. Sitting in the broiling sun, and perishing with thirst, he dropped his Maya, and by signs made her understand what he wanted, when she brought him water.

Our host, who was a Mestizo and ex-alcalde, procured for us another empty hut, which, by the time our carriers arrived, we had swept out and made comfortable.

The situation of this rancho was on a fine open plain; the land was good, and water abundant, though not very near at hand, the supply being derived from an aguada, to which we sent our horses; and they were gone so long that we determined the next morning, as the aguada lay but little out of our road, to ride by it and water them ourselves.

From this place we intended to visit the ruins of Mankeesh, but we learned that it would require a large circuit to reach them, and, at the same time, we received intelligence of other ruins of which we had not heard before, at the rancho of Yakat-zib, on the road we had intended taking. We determined for the present to continue on the route we had marked out, and it so happened that we did not reach the ruins of Mankeesh at all, which, according to more particular accounts received afterward, when it was too late to profit by them, merit the attention of the future traveller.

CHAPTER XIII

At seven o'clock the next morning we started, and at the distance of a league reached the rancho of Jalal, from which we turned off to the aguada to water our horses. Plate XXIV represents this aguada. When we first came down upon its banks it presented one of the most beautifully picturesque scenes we met with in the country. It was completely enclosed by a forest, and had large trees growing around the banks and overhanging the water. The surface was covered with water weeds like a carpet of vivid green, and the aguada had a much higher interest than any derived from mere beauty. According to the accounts we had received at the rancho, ten years before it was dry, and the bottom covered with mud several feet deep. The Indians were in the habit of digging pits in it for the purpose of collecting the water which filtered through, and in some of these excavations they struck upon an ancient well, which, on clearing it away, was found to be of singular form and construction. It had a square platform at the top, and beneath was a round well, faced with smooth stones, from twenty to twenty-five feet deep. Below this was another square platform, and under the latter another well of less diameter, and about the same depth. The discovery of this well induced farther excavations, which, as the whole country was interested in the matter, were prosecuted until upward of forty wells were discovered, differing in their character and construction, and some idea of which may

Plate XXIV

be formed from Figure 9. These were all cleared out, and the whole aguada repaired, since which it furnishes a supply during the greater part of the dry season, and when this fails the wells appear, and continue the supply until the rains come on again.

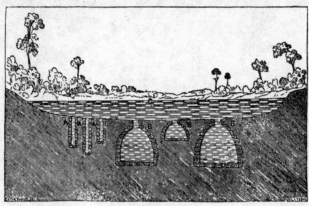

FIG. 9

Leaving this, we continued again upon a plain. Albino had not come up with us, and passing through one Indian rancho, we came to another, in which were many paths, and we were at a loss which to take. The men were all away, and we were obliged to chase the women into their very huts to ask directions. At the last hut we cornered two, who were weaving cotton, and came upon them with our great effort in the Maya language, "Tush y am bé—" "Is this the way to—" adding Yakatzib, the name of the rancho at which we were told there were ruins. We had acquired great facility in asking this question, but if the answer went beyond "yes" or "no," or an indication with the hand, as was the case on this occasion, it was entirely beyond our attainments. The woman gave us a very long, and probably a very civil answer, but we could not understand a word of it; and finding it impossible to bring them to monosyllables, we asked for a draught of water and rode on.

When we had gone some distance beyond the rancho, it occurred to us that this might be Yakatzib itself, and we turned back. Before reaching it, however, we turned off into a grove of large orange trees at one side of the road, dismounted, and tied our horses under the shade to wait for Albino. The trees were loaded and the ground covered with fruit, but the oranges were all of the sour kind. We could not sit down under the trees, for the ground was teeming with garrapatas, ants, and other insects,

166

and while standing we were obliged to switch them off with our riding whips. Soon Albino came thundering along on the trotter, and we learned that we had really passed Yakatzib, as the women had no doubt told us. While we were mounting to go back, a boy passed on a miserable old horse, his bare body perched between two water-kegs, with which he was going to the aguada. For a medio he slipped off, tied his horse to a bush, and ran before us as our guide through the rancho, beyond which, turning off to the right, we soon reached a ruined edifice.

It was small, and the whole front was gone; the door had been ornamented with pillars, which had fallen, and lay on the ground. The boy told us that there were ruined mounds, but no other remains of buildings. We turned back without dismounting, and continued our journey.

At two o'clock we reached the foot of a stony sierra, or mountain range, toilsome and laborious for the horses, but Mr. Catherwood remarked that his pricked up his ears and trod lightly, as if just beginning a journey. From the top of the same sierra we saw at its foot, on the other side, the village of Becanchen, where, on arriving, we rode through the plaza, and up to a large house, the front of which was adorned with a large red painting of a major domo on horseback, leading a bull into the ring. We inquired for the casa real, and were directed to a miserable thatched house, where a gentleman stepped out and recognized Mr. Catherwood's horse, which had belonged to Don Simon Peon, and through the horse he recognised me, having seen me with Don Simon at the fair at Jalacho, on the strength of which he immediately offered his house for a posada, or inn, which offer, on looking at the casa real, we did not hesitate to accept.

We were still on the great burial-ground of ruined cities. In the corridor of the house were sculptured stones, which our host told us were taken from the ancient buildings in the neighbourhood; they had also furnished materials for the foundation of every house on the plaza; and besides these there were other memorials. In the plaza were eight wells, then furnishing an abundant supply of water, and bearing that stamp which could not be mistaken, of the hand of the ancient builders. Below the plaza, on the declivity of the hill, was water gushing from the rocks, filling a clear basin beneath, and running off till it was lost in the woods. It was the first time in our whole journey that we had seen anything like a running stream, and after the parched regions through which we had passed, of almost inaccessible caves, muddy aguadas, and little pools in the hollows of rocks, it was a refreshing and delightful spectacle. Our Indian carriers had taken up their quarters under a brush fence, in sight and within reach of the stream, and to them and the muleteers it was like the fountain to the Arab in the desert, or the rivers of sweet water promised to the faithful in the paradise of Mohammed.

The history of this village has all the wildness of romance, and, indeed, throughout this land of sepulchred cities the genius of romance sits enthroned. Its name is derived from this stream of water, being compounded of the Maya words *Becan*, running, and *chen*, a well. Twenty years ago the country round about was a wilderness of forest. A solitary Indian came into it, and made a clearing for his milpa. In doing so he struck upon the running stream, followed it until he found the water gushing from the rock, and the whole surface now occupied by the plaza pierced with ancient wells. The Indians gathered round the wells, and a village grew up, which now contains six thousand inhabitants; a growth, having regard to the difference in the resources of the country and the character of the people, equal in rapidity to that of the most prosperous towns in ours.

These wells are all mere excavations through a stratum of limestone rock, varying in depth according to the irregularity of the bed, and in general not exceeding four or five feet. The source of the water is considered a mystery by the inhabitants, but it seems manifest that it is derived from the floods of the rainy season. The village is encompassed on three sides by hills. On the upper side of the plaza, near the corner of a street running back to the elevated range, is a large hole or natural opening in the rock, and during the whole of the rainy season a torrent of water collects into a channel, pours down this street, and empties into this hole. As we were told, the body of water is so great that for a week or ten days after the last rains the stream continues to run; and at the time of our visit it was eighteen inches in diameter. The water in the wells is always at the same level with that in the hole. They rise and fall together; and there is another conclusive proof of direct connexion, for, as we were told, a small dog that had been swept into the hole appeared some days afterward dead in one of the most distant wells.

Doctor Cabot and I descended into one of the wells, and found it a rude, irregular cavern, about twenty-five feet in diameter; the roof had some degree of regularity, and perhaps, to a certain extent, was artificial. Directly under the mouth the water was not more than eighteen inches deep, but the bottom was uneven, and a step or two beyond the water was so deep that we could not examine it thoroughly. By the light of a candle we could see no channel of communication with the other wells, but on one side the water ran deep under a shelving of the rock, and here there were probably some crevices through which it passed; indeed, this must have been the case, for this was the well in which the dog had come to light.

When we emerged from this well other business offered. Having little or no intercourse with the capital, this village was the first which Doctor Cabot's fame had not reached, and our host took me aside to ask me in confidence whether Doctor Cabot was a real medico; which fact being easily established by my evidence, he wanted the medico to visit a young Indian whose hand had been mangled by a sugar-mill. Doctor Cabot made some inquiries, the answers to which led to the conclusion that it would be necessary to cut off the hand; but, unluckily, at the last reduction of our luggage he had left his amputating instruments behind. He had a hand-saw for miscellaneous uses, which would serve in part, and Mr. Catherwood had a large spring-knife of admirable temper, which Doctor Cabot said would do, but the former flatly objected to its conversion into a surgical instrument. It had been purchased at Rome twenty years before, and in all his journeyings had been his travelling companion; but after such an operation he would never be able to use it again. Strong arguments were urged on both sides, and it became tolerably manifest that, unless amputation was necessary to save the boy from dying, the doctor would not get the knife.

Reaching the house, we saw the Indian sitting in the sala, the hand torn off to within about an inch of the wrist, and the stump swollen into a great ball six inches in diameter, perfectly black, and literally alive with vermin. At the first glance I retreated into the yard, and thence into the kitchen, when a woman engaged in cooking ran out, leaving her vessels boiling over the fire. I superintended her cooking, and dried my damp clothes, determined to avoid having anything to do with the operation; but, fortunately for me and Mr. Catherwood's knife, Doctor Cabot considered that it was not advisable to amputate. It was ten days since the accident happened, and the wound seemed to be healing. Doctor Cabot ascribed the lad's preservation to the sound and healthy state of the blood, arising from the simple diet of the Indian.

At this place we determined to separate; Mr. Catherwood to go on direct to Peto, a day and a half's journey distant, and lie by a few days to recruit, while Doctor Cabot and I made a retrograde and circuitous movement to the village of Mani. While speaking of our intention, a by-stander, Don Joaquin Sais, a gentleman of the village, told us of ruins on his hacienda of Zaccacal, eight leagues distant by a milpa road, and said that if we would wait a day, he would accompany us to visit them; but as we could not, he gave us a letter to the major domo.

Early the next morning Doctor Cabot and I set out with Albino and a single Indian, the latter carrying a petaquilla and hammocks. We left the village by the running stream, and rode for some time along a deep gully made by the great body of water which rushes through it in the rainy season. At half past nine we reached a large aguada, the banks of which were so muddy that it was impossible to get down to it to drink. A league beyond we reached another, surrounded by fine shade trees, with a few ducks floating quietly upon its surface. As we rode up Dr. Cabot shot a trogan, one of the rare birds of that country, adorning by its brilliant plumage the branches of an overhanging teee. We lost an hour of hard riding by mistaking our road among the several diverging tracks that led from the aguada. It was very hot; the country was desolate, and, suffering from thirst, we passed some Indians under the shade of a large seybo tree eating tortillas and chili, to whom we rode up, confident of procuring water; but they either had none, or, as Albino supposed, hid it away as we approached. At one o'clock we came to another aguada, but the bank was so muddy that it was impossible to get to the water without miring our horses or ourselves, and we were obliged to turn away without relief from our distressing thirst. Beyond this we turned off to the left, and, unusually fatigued with the heat and hard riding, although we had come but eight leagues, to our great satisfaction we reached the hacienda of Zaccacal.

Toward evening, escorted by the major domo and a vaquero to show the way, I set out for the ruins. At the distance of half a mile on the road to Tekax, we turned off into the woods to the left, and very soon reached the foot of a stone terrace. The vaquero led the way up it on horseback, and we followed, dismounting at the top. On this terrace was a circular hole like those before referred to at Uxmal and other places, but much larger; and, looking down into it till my eyes became accustomed to the darkness, I saw a large chamber with three recesses in different parts of the wall, which the major domo said were doors opening to passages that went under ground to an extent entirely unknown. By means of a pole with a crotch I descended, and found the chamber of an oblong form. The doors, as the major domo called them, were merely recesses about two feet deep. Touching one of them with my feet, I told him that the end of his passage was there, but he said it was tapado, or closed up, and persisted in asserting that it led to an indefinite extent. It was difficult to say what these recesses were intended for. They threw a mystery around the character of these subterranean chambers, and unsettled the idea of their being all intended for wells.

Beyond this, on a higher terrace, among many remains, were two buildings, one of which was in a good state of preservation, and the exterior was ornamented all around with pillars set in the wall, somewhat different from those in the façades of other buildings, and more fanciful. The interior consisted of but a single apartment, fifteen feet long and nine feet wide. The ceiling was high, and in the layer of flat stones along the centre of the arch was a single stone, like that seen for the first time at Kewick, ornamented with painting.

This building stood in front of another more overgrown and ruined, which had been an imposing and important edifice. The plan was complicated, and the exterior of one part was rounded, but the rounded part was a solid mass, and within the wall was straight. In the back wall was a recess, once occupied, perhaps, by a statue. Altogether, there was much about this edifice that was new and curious; and there were other cerros, or mounds, of undistinguishable ruins.

Short as my visit was, there were few considerations that could have tempted me to remain longer. The garrapatas would soon be over, but they continued with the rainy season, and, in fact, increased and multiplied. I discovered them the moment I dismounted, and at first attempted to whip them off, but wishing to get through before night, I hurried round this building, creeping under branches and tearing aside bushes, and, actually covered with the abominable insects, started for the road.

In hurrying forward I unwittingly crossed the track of a procession of large black ants. These processions are among the extraordinary spectacles of that country, darkening the ground for an hour at a time; and the insect has a sting equal to that of hornets, as I quickly learned on this occasion. When I reached the road I was almost numbed with pain, and when I mounted I felt that nothing could tempt me to live in such a country. The hacienda was in an unusually pretty situation. Opposite was a long line of hills; the sun was setting, and it was precisely the hour and the scene for a country ramble; but the owner of thousands of acres could never diverge from the beaten path without bringing these pests upon him.

I returned to the house, where the major domo kindly provided me with warm water for a bath, which cooled the fever of my blood. At night, for the first time in the country, we had at one end of the room the hammocks of the women, but this was not so bad as ants or garrapatas.

CHAPTER XIV

March 5. Early the next morning we set out
for the ruins of San José. At seven o'clock we reached the pueb-
locito, or little village, of that name, pleasantly situated between
a range of hills and a sierra, containing about two hundred inhabitants, among whom, as we rode into the plaza, we saw
several white men. At the casa real we found a cacique of respectable appearance, who told us that there were no "old walls"
in that village, which report of his, other Indians standing round
confirmed. We were not much disappointed, nor at all anxious
to find anything that would make it necessary to change our
plans; to lose no time, we determined to push on to Mani, eight
leagues distant, and applied for an Indian to carry our hammocks, which the cacique undertook to provide.

On the opposite side of the square was a thatched church,
the bell of which was tolling for morning mass, and before the
door was a group of men, surrounding a portly old gentleman
in a round jacket, who I knew must be the padre. They all confirmed the accounts we had received at the casa real, that there
were no ruins; but the cura, enforcing his words with an Ave
Maria, said that at Ticul, the head of his curacy, there were
bastante, or enough of them. He intended to return immediately
after mass, and wanted us to go with him to see them, and write
a description of them. I felt a strong disposition to do so, if it

173

was only to pass a day with him at the convent; but, on inquiring, I learned that the "old walls" were entirely in ruins; they had furnished materials for that church and convent, and all the stone houses of the village.

While this was going on at the door of the church, an Indian sexton was pulling lustily at the bell-rope, ringing for mass, and, as if indignant that his warning was not attended to, he made it so deafening that it was really a labour for us to hear each other. The cura seemed in no hurry, but I had some scruples about keeping the congregation waiting, and returned to the casa real.

Here a scene had just taken place, of which nothing but the noise of the bell prevented my having some previous knowledge. The cacique had sent for an Indian to carry our load, but the latter refused to obey, and was insolent to the cacique, who, in a rage, ordered him to be put into the stocks. When I entered, the recusant, sullen and silent, was waiting the execution of his sentence, and in a few minutes he was lying on his back on the ground, with both legs secured in the stocks above his knees. The cacique sent for another, and in the mean time an old woman came in with a roll of tortillas, and a piteous expression of face. She was the mother of the prisoner, and took her seat on the stocks to remain with him and comfort him; and, as the man rolled his head on the ground, and the woman looked wonderingly at us, we reproached ourselves as the cause of his disaster, and endeavoured to procure his release, but the cacique would not listen to us. He said that the man was punished, not for refusing to go with us, although bound to do so on account of indebtedness to the village, but for insolence to himself. He was evidently one who would not allow his authority to be trifled with; and seeing that, without helping the Indian, we might lose the benefit of the cacique's good dispositions in our favour, we were fain to desist. At length, though evidently with some difficulty, he procured another Indian. As we mounted, we made a final effort in behalf of the poor fellow in the stocks; and, though apparently unable to comprehend why we should take any interest in the matter, the cacique promised to release him.

This over, we found that we had thrown another family into confusion. The wife and a little daughter of our carrier accompanied him to the top of a hill beyond the village, where they bade him farewell as if he was setting out on a long and dangerous journey. The attachment of the Indian to his home is a striking feature of his character. The affection which grows up between the sexes was supposed by the early writers upon the character of the Indians not to exist among them, and probably the sentiment and refinement of it do not; but circumstances and habit bind together the Indian man and woman as strongly as any known ties. When the Indian grows up to manhood he requires a woman to make him tortillas, and to provide him warm water for his bath at night. He procures one, sometimes by the providence of the master, without much regard to similarity of tastes or parity of age; and though a young man is mated to an old woman, they live comfortably together. If he finds her guilty of any great offence, he brings her up before the master or the alcalde, gets her a whipping, and then takes her under his arm and goes quietly home with her. The Indian husband is rarely harsh to his wife, and the devotion of the wife to her husband is always a subject of remark. They share their pleasures as well as their labours; go up together with all their children to some village fiesta, and one of the most afflicting incidents in their lot is a necessity that takes the husband from his home.

In the suburbs of the village we commenced ascending the sierra, from the top of which we saw at the foot the hacienda of Santa Maria. Behind it rose a high mound, surrounded by trees, indicating that here too were the ruins of an ancient city.

Descending the sierra, we rode up to the hacienda, and saw three gentlemen sitting under a shed breakfasting. One of them had on a fur hat, a mark of civilization which we had not seen for a long time; an indication that he was from the city of Tekax, and had merely come out for a morning ride.

The proprietor came out to receive us, and, pointing to the mound, we made some inquiry about the building, but he did not comprehend us, and, supposing that we meant some old ranchos in that direction, said that they were for the servants. Albino explained that we were travelling over the country in search of ruins, and the gentleman looked at him perhaps somewhat as the inn-keeper looked at Sancho Panza when he explained that his master was a knight-errant travelling to redress grievances. We succeeded, however, in coming to an understanding about the mound, and the master told us that he had never been to it; that there was no path; that if we attempted to go to it we should be eaten up by garrapatas, and he called some Indians, who said that it was entirely in ruins. This was satisfactory, for the idea of being loaded with garrapatas to carry about till night had almost made me recoil. At the same time, the other gentlemen told us of other ruins at a league's distance from Tekax, on the hacienda of Señor Calera. I felt strongly disposed to turn off and visit the latter, but our carrier had gone on, and the little difficulties of overtaking him, procuring another for a change of route, and perhaps losing a day, were now serious objections; besides, there was no end to the ruins.

Leaving the hacienda, we entered, with a satisfaction that can hardly be described, upon a broad road for carretas and calesas. We had emerged from the narrow and tangled path of milpas and ranchos, and were once more on a camino real. We had accomplished a journey which we were assured, on setting out, was impracticable; and now we were coming upon the finest portion of the state, famed for its rich sugar plantations. We met heavy, lumbering vehicles drawn by oxen and horses, carrying sugar from the haciendas. Very soon we reached Tekax, one of the four places in Yucatan bearing the name of a city, and I must confess that I felt some degree of excitement. Throughout Yucatan our journey had been so quiet, so free from danger or interruption of any kind, that, after my Central American experience, it seemed unnatural. Yucatan was in a state of open rebellion against Mexico; we had heard of negotiations, but there had been no tumult, confusion, or bloodshed. Tekax alone had broken the general stillness, and while the rest of the country was perfectly quiet, this interior city had got up a small revolution on its own account, and for the benefit of whom it might concern.

According to the current reports, this revolution was got up by three patriotic individuals, whose names, unfortunately, I have lost. They belonged to the party called Los Independientes, in favour of declaring independence of Mexico. The elections had gone against their party, and alcaldes in favour of a reannexation to Mexico were installed in office. In the mean time commissioners arrived from Santa Ana to negotiate with the government of Yucatan, urging it not to make any open declaration, but to continue quietly in its state of independence de facto until the internal difficulties of Mexico were settled, when its complaints would be attended to and its grievances redressed. Afraid of the influence which these commissioners might exercise, the three patriots of Tekax resolved to strike for liberty, went round among the ranchos of the sierra, and collected a band of more than half-naked Indians, who, armed with machetes, a few old muskets, and those primitive weapons with which David slew Goliath, descended upon Tekax, and, to the great alarm of the women and children, took possession of the plaza, set up the figure of Santa Ana, pelted him with stones, put some bullets into him, burned him to ashes, and shouted "Viva la independencia." But few of them had ever heard of Santa Ana, but this was no reason why they should not pelt him with stones and burn him in effigy. They knew nothing of the relations between Yucatan and Mexico, and by the cry of independencia they meant a release from tribute to the government and debts to masters. With but little practice in revolutions, they made a fair start by turning out the alcaldes and levying contributions upon political opponents, and threw out the formidable threat that they would march three hundred men against the capital, and compel a declaration of independence. Intelligence of these movements soon reached Merida, and fearful menaces of war were bandied from one city to the other. Each waited for the other to make the first demonstration, but at length the capital sent forth its army, which reached Ticul the day after I left at the conclusion of my first visit, and while Doctor Cabot was still there. It was then within one day's march of the seat of rebellion, but halted to rest, and to let the moral effect of its approach go on before. The reader has perhaps never before heard of Tekax; nevertheless, a year has not elapsed since the patriotic, half-naked band in arms for independence thought that the eyes of the whole world were upon them. In three days the regular army resumed its march, with cannon in front, colours flying, drums beating, and the women of Ticul laughing, sure that there would be no bloodshed. The same day it reached Tekax, and the next morning, instead of falling upon each other like so many wild beasts, the officers and the three patriot leaders were seen walking arm in arm together in the plaza. The former promised good offices to their new friends, two reales apiece to the Indians, and the revolution was crushed. All dispersed, ready to take up arms again upon the same terms whenever their country's good should so require.

Such were the accounts we had received, always coupled with sweeping denunciations of the population of Tekax as revolutionary and radical, and the rabble of Yucatan. Having somewhat of a leaning to revolutions in the abstract, I was happy to find that, with such a bad reputation, its appearance was finer, and more promising than that of any town I had seen, and I could not but think it would be well for Yucatan if many of her dead-and-alive villages had more such rabble.

The city stands at the foot of the sierra. Riding up the

street, we had in full view the church of La Hermita, with a broad flight of stone steps scaling the side of the mountain. The streets were wide, the houses large and in fine order, and one had three stories, with balconies overhanging the street; and there was an appearance of life and business, which, coming as we did from Indian ranchos, and so long away from anything that looked like a city and the comforts and elegances of living, was really exciting.

As we rode along a gay calesa approached us, occupied by a gentleman and lady, well dressed and handsome, and, to our surprise, in the lady we recognised the fair subject upon whom we had begun business as Daguerreotype portrait takers, and whose gift of a cake had penetrated the very leather of my saddle-bags. A few short weeks had made a great change in her condition; she was now riding by the side of her lawful proprietor. We attempted, by the courtesy of our salute, to withdraw attention from our wearing apparel. Unluckily, Doctor Cabot's sombrero was tied under his chin, so that he could not get it off. Mine, with one of the strings carried away, described a circle in the air, and, as the doctor maliciously said, disappeared under my horse. The gentleman nodded condescendingly, but it was flattering ourselves to believe that the lady took any notice of us whatever.

But though old friends forgot us, we were not unnoticed by the citizens of Tekax. As we rode along all eyes were turned upon us. We stopped in the plaza, which, with its great church and the buildings around it, was the finest we had seen in the country, and all the people ran out to the corridors to gaze at us. It was an unprecedented thing for strangers to pass through this place. European saddles, holsters, and arms were strange, and, including Albino, we made the cabalistic number of three which got up the late revolution. Knowing the curiosity we excited, and that all were anxious to speak to us, without dismounting or exchanging a word with an inhabitant, we passed through the plaza and continued our journey. The people were bewildered, as if the ragged tail of a comet had passed over their heads; and afterward, at a distant village, we heard the report that we had passed through Tekax *vestidos como Moros*, or dressed like Moors. The good people, having never seen a Moor, and not being very familiar with Moorish costume, had taken our blouzes for such. The strange guise in which we appeared to them alleviated somewhat the mortification of not being recognised by the fair lady of Merida.

178

Our road lay for some distance along the sierra. It was broad, open, and the sun beat fiercely upon us. At half past ten we reached Akil, and rode up to the casa real. At the door was a stone hollowed out like those often before referred to, called pilas. In the steps and foundation were sculptured stones from ruined mounds in the immediate neighbourhood, and the road along the yard of the church ran through a mound, leaving part on each side, and the excavated mass forming on one side the wall of the convent yard. The rest of the wall, the church, and the convent were built with stones from the ancient buildings. We were on the site of another ruined city, of which we had never heard, and might never have known, but for the tell-tale memorials at the door of the casa real.

At a quarter before three we resumed our journey. The sun was still very hot; the road was straight, stony, and uninteresting, a great part of the way through overgrown milpas. At half past five we reached Mani, again finding over the door and along the sides of the casa real sculptured stones, some of them of new and curious designs; in one compartment was a seated figure, with what might seem a crown and sceptre, and the figures of the sun and moon on either side of his head, curious and interesting in themselves, independent of the admonition that we were again on the site of an aboriginal city.

In all our journey through this country there were no associations. Day after day we rode into places unknown beyond the boundaries of Yucatan, with no history attached to them, and touching no chord of feeling. Mani, however, rises above the rest, and, compared with the profound obscurity or the dim twilight in which other places are enveloped, its history is plainly written.

When the haughty caciques of Maya rebelled against the supreme lord, and destroyed the city of Mayapan, the reigning monarch was left with only the territory of Mani, the people of which had not joined in the rebellion. Here, reduced in power to the level of the other caciques, the race of the ancient lords of Maya ruled undisturbed until the time of the Spanish invasion; but the shadow of the throne rested over it; it was consecrated in the affections of the Indians, and long after the conquest it bore the proud name of la Corona real de Mani.

It has been mentioned that on their arrival at Tihoo the Spaniards encamped on a cerro, or mound, which stood on the site now occupied by the plaza of Merida. While in this position, surrounded by hostile Indians, their supplies cut off and strait-

179

ened for provisions, one day the scouts brought intelligence to Don Francisco Montejo of a great body of Indians, apparently warlike, advancing toward them. From the top of the cerro they discovered the multitude, and among them one borne on the shoulders of men, as if extended on a bier. Supposing that a battle was certain, the Spaniards recommended themselves to God, the chaplain held up a holy cross, and, prostrating themselves before it, they took up their arms. As the Indians drew near to the cerro, they lowered to the ground the person whom they carried on their shoulders, who approached alone, threw down his bow and arrow, and, raising both hands, made a signal that he came in peace. Immediately all the Indians laid their bows and arrows on the ground, and, touching their fingers to the earth, kissed them, also in token of good-will.

The chief advanced to the foot of the mound, and began to ascend it. Don Francisco stepped forward to meet him, and the Indian made him a profound reverence; Don Francisco received him with cordiality, and, taking him by the hand, conducted him to his quarters.

This Indian was Tutul Xiu, the greatest lord in all that country, the lineal descendant of the royal house which once ruled over the whole land of Maya, and then cacique of Mani. He said that, moved by the valour and perseverance of the Spaniards, he had come voluntarily to render obedience, and to offer his aid and that of his subjects for the pacification of the rest; and he brought a large present of turkeys, fruits, and other provisions. He had come to be their friend; he desired, also, to be a Christian, and asked the adelantado to go through some Christian ceremonies. The latter made a most solemn adoration to the holy cross, and Tutul Xiu, watching attentively, imitated the Spaniard as well as he could until, with many demonstrations of joy, he came to kiss the cross on his knees. The Spaniards were delighted, and, the adoration over, they remarked that this fortunate day for them was that of the glorious San Ildefonso, whom they immediately elected for their patron saint.

Tutul Xiu was accompanied by other caciques, whose names, as found in an Indian manuscript, have been handed down. They remained with the Spaniards seventy days, and on taking leave, Tutul Xiu promised to send ambassadors to solicit the other chiefs, though they were not his vassals, to render obedience to the Spaniards; when, leaving them a great supply of provisions and many Indian servants, he returned to Mani.

He convoked all his Indians, and gave them notice of his

intentions, and of the agreement he had made with the Spaniards; to which they all assented.

Afterward he despatched the caciques who went with him to render submission to the Spaniards, as ambassadors to the Lords of Zotuta, called the Cocomes, and the other nations to the east as far as the region where now stands the city of Valladolid, making known to them his resolution, and the friendship he had contracted with the Spaniards, and beseeching them to do the same; representing that the Spaniards were determined to remain in the land, had established themselves in Campeachy, and were preparing to do so in Tihoo; reminding them how many battles they had fought, and how many lives of the natives had been lost; and informing them that he had experienced from the Spaniards while he remained with them good-will, and that he held it better for all his countrymen to follow his example, considering the dangers of the opposite course.

The ambassadors proceeded to the district of Zotuta, and made known their embassy to Nachi Cocom, the principal lord of that territory. The latter requested them to wait four or five days for their answer, and in the mean time convoked all his dependant caciques, who, in concert with this chief, determined to make a great wild-boar hunt, ostensibly to fête the ambassadors. Under this pretext, they enticed them from the inhabited parts of the country into a dense forest, and feasted them three days. On the fourth they assembled to eat beneath a large sapote tree, and the last act of the feast was to cut the throats of the ambassadors, sparing but one, whom they charged to inform Tutul Xiu of their reception of his embassy, and to reproach him with his cowardice; but though they spared the life of this one, they put out his eyes with an arrow, and sent him, under the charge of four captains, to the territory of Tutul Xiu, where they left him and returned to their own country.

Such were the unfortunate circumstances under which Mani became known to the Spaniards. It was the first interior town that submitted to their power, and by referring to the map, the reader will see that after our long, irregular, and devious route, we are at this moment but four leagues from Ticul, and but eleven from Uxmal by the road of the country, while the distance is much less in a straight line.

Among the wonders unfolded by the discovery of these ruined cities, what made the strongest impression on our minds was the fact that their immense population existed in a region so scantily supplied with water. Throughout the whole country there is no stream, or spring, or living fountain, and, but for the extraordinary caves and hollows in the rocks from which the inhabitants at this day drink, they must have been entirely dependant upon artificial fountains, and literally upon the rain that came down from heaven. But on this point there is one important consideration. The aborigines of this country had no horses, or cattle, or large domestic animals, and the supply required for the use of man only was comparatively small. Perhaps at this day, with different wants and habits, the same country would not support the same amount of population. And, besides, the Indian now inhabiting that dry and thirsty region illustrates the effect of continual scarcity, habit, and training, in subduing the appetites. Water is to him, as to the Arab of the Desert, a scarce and precious commodity. When he puts down the load from his back, his body streaming with perspiration, a few sips of water dipped up in the palm of his hand from a hollow rock suffice to quench his thirst. Still, under any circumstances, the sources of supply present one of the most interesting features connected with the discovery of these ruined cities, and go to confirm belief in the vast numbers and power, as well as the laborious industry of the ancient inhabitants.

It was late on Saturday afternoon when we reached Mani. The guarda of Indians had served their term of a week in attendance at the casa real, and were now retiring from office, as usual all intoxicated, but we got a large room swept out, had it furnished with chairs and tables, and our hammocks hung up; and here, amid the wrecks of cities, we were almost in ruins ourselves. Before resorting to our hammocks we made an important and touching discovery, which was that we had but one clean camisa between us; and if the reader knew the extent of our travelling wardrobe, he would, perhaps, be somewhat astonished that we had that. Nevertheless, the discovery perplexed us. The next day was Sunday; all the village would appear in clean clothes; it was mortifying that we could not do so too, and, besides, we had some little feeling on the score of personal comfort. In Europe, with a frock-coat buttoned tight across the breast, black stock, and one pair of pantaloons, hat, and boots, the traveller is independent of the world, but not so under the hot sun of Yucatan. We sent Albino out to look for supplies, but he returned unsuccessful, though he did succeed in making a bargain with a woman to wash an entire change for us the next day; but she could hardly be made to understand that stockings and sheets were included in a change.

CHAPTER XV

Early in the morning Albino was in quest of some gentleman who might have a spare camisa and pantaloons which he would be willing to part with, and, by one of those rare pieces of good luck that sometimes illuminate the path of a traveller, he procured both, the latter having an elegantly embroidered bosom, which fell to Doctor Cabot; and, with my cast-off blouse, which was in better condition than his, and a thin frock-coat, that considered itself cast-off some time before, for myself, we were able to make a dashing appearance in the streets.

Notwithstanding our perplexities, I had an uncommon degree of satisfaction at waking up in Mani. I had heard of this place on my first visit to Uxmal, of relics and heirlooms in the hands of the cacique, and of ruins, which, however, we were advised were not worth visiting. The morning, nevertheless, did not open with much promise. On first emerging we found about the door of the casa real a crowd of loungers, of that mixed race who might trace their ancestry to the subjects of Tutul Xiu and the conquerors, possessing all the bad qualities of both, and but few of the good traits of either. Some of them were intoxicated, and there were many half-grown, impudent boys, who kept close to us, watching every movement, and turning aside to laugh when they could do so unobserved.

We set out to look at the ruins, and the crowd followed at our heels. At the end of a street leading to the well we saw a long building, pierced in the middle by the street, and part still standing on each side. We saw at a glance that it was not the work of the antiguos, but had been erected by the Spaniards since the conquest, and yet we were conducted to it as one of the same class with those we had found all over the country; though we did meet with one intelligent person, who smiled at the ignorance of the people, and said that it was a palace of *El Rey*, or the *king*, Montejo. Its true history is perhaps as much unknown as that of the more ancient buildings. In its tottering front were interspersed sculptured stones taken from the aboriginal edifices, and thus, in its own decay, it publishes the sad story that it had risen upon the ruins of another race.

Near this building, and at the corner of the street, is the well referred to in the conclusion of my legend of the House of the Dwarf at Uxmal. "The old woman (the mother of the Dwarf) then died, but at the Indian village of Mani there is a deep well, from which opens a cave that leads under ground an immense distance to Merida. In this cave, on the bank of a stream, under the shade of a large tree, sits an old woman, with a serpent by her side, who sells water in small quantities, not for money, but only for a criatura, or baby, to give the serpent to eat; and this old woman is the mother of the Dwarf." The entrance to the well was under a great shelf of overhanging rock, forming the mouth of a magnificent cavern, will enough to sustain the legend. The roof was high, and the villgers had constructed steps, by which, walking erect, we reached a large pool of water, whence women were filling their cantaros. At one side was an opening in the rock above, which should have been, and was intended to be, made directly over the water, for the purpose of drawing it up in buckets; and as this mistake occurred in a cave where the water is but a short distance from the mouth, and the passage is wide, it shows the difficulty, without any knowledge of the use of instruments, of fixing on the surface the precise point over the water in the other caves, which have long, narrow, and winding passages.

In the yards of some houses on a street at the rear of the casa real were the remains of large mounds. In the wall round the square of the church was a large circular upright stone, like those heretofore called picotes, or whipping-posts, and our guide told us that in the suburbs there were other mounds; but, without leaving the streets, we saw enough to satisfy us that Mani stood on the site of an ancient town of the same general character with all the others.

Returning to the casa real, we found a new guarda, who came into office rather more intoxicated than their predecessors in going out. Albino had inquired of the cacique for the ancient relics of which we had heard accounts, and the Indians brought a copy of Cogolludo, wrapped up and treasured with great care in the casa real. This did not astonish us much, and they opened the book and pointed out a picture, the only one in it, being a representation of the murder of the ambassadors of Tutul Xiu; and while we were looking at it they brought out and unrolled on the floor an old painting on cotton cloth, being the original from which Cogolludo had the engraving made. The design was a coat of arms bordered with the heads of the murdered ambassadors, one of which has an arrow fixed in the temple, intended to represent the ambassador who had his eyes put out with this weapon. In the centre is a tree growing out of a box, representing the sapote tree at Zotuta, under which the murder was committed, and which, the Indians say, is still standing. This tree I shall have occasion to mention again hereafter. The painting had evidently been executed by an Indian, and probably very near the time of the occurrence which it was intended to commemorate. Cogolludo refers to it as an ancient and interesting relic in his time, and, of course, it is much more so now. It is an object of great reverence among the Indians of Mani. In fact, throughout our whole journeyings, either in Central America or Yucatan, it was the first and only instance in which we met with any memorial in the hands of the Indians, tending to keep alive the memory of any event in their history; but this must not be imputed to them as a reproach. History, dark as it is on other points, shows clearly enough that this now abject and degraded race did cling with desperate and fatal tenacity to the memory of those ancestors whom they know not now; the records of their conquerors show the ruthless and savage policy pursued by the Spaniards to root this memory from their minds; and here, in this very town of Mani, we have a dark and memorable instance.

In 1571, twenty-nine years after the foundation of Merida, some Indians of Mani relapsed and became idolaters, practising in secret their ancient rites.

Intelligence of their backsliding reached the ears of the provincial in Merida, who came to Mani in person, and forthwith established himself as inquisitor. Some who had died obstinately in the secret practice of idolatrous rites had been buried in sacred ground; he ordered their bodies to be dug up, and their bones thrown into the fields; and, in order to strike terror into the minds of the Indians, and root out the memory of their ancient rites, on a day appointed for that purpose, attended by the principal of the Spanish nobility, and in the presence of a great multitude of Indians, he made them bring together all their books and ancient characters, and publicly burned them, thus destroying at once the history of their antiquities. Those envious of the blessed father, says the historian, gave him the title of cruel; but very differently thought of the action the Doctor Don Pedro Sanchez de Aguilar, in his information against the idolaters of this country.

The sight of this painting made me more earnest in pushing my inquiries for other memorials, but this was all; the Indians had no more to show, and I then inquired of the alcalde for ancient archives. He knew nothing about them, but said we could examine for ourselves, and the key of the apartment in which they were kept was with the second alcalde.

The schoolmaster of the village, who had received a letter in our behalf from our friend the cura Carillo of Ticul, accompanied me to look for the second alcalde, and, after tracing him to several places, we procured the keys, and returned to the casa real, and when we unlocked the door we had thirty or forty persons to enter with us. The books and archives of the municipality were in the back room, and among them was one large volume which had an ancient and venerable appearance, being bound in parchment, tattered, and worm-eaten, and having a flap to close like that of a pocket-book. Unhappily, it was written in the Maya language, and perfectly unintelligible. The dates, however, showed that these venerable pages were a record of events which had taken place within a very few years after the entry of the Spaniards into the country; and as I pored over them, I was strongly impressed with the belief that directly, or in some incidental expressions, they contained matter which might throw some light upon the subject of my investigations.

Being Sunday, a crowd of curious and lazy lookers-on surrounded the table, but they could not distract my attention. I found that, though all could speak the Maya, none could read it. Nevertheless, I continued to turn over the pages. On the 157th page, in a document which bore the date of 1557, I saw the word *Vxmal*. Here I stopped, and called upon the by-standers. The schoolmaster was the only one who could even attempt to give me any assistance, but he was not familiar with the Maya as a written tongue, and said that this, having been written nearly three hundred years before, differed somewhat from that of the present day, and was more difficult to comprehend. Other places were referred to in the document, the names of which were familiar to me, and I observed that the words immediately preceding Vxmal were different from those preceding the other names. The presumption was that Uxmal was referred to in some different sense.

In turning to the end of the document I found a sheet of foolscap paper, which had been secured in the book, but was then loose; and upon it was a curious map, also dated in 1557, of which Mani was the centre. Vxmal was laid down upon it, and indicated by a peculiar sign, different from that of all the other places named. On the back of the map was endorsed a long instrument of the same date, in which the word *Vxmal* again occurred, and which, beyond doubt, contained matter relating to other places named in the map, and to their condition or state of being at that time. With the assistance of the schoolmaster I compared this with the one written in the book, and ascertained that the latter was a recorded copy of the other.

A few pages beyond was another document, bearing date in 1556, one year earlier, and in this, again, the word Vxmal appeared. The schoolmaster was able to give me some general idea of the contents, but he could not translate with facility, nor, as he said, very accurately. The alcalde sent for an Indian escribano, or clerk, of the municipality; but he was not in the village, and an old Indian was brought who had formerly served in that capacity; but, after staring stupidly at the pages as if looking at a row of machetes, he said he had grown so old that he had forgotten how to read. My only course was to have copies made, which the schoolmaster set about immediately, and late in the afternoon he placed them in my hands. In the evening, by the permission of the alcalde, I took the book to my quarters, and looked over every page, running my finger along every line, in search of the word Uxmal, but I did not meet with it in any other place, and probably the documents referred to are the most ancient, if not the only ones in existence of ancient date, in which that name is mentioned.

The copies I carried with me to my friend Don Pio Perez, who discovered some errors, and, at his instance, my good friend the cura Carillo went over to Mani, and made exact copies of the map and documents. He also made diligent search through the Maya archives for other papers mentioning Uxmal, or referring to it in any way, but found none. He added to his copies a translation, which was revised by Don Pio, and it is from his version that what follows is prepared.

Plate XXV is a copy of the ancient map, the original of which covers one side of a sheet of foolscap paper.

The instrument endorsed on the back, as translated, reads as follows:

"Memorandum of having divided the lands by D. Francisco Montejo Xiu, governor of this pueblo of Mani, and the governors of the pueblos who are under him.

"There met together Don Francisco Montejo Xiu, governor of this pueblo, and of the jurisdiction of Tutul Xiu; Don Francisco Che, governor of Ticul, Don Francisco Pacab, governor of Oxcutzcab, Don Diego Vs, governor of Tekax, Don Alonzo Pacab, governor of Jan-monal, Don Juan Che, governor of Mama, Don Alonzo Xiu, governor of Tekit, and the other governors within the jurisdiction of Mani, together with the regidores, for the purpose of regulating the landmarks, and maintaining the right of each village respecting the felling of trees, and to fix and settle with crosses the boundaries of the milpas of their respective villages, dividing them into parts according to their situation, showing the lands pertaining to each. The people of Canul, those of Acanceh, of Ticoh, those of Cosuma, those of Zotuta and its jurisdiction, those of Tixcacab, a part of those of Peto, Colotmul, and Zuccacab, after having conferred together, declared it necessary to cite the governors of the villages, and we answered that they should come to this audiencia of Mani, each one bringing with him two regidores to be present at the division of the lands. Don Juan Canul, governor of Nunkini, and Francisco Ci, his colleague; D. Juan Cocom, governor of Ticoh, D. Gaspar Tun of Cosuma, Don Juan Cocom, governor of Zotuta, D. Gonzalo Tuyn, governor of Tixcacab, D. Juan Han of Yaxcacab; these received the donation on the fifth day from Merida, consisting of one hundred 'paties' of fine sheets, each pati or cotton cloth, and thus they continued receiving by twenties for a beginning, being rolled up by Juan Nic, Pedro May, and Pedro Coba, assembled in the house of Don Francisco Montejo Xiu, governor of the village of Mani; three arrobas of wax, which were sold by them, Don Juan Cocom of Zotuta having first received them. In Talchaquillo, on the road to Merida, toward the north of said village, the cross was planted, and called Hoal. In Sacmuyalna they put a cross; this is the limit of the lands of those of Ticoh. In Kochilha a cross

Plate XXV

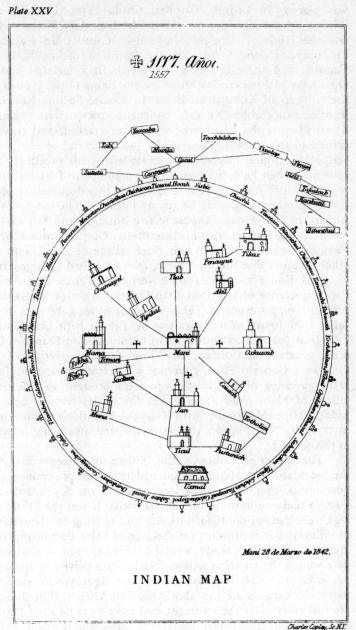

INDIAN MAP

was placed. In Cisinil, Toyotha, Chulul Ytza, Ocansip, and Tiphal, crosses were placed; this is the boundary of the milpas and the lands of those of Maxcanú-al Canules. In Kaxabceh Chacnocac, Calam, Sactos, are the limits of the fields of the Canules, and there crosses were placed. In Zemesahal and in Opal were planted crosses: these are the limits of the grounds of the villagers of Kilhini and Becal. In Yaxche Sucilha Xcalchen, Tehico Sahcabchen Xbacal, Opichen, crosses were planted. Twenty-two is the number of the places marked, and they returned to raise new landmarks, by the command of the judge, Felipe Manriques, specially commissioned by his excellency the governor, when he arrived at *Uxmal*, accompanied by his interpreter, Gaspar Antonio," &c. The rest of this document I omit.

The other document begins as follows: "On the tenth of August, in the year one thousand five hundred and fifty-six, the special judge arrived with his interpreter, Gaspar Antonio, *from Vxmal*, when they reached this chief village of Mani, with the other caciques that followed them, Don Francisco Che, governor of Ticul, Don Francisco Pacab, governor of Tekax, Don Alonzo Pacab, governor of Jan, Don Juan Che, governor of Mama, Don Alonzo Xiu, governor of Tekit, with the other governors of his suite, Don Juan Cacom, governor of Tekoh, with Don Gaspar Fun, Don Juan Camal, governor of Nunhini, Don Francisco Ciz, other governor of Cosuma, Don Juan Cocom, governor of Zotuta, Don Gonzalo Fuyú, governor of Tixcacaltuyú, Don Juan Han, governor of Yaxcaba; those were brought to this chief village of Mani *from Vxmal*, with the others named, and the judge Felipe Manrique, with Gaspar Antonio, commissioned interpreter." Of this, too, the rest is omitted, not being relevant to this subject.

The reader will observe that, fifteen or sixteen years after the foundation of Merida, Mani had the same pre-eminence of position as when Tutul Xiu went up with his dependant caciques to make submission to the Spaniards. It was the "chief village," the central point for meeting and settling the boundaries of villages; but it appears, on the face of these documents, that great changes had already occurred. In fact, even at that early date we see the entering wedge, which, since driven to its mark, has overturned all the institutions and destroyed forever the national character of the aboriginal inhabitants. The Indians are still rulers over their villages, and meet to settle their boundary lines, but they meet under the direction of Don Felipe Manriques, a Spanish officer, specially commissioned for that purpose; they establish their boundaries by planting *crosses,* symbols introduced by the Spaniards; they have lost their proud and independent national title of cacique, and are styled *Dons* and *Gobernadores*; under the gentle patting of the hand destined soon to crush their race, they have abandoned even the names received from their fathers, and have adopted, either voluntarily or by coercion, the Christian names of the Spaniards; and the Lord of Mani himself, the lineal descendant of the royal house of Maya, either that same Tutul Xiu who first submitted himself and his vassals to the dominion of Don Francisco Montejo, or his immediate descendant, in compliment to the conqueror and destroyer of his race, appears meekly and ingloriously under the name of *Don Francisco* Xiu.

But it is not for the sake of this melancholy tale that I have introduced these documents; they have another and a more important bearing. By this act of partition it appears that, in 1557, "the judge *arrived at Uxmal,* accompanied by his interpreter Don Antonio Gaspar." And by the agreement it appears that in 1556, one year previous, the special judge *arrived* with his interpreter, Gaspar Antonio, *from Uxmal,* when they reached the chief village of Mani with the other caciques who followed them. The names are all given, and it is said these *"were brought to this* chief village of Mani *from Uxmal,* with the others named, and the judge Felipe Manrique and Gaspar Antonio, commissioned interpreter."

Now what was Uxmal? It is clear, beyond all question, that it was a place at which persons could arrive, at which they could be, and from which they could come. I am safe in supposing that it was not a mere hacienda, for at that early period of the conquest haciendas had not begun to be established; and, besides, the title papers of Don Simon Peon show that the first grant of it was made for the purposes of a hacienda one hundred and forty-four or one hundred and forty-five years afterward, at which time the land was waste and belonged to the crown, and had small settlements of Indians upon it, who were publicly and notoriously worshipping the devil in the ancient buildings. It was not, then, a hacienda. Was it a Spanish town? If so, some remains would have been visible at the time of the grant, and the great object of driving away the Indians and breaking up their idolatrous worship would already have been accomplished. There is no indication, record, or tradition that a Spanish town was ever established at Uxmal; the general belief is that there never was any; Don Simon is sure of it, and in that confidence I fully participate. But as the strongest proof on this point, I call in this ancient map. It is a fact perhaps more clearly established than any other in the history of the conquest, that in every Indian village in which the Spaniards made a settlement, with that strong religious enthusiasm which formed so remarkable a feature in their daring and unscrupulous character, their first act was the erection of a church. Now it will be remarked that nearly all the places laid down on the map are indicated by the sign of a church; most of them now exist, all have aboriginal names, and the inference is that they were at that time existing aboriginal towns, in which the Spaniards had erected churches, or had taken the preliminary steps for doing so. Several of these places we had visited; we had seen their churches reared upon the ruins of ancient buildings, and in their immediate vicinity vestiges and extensive ruins of the same general character with those at Uxmal.

But Uxmal, it will be seen, is not indicated by the sign of a church. This I consider evidence that no church was erected there, and that while the Spaniards were establishing settlements in other Indian towns, for some reason, now unknown, perhaps on account of its unhealthiness, at Uxmal they made none. But it will be seen farther, that Uxmal not only is not indicated by the sign of a church, but is indicated by one entirely different, of a peculiar and striking character, which was manifestly never adopted from caprice or without cause. In my opinion, this sign was intended to represent what would most clearly distinguish a large place without a church from those in which churches had been erected, the characteristic ornaments on the fronts of the aboriginal buildings, as now seen at Uxmal. It is the same obvious character or symbol which might serve at this day to indicate on a map a city like Uxmal, and to my mind the conclusion is irresistible that at the time when the Judge Don Felipe Manriques arrived *at* Uxmal and arrived *from* Uxmal, it was an existing inhabited aboriginal town. Farther, in the scanty light that we have on this subject, the slightest incidental circumstance is not to be disregarded. In each reference to his arrival at or from Uxmal, it is mentioned that he was accompanied by his interpreter. He would not need an interpreter if the place was desolate, or if it was a hacienda, or a Spanish town. He could need an interpreter only when the place was occupied by the aborigines, whose language he did not understand, and such, I cannot help believing, was actually the case. I can easily believe, too, that its depopulation and desolation within the hundred and forty years preceding the royal grant for the purposes of a hacienda, were the inevitable consequence of the policy pursued by the Spaniards in their subjugation of the country. I would remark that there is no doubt of the authenticity of these documents. They are true records of events which occurred at that early period of the conquest. To this day the map and act of partition are good evidence in all legal proceedings affecting the title to lands in that neighbourhood, and I afterward saw them enrolled as proofs and forming part of the record in a contested and protracted lawsuit.

I make no apology for dwelling so long upon this ancient map. Perhaps, however, it will not interest the reader so much as it did ourselves and the half-breeds of Mani. These ascribed our curiosity to a much less innocent motive than that of investigating the history of ancient cities. In consequence of some recent difficulties, los Ingleses were somewhat objects of suspicion; the idlers of Mani made close inquiries of Albino touching our reasons for wanting the map, and, not being able to comprehend his explanations, which were, perhaps, not very clear, they said that we intended to seek out and seize the strong points for fortifications; and, with a spirit unlike that of their warlike sires, Spanish or Indian, quietly made up their minds that we intended to reduce the country and make slaves of them.

Toward evening we strolled over to the church and convent, which are among the grandest of these early structures erected in Yucatan, proud monuments of the zeal and labour of the Franciscan friars. They were built under the direction of Friar Juan of Merida, distinguished as a warrior and conqueror, but who threw aside the sword and put on the habit of a monk. According to Cogolludo, they were both finished in the short space of seven months, the cacique who had been lord of that country furnishing six thousand Indians. Built upon the ruins of another race, they are now themselves tottering and going to decay.

The convent had two stories, with a great corridor all round; but the doors were broken and the windows wide open, rain beat into the rooms, and grass grew on the floor.

The roof of the church formed a grand promenade, commanding an almost boundless view of the great region of country of which it was once the chief place and centre. Far as the eye could reach was visible the great sierra, running from east to west, a dark line along the plain. All the rest was plain, dotted only by small clearings for villages. My guide pointed out and named Tekax, Akil, Oxcutzcab, Schochnoche, Pustonich, Ticul, Jan, Chapap, Mama, Tipika, Teab, the same villages laid down in the ancient map, whose caciques came up, three hundred years before, to settle the boundaries of their lands; and he told me that, under a clearer atmosphere, more were visible. Some I had visited, and had seen the crumbling remains of the ancient town; and looking at them from the roof of the church, the old map gave them a vividness, reality, and life, as they had been three hundred years before, more exciting than the wildest speculations in regard to lost and unknown races. The sun went down, and the gloom of night gathered over the great plain, emblematic of the fortunes and the fate of its ancient inhabitants.

CHAPTER XVI

Monday, March 7. Before daylight the next morning we left Mani.

Our present mode of travelling favoured Doctor Cabot's particular objects. His best chance for procuring birds was always on the road, the time passed at ruins, on account of the density of the woods and underbrush, being in a great measure lost to him. Yucatan had never before been explored ornithologically; or, to speak more correctly, the only person who had given any attention to that branch of its natural history, a German, died in the country; his collections were scattered and his notes lost. Doctor Cabot's field of operations, therefore, was, like our own, entirely new; and our attention being constantly directed to the brilliant plumage of the birds and their interesting habits, they became identified with the purposes of our journey. It was my intention to obtain from Doctor Cabot, and publish in this work, a full essay on the ornithology of the country, but I find my materials so abundant and my volumes growing to such a bulk that compression has become a work of serious necessity.

Doctor Cabot has published, in the Boston Journal of Natural History, an account of his observations upon one rare and splendid bird, the ocellated turkey, of which one stuffed specimen at the Jardin des Plantes, and another in the collection of the Earl of Derby, are the only two known to exist, and of which, besides obtaining a stuffed specimen, we succeeded in transporting two living birds from the interior, and embarking them for home, but lost them overboard on the voyage. I have hopes that he may be induced to publish a full account of his observations upon the ornithology of Yucatan. In the mean time I give in the Appendix a memorandum of about one hundred birds observed by him in that country, which are also found within the United States, and have been figured and described by Wilson, Bonaparte, Audubon, and Nuttall; of others, which are well known to the scientific world for their striking brilliancy of plumage, having been observed in different parts of South and Central America, but are known only by skins prepared and sold in the country, and whose habits have never been described; and a third class, more important to the naturalist than either of the others, comprising birds entirely unknown until discovered by him in Yucatan. The memorandum is accompanied by a few notes referring to the places and circumstances under which they were procured; and in referring to them in the Appendix, I would take occasion to say that some of the most really important matter in this work is to be found in that place, for the sake of which I have considered it expedient materially to abridge my narrative.

But to resume. We stopped that night at Tixmeach, eight leagues distant, a neat village with a well one hundred and forty-four feet deep, at which every woman drawing from it left a handful of maize for a cantaro of water, and we paid a medio for watering our horses; and setting out before daylight the next morning, at half past nine we reached Peto, where we found Mr. Catherwood and our luggage on the hands of our friend Don Pio Perez.

Peto is the head of a department, of which Don Pio Perez was gefe politico. It was a well-built town, with streets indicated, as at Merida, by figures on the tops of the houses. The church and convent were large and imposing edifices, and the living of the cura one of the most valuable in the church, being worth six or seven thousand dollars per annum.

At this place we found letters and packets of newspapers from home, forwarded to us from Merida, and, except attending to them, our time was devoted almost exclusively to long and interesting conversations with Don Pio on matters connected with the antiquities of the country. I cannot sufficiently express my obligations to this gentleman for the warm interest he took in facilitating our pursuits, and for the labour he bestowed ungrudgingly in our behalf. Besides preparing a series of verbal forms and other illustrations of the grammar of the Maya language, according to memoranda made by the same distinguished gentleman before referred to, he gave me a vocabulary in manuscript, containing more than four thousand Maya words, and an almanac, prepared by himself, according to the Indian system of computation, for the year from the 16th of July, 1841, to the 15th of July, 1842, a translation of which is published in the Appendix, as a key or supplement to his calendar.*

Besides these, he furnished me with the copy of one other document, which, if genuine and authentic, throws more light upon aborginal history than any other known to be in existence. It is a fragment of a Maya manuscript, written from memory by an Indian, at some time not designated, and entitled "Principal epochs of the ancient history of Yucatan."

It purports to give the series of "katunes," or epochs, from the time of the departure of the Toltecs from the country of Tulapan until their arrival at this, as it is called, island of Chacno-uitan, occupying, according to Don Pio's computation of katunes, the lapse of time corresponding with that between the years 144 and 217 of the Christian era.

It assigns dates to the discovery of Bacalar and then of Chichen Itza, both within the three epochs corresponding with the time between A.D. 360 and A.D. 432; the colonization of Champoton, and its destruction; the times of wandering through the uninhabited forests, and establishing themselves a second time at Chichen Itza, within epochs corresponding with the lapse between A.D. 888 and A.D. 936.

The epoch of the colonization of Uxmal, corresponding with the years between A.D. 936 and 1176 A.D.; the epochs of wars between the governors of Chichen Itza and Mayapan; the destruction of the latter city by the Uitzes of the Sierras, or highlanders; and the arrival of the Spaniards, adding that "Holy men from the East came with them;" and the manuscript terminates with the epoch of the first baptism and the arrival of the first bishop.

I shall make no comment upon the subject matter of this manuscript. How far it is to be regarded as authentic I am not able to say, but as the only known manuscript in existence that purports to be written by an Indian in his native language, giving an account of the events in the ancient history of this country, I publish it entire in the Appendix. It may conflict in

*See Appendix to vol. i.

some particulars with opinions expressed by me, but I consider the discovery of the truth on this subject as far more important than the confirmation of any theory of my own; and I may add that, in general, it bears out and sustains the views presented in these pages.

On the afternoon of the 11th of March we bade farewell to Don Pio Perez, and set out for Chichen. Ever since we left home we had had our eyes upon this place. We had become eager to reach it, and the increasing bulk of these volumes warns me that I must not now linger on the road. I shall therefore barely say that the first night we stopped at the village of Taihxiu, the second at Yaxcaba, and at noon of the third day we reached Pisté, about two miles distant from Chichen. We had heard some unpropitious accounts concerning the hospitality of the proprietor of the hacienda, and thought it safer not to alarm him by going upon him with appetites sharpened by a hard day's ride, but first to lay the village under a moderate contribution.

At four o'clock we left Pisté, and very soon we saw rising high above the plain the Castillo of Chichen. In half an hour we were among the ruins of this ancient city, with all the great buildings in full view, casting prodigious shadows over the plain, and presenting a spectacle which, even after all that we had seen, once more excited in us emotions of wonder. The camino real ran through the midst of them, and the field was so open that, without dismounting, we rode close in to some of the principal edifices. Involuntarily we lingered, but night was approaching, and, fairly dragging ourselves away, we rode on, and in a few minutes reached the hacienda. Vaqueros were shouting, and a large drove of cattle was pouring in at the gate. We were about following, but a crowd of men and women on the steps of the hacienda shouted to us not to come in, and a man ran toward us, throwing up both hands, and shut the gate directly in our faces. This promised us another Don Gregorio welcome; but this ominous demonstration did not mean anything churlish; on the contrary, all was done out of kindness. We had been expected for three months. Through the agency of friends the proprietor had advised the major domo of our intended visit, directing him to do all in his power to make us comfortable, and it was for this reason that the latter had ordered the gate to be shut upon us, for, as the man who did it told us, the hacienda was overrun with women and children, and there was no room for another hammock. He conducted us to the church, standing in a fine situation, and offered us the sacristia, or vestry-room, which was new, clean, and had plastered walls, but it was small, and had only knobs for two hammocks. It had a door of communication with the church, and he said we might swing a third hammock in the latter, but it was toward the end of a fiesta, the Indians might want to use the altar, and we had some scruples.

Our alternative was a house directly opposite the gate of the hacienda, to which there was no objection on the score of size, for as yet its dimensions were unlimited, as it was merely a frame of poles supporting a thatched roof, with a great pile of lime and sand in the centre, intended to be made into walls. The proprietor was erecting it expressly for the accommodation of travellers. While we resided in it, the pile of lime and sand was converted to its destined purpose, and we were plastered in; so that the next visiter to these ruins will find a good house ready for his reception. The major domo wished us to take our meals at the hacienda, but as we had all our travelling equipage, we again organized for housekeeping, and to that end we had an unusual proportion of comforts. Besides the resources of the hacienda, we had the village of Pisté at command, and Valladolid being but six hours' distance, we prepared an order for supplies to be sent off the next day.

The next morning, under the guidance of an Indian of the hacienda, we prepared for a preliminary survey. The ruins of Chichen lie on a hacienda, called by the name of the ancient city. It is the property of Don Juan Sosa, and was set off to him, on the decease of his father and an apportionment of his estate, with cattle, horses, and mules, at a valuation of between five and six thousand dollars. As with most of the lands in that neighbourhood, the fee is in the government, and the proprietor is entitled only to the majores, or improvements.

The ruins are nine leagues from Valladolid, the camino real to which passes directly through the field. The great buildings tower on both sides of the road in full sight of all passers-by, and from the fact that the road is much travelled, the ruins of Chichen are perhaps more generally known to the people of the country than any other in Yucatan. It is an interesting fact, however, that the first stranger who ever visited them was a native of New-York, whom we afterward met at Valladolid, and who is now again residing in this city.

Immediately on our arrival at Chichen we heard of a pay-sanno, or countryman, Don Juan Burque, enginero en la machina de Valladolid, the English of which is, Mr. John Burke, engineer in the factory. In 1838 Mr. Burke came from Valladolid to the village of Cawa, six leagues distant from Chichen. While making excursions in the neighbourhood, one of the young men told him of old buildings on this hacienda, from one of which Valladolid was visible. Mr. Burke rode over, and on the fourth of July stood on the top of the Castillo, spyglass in hand, looking out for Valladolid. Two years afterward, in 1840, they were visited by the Baron Frederichstahl, and by him first brought to the notice of the public, both in Europe and this country; and I take occasion to say that this visit was made in the prosecution of a route recommended to him by me after my return from my former interrupted journey of exploration among the ruins of Yucatan.

But to return. From the door of our hut some of the principal buildings were in sight. We went first to those on the opposite side of the camino real. The path led through the cattle-yard of the hacienda, from which we passed out at one end by a range of bars into the field of ruins, partially wooded, but the greater part open and intersected by cattle-paths. Garrapatas were as abundant as ever, and perhaps more so from the numerous cattle running over the plain, but the luxuries of an open country, and the facility of moving from place to place, were so great, that these could not mar our satisfaction, which was raised to the highest pitch by the ruins themselves. These were, indeed, magnificent. The buildings were large, and some were in good preservation; in general, the façades were not so elaborately ornamented as some we had seen, seemed of an older date, and the sculpture was ruder, but the interior apartments contained decorations and devices that were new to us, and powerfully interesting. All the principal buildings were within a comparatively small compass; in fact, they were in such proximity, and the facilities for moving among them were so great, that by one o'clock we had visited every building, examined every apartment, and arranged the whole plan and order of work. This over, we went to join Doctor Cabot, who was in the mean time pursuing an independent occupation, but on joint account, and for joint benefit.

The name of Chichen is another instance added to those already given, showing the importance attached in that dry country to the possession of water. It is compounded of the two Maya words *chi*, mouth, and *chen*, well, and signifies the mouth of the well. Among the ruins are two great senotes, which, beyond doubt, furnished water to the inhabitants of the ancient city. Since the establishment of a hacienda and the construction of a well, these had fallen into disuse. Doctor Cabot had undertaken to open a path in one of them down to the water, for the purpose of bathing, which, in that hot climate, was as refreshing as food. We came upon him just as he had finished, and, besides his Indian workmen, he had the company of a large party of Mestizo boys from the village of Pisté, who were already taking advantage of his labours, and were then swimming, diving, and perched all about in the hollows of the rocks.

On our journey from Peto, the particulars of which I was obliged to omit, we had entered a region where the sources of the supply of water again formed a new and distinctive feature in the face of the country, wilder, and, at first sight, perhaps creating a stronger feeling of admiration and wonder than even the extraordinary cuevas, aguadas, and senotes we had formerly encountered. These, too, are called senotes, but they differ materially from those before presented, being immense circular holes, from sixty to two hundred feet in diameter, with broken, rocky, perpendicular sides from fifty to one hundred feet deep, and having at the bottom a great body of water, of an unknown depth, always about the same level, supposed to be supplied by subterranean rivers. We had seen ranchos of Indians established near these senotes, with a railing on one side, over which Indian women were drawing up water in little bark buckets; probably the two great senotes at this place were the inducements to the foundation of the ancient city.

Figure 10 represents this senote among the ruins of Chichen. Though wild enough in its appearance, it had less of that extraordinary regularity than the others we had seen. Those were all circular, and it was impossible to get access to the water except by means of a rope. This was oblong, about three hundred and fifty feet in length and one hundred and fifty wide. The sides were between sixty and seventy feet high, and perpendicular, except in one place, which was broken so as to form a steep, winding descent to the water. The view is taken from the edge of the water. The path is evidently, to a certain extent, artificial, as we saw in one place the vestiges of a stone wall along the brink. On this side Doctor Cabot had erected a railing for protection, which the mischievous boys of Pisté afterward pulled down; we tempted them with a reward of two reales apiece for the discovery of the offenders, but none of them ever accepted the offer. These boys, by-the-way, with the inhabitants

Fig. 10

of Pisté generally, both men and women, seemed to consider that the opening of this path was for their especial benefit, and at first they made it a point to be on the spot at the same hour with us. Upon one occasion we were so annoyed by the presence of two ladies of that village, who seemed determined not to go away, that we were obliged to come to an amicable understanding by means of a peremptory notice that all persons must give us the benefit of their absence at that hour; and every day, when the sun was vertical and scarcely endurable on the surface of the earth, we bathed in this deep senote.

We returned to the hut well satisfied with our first day at Chichen; and there was another circumstance which, though painful in itself, added materially to the spirit with which we

202

commenced our labours at this place. The danger apprehended from the rainy season was coming to pass, and under the anticipation of a failure of the next crop, corn had risen from two reales to a dollar the load. The distress occasioned in this country by the failure of the corn crop cannot well be imagined. In 1836 this calamity occurred, and from the same cause that threatened to produce it now. Along the coast a supply was furnished from the United States, but it would not bear the expense of transportation into the interior, and in this region corn rose to four dollars a load, which put the staff of life completely beyond the reach of the Indians. Famine ensued, and the poor Indians died of starvation. At the time of our arrival, the criados, or servants, of the hacienda, always improvident, had consumed their small stock, and, with no hope from their milpas, with the permission of the master were about moving away to regions where the pressure would be less severe. Our arrival, as the major domo told us, arrested this movement; instead of our being obliged to hunt them up, the poor Indians crowded round the door of our hut, begging employment, and scrambling for the reales which Albino distributed among them; but all the relief we could afford them was of short duration, and it may not be amiss to mention that at the moment of writing the calamity apprehended has come to pass; the ports of Yucatan are thrown open and begging for bread, and that country in which, but a few short months since, we were moving so quietly and experiencing continual acts of kindness, is now groaning under famine superadded to the horrors of war.

CHAPTER XVII

Plate XXVI represents the general plan of the
ruins of Chichen. This plan is made from bearings taken with
the compass, and the distances were all measured with a line.
The buildings are laid down on the plan according to their
exterior form. All now standing are comprehended, and the
whole circumference occupied by them is about two miles, which
is equal to the diameter of two thirds of a mile, though ruined
buildings appear beyond these limits.

By referring to the plan the reader will see the position of
the hut in which we lived, and, following the path from our
door through the cattle-yard of the hacienda, at the distance of
two hundred and fifty yards he will reach the building represented in Plate XXVII. It does not stand on an artificial terrace,
but the earth seems to have been excavated for some distance
before it, so as to give it elevation of position. It faces the east,
and measures one hundred and forty-nine feet in front by forty-

Plate XXVI

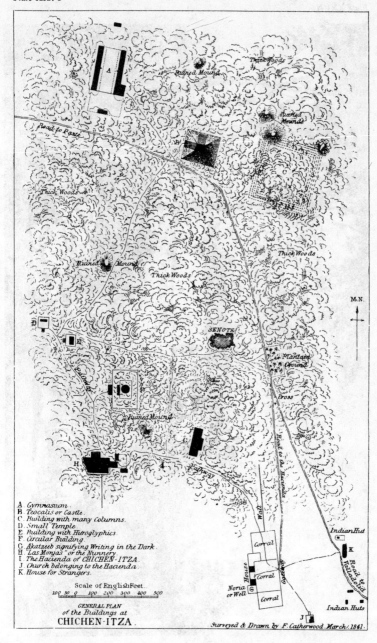

A. Gymnasium.
B. Teocalis or Castle.
C. Building with many Columns.
D. Small Temple.
E. Building with Hieroglyphics.
F. Circular Building.
G. Akatzeeb signifying Writing in the Dark.
H. "Las Monjas" or the Nunnery.
I. The Hacienda of CHICHEN-ITZA.
J. Church belonging to the Hacienda.
K. House for Strangers.

Scale of English Feet.
100 50 0   100   200   300   400   500

GENERAL PLAN
of the Buildings at
CHICHEN-ITZA.

Surveyed & Drawn by F. Catherwood March 1841.

Plate XXVII

CHICHEN

eight feet deep. The whole exterior is rude, and without ornament of any kind. A grand staircase, forty-five feet wide, now
entirely in ruins, rises in the centre to the roof of the building.
On each side of the staircase are two doorways; at each end is a
single doorway, and the front facing the west has seven. The
whole number of apartments is eighteen. The west front opens
upon a large hollow surface, whether natural or artificial it is
not easy to say, and in the centre of this is one of those features
before referred to, a solid mass of masonry, forty-four feet by
thirty-four, standing out from the wall, high as the roof, and
corresponding, in position and dimensions, with the ruined
staircase on the eastern front. This projection is not necessary for
the support of the building; it is not an ornament, but, on the
contrary, a deformity; and whether it be really a solid mass, or
contain interior chambers, remains to be ascertained by the future explorer.

At the south end the doorway opens into a chamber, round
which hangs a greater and more impenetrable mystery. This
chamber is nineteen feet wide by eight feet six inches deep, and
in the back wall a low, narrow doorway communicates with another chamber in the rear, of the same dimensions, but having
its floor one step higher. The lintel of this doorway is of stone,
and on the soffite, or under part, is sculptured the subject represented in Plate XXVIII. This tablet, and the position in which it
exists, have given the name to the building, which the Indians
call Akatzeeb, signifying the writing in the dark; for, as no light
enters except from the single doorway, the chamber was so dark
that the drawing could with difficulty be copied. It was the first
time in Yucatan that we had found hieroglyphics sculptured on
stone, which, beyond all question, bore the same type with those
at Copan and Palenque. The sitting figure seems performing
some act of incantation, or some religious or idolatrous rite,
which the "writing in the dark" undoubtedly explains, if one
could but read it. Physical force may raze these buildings to the
ground, and lay bare all the secrets they contain, but physical
force can never unravel the mystery that involves this sculptured
tablet.

Leaving this building, and following the path indicated in
the map, at the distance of one hundred and fifty yards westward
we reach a modern stone fence, dividing the cattle-field of the
hacienda, on the other side of which appears through the trees,
between two other buildings, the end façade of a long, majestic
pile, called, like one of the principal edifices at Uxmal, the

Plate XXVIII

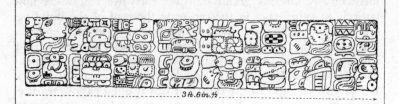

3 ft. 6 in. ½

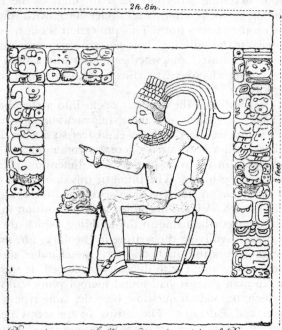

2 ft. 8 in.

3 Feet

Drawing on Soffite or under side of Doorway

Sculptured Figure and Hieroglyphics in low relief on the Soffite and upper part of a Doorway of a Building called AKATZEEB at CHICHEN-ITZA

3 ft. 10 in.

1 ft. 8 in.
Step

DOORWAY

This Building is of Stone well put together and the Sculpture has been painted. Red, Blue and Yellow, are still visible.

Level of Floor

F. Catherwood.

J. N. Gimbrede.

208

Monjas, or Nuns; it is remarkable for its good state of preservation, and the richness and beauty of its ornaments, as represented in Plate XXIX. The view comprehends the corner of a building on the right, at a short distance, called the Eglesia, or Church. The height of this façade is twenty-five feet, and its width thirty-five. It has two cornices of tasteful and elaborate design. Over the doorway are twenty small cartouches of hieroglyphics in four rows, five in a row, barely indicated in the engraving, and to make room for which the lower cornice is carried up. Over these stand out in a line six bold projecting curved ornaments, like that presented from the House of the Governor at Uxmal, resembling an elephant's trunk, and the upper centre space over the doorway is an irregular circular niche, in which portions of a seated figure, with a head-dress of feathers, still remain. The rest of the ornaments are of that distinctive stamp, characteristic of the ancient American cities, and unlike the designs of any other people, with which the reader must now be familiar. The tropical plants and shrubs growing on the roof, which, when we first saw it, hung over the cornice like a fringe-work, added greatly to the picturesque effect of this elegant façade.

Plate XXX represents the front of the same building. It is composed of two structures entirely different from each other, one of which forms a sort of wing to the principal edifice, and has at the end the façade before presented. The whole length is two hundred and twenty-eight feet, and the depth of the principal structure is one hundred and twelve feet. The only portion containing interior chambers is that which I have called the wing. This has two doorways opening into chambers twenty-six feet long and eight feet deep, behind each of which is another of corresponding dimensions, now filled up several feet with mortar and stones, and appearing to have been originally filled up solid to the ceiling, making again casas cerradas, or closed houses. The whole number of chambers in this wing is nine, and these are all the apartments on the ground floor. The great structure to which the wing adjoins is apparently a solid mass of masonry, erected only to hold up the two ranges of buildings upon it. A grand staircase fifty-six feet wide, the largest we saw in the country, rises to the top. On one side of the staircase a huge breach, twenty or thirty feet deep, has been made by the proprietor, for the purpose of getting out building stone, which discloses only solid masonry. The grand staircase is thirty-two feet high, and has thirty-nine steps. On the top of

Plate XXIX

F. Catherwood.

Gambreda.

MONJAS. CHICHEN ITZA.

Plate XXX

CASA DE LAS MONJAS . CHICHEN.

the structure stands a range of buildings, with a platform of fourteen feet in front extending all round.

From the back of this platform the grand staircase rises again, having the same width, fifteen steps to the roof of the second range, which forms a platform in front of the third range; this last is, unfortunately, in a ruinous condition, and it is to be observed that in this, as in all the other cases, these ancient architects never placed an upper building on the roof of a lower one, but always back, so as to rest on a structure solid from the ground, the roof of the lower range being merely a platform in front of the upper one.

The circumference of this building is six hundred and thirty-eight feet, and its height, when entire, was sixty-five feet. It seems to have been constructed only with reference to the second range of apartments, upon which the art and skill of the builders have been lavishly expended. It is one hundred and four feet long and thirty feet wide, and the broad platform around it, though overgrown with grass several feet high, formed a noble promenade, commanding a magnificent view of the whole surrounding country.

On the side of the staircase are five doorways, of which the three centre ones are what are usually called false doors, appearing to be merely recesses in the wall. The compartments between the doorways contained combinations of ornaments of unusual taste and elegance, both in arrangement and design. The two extreme doorways open into chambers, in each of which are three long recesses in the back wall, extending from the floor to the ceiling, all of which, from the remains still visible, were once ornamented with paintings. At each end of the building was another chamber, with three niches or recesses, and on the other side, facing the south, the three centre doorways, corresponding with the false doors on the north side, opened into an apartment forty-seven feet long and nine deep, having nine long niches in the back wall; all the walls from the floor to the peak of the arch had been covered with painted designs, now wantonly defaced, but the remains of which present colours in some places still bright and vivid; and among these remains detached portions of human figures continually recur, well drawn, the heads adorned with plumes of feathers, and the hands bearing shields and spears. All attempt at description would fail, and much more would an attempt to describe the strange interest of walking along the overgrown platform of this gigantic and desolate building.

Plate XXXI

EGLESIA, CHICHEN ITZA

Descending again to the ground, at the end of the wing stands what is called the Eglesia, or Church, a corner of which was comprehended in a previous view, and the front of which is represented in Plate XXXI. It is twenty-six feet long, fourteen deep, and thirty-one high, its comparatively great height adding very much to the effect of its appearance. It has three cornices, and the spaces between are richly ornamented. The sculpture is rude but grand. The principal ornament is over the doorway, and on each side are two human figures in a sitting posture, but, unfortunately, much mutilated. The portion of the façade above the second cornice is merely an ornamented wall, like those before mentioned at Zayi and Labnà.

The whole of this building is in a good state of preservation. The interior consists of a single apartment, once covered with plaster, and along the top of the wall under the arch are seen the traces of a line of medallions or cartouches in plaster, which once contained hieroglyphics. The Indians have no superstitious feelings about these ruins, except in regard to this building; and in this they say that on Good Friday of every year music is heard sounding; but this illusion, brought with us from Santa Cruz del Quiché, was here destined to be broken. In this chamber we opened our Daguerreotype apparatus, and on Good Friday were at work all day, but heard no music. This chamber, by-the-way, was the best we had found for our Daguerreotype operations. Having but one door, it was easily darkened; we were not obliged to pack up and carry away; the only danger was of cattle getting in and breaking; and there was no difficulty in getting an Indian to pass the night in the room and guard against this peril.

South of the end of the Monjas, and twenty-two feet distant, is another building, measuring thirty-eight feet by thirteen, having the exterior above the cornice decorated in the usual manner, but which I do not think it worth while to present.

Leaving this pile of buildings, and passing on northward from the Monjas, at the distance of four hundred feet we reach the edifice represented in Plate XXXII, conspicuous among the ruins of Chichen for its picturesque appearance, and unlike any other we had seen, except one at Mayapan much ruined. It is circular in form, and is known by the name of the Caracol, or winding staircase, on account of its interior arrangements. It stands on the upper of two terraces. The lower one measures in front from north to south two hundred and twenty-three feet, and in depth from east to west one hundred and fifty feet, and

Plate XXXII

Catherwood.

Johnson.

CHICHEN
Circular Building

is still in good preservation. A grand staircase forty-five feet wide, and containing twenty steps, rises to the platform of this terrace. On each side of this staircase, forming a sort of balustrade, were the entwined bodies of two gigantic serpents, three feet wide, portions of which are still in place; and among the ruins of the staircase we saw a gigantic head, which had terminated at one side the foot of the steps.

The platform of the second terrace measures eighty feet in front and fifty-five in depth, and is reached by another staircase forty-two feet wide, and having sixteen steps. In the centre of the steps, and against the wall of the terrace, are the remains of a pedestal six feet high, on which probably once stood an idol. On the platform, fifteen feet from the last step, stands the building. It is twenty-two feet in diameter, and has four small doorways facing the cardinal points. A great portion of the upper part and one of the sides have fallen. Above the cornice the roof sloped so as almost to form an apex. The height, including the terraces, is little short of sixty feet, and, when entire, even among the great buildings around, this structure must have presented a striking appearance. The doorways give entrance to a circular corridor five feet wide. The inner wall has also four doorways, smaller than the others, and standing at intermediate points of the compass, facing northeast, northwest, southwest, and southeast. These doors give entrance to a second circular corridor, four feet wide; and in the centre is a circular mass, apparently of solid stone, seven feet six inches in diameter; but in one place, at the height of eight feet from the ground, was a small square opening choked up with stones, which I endeavoured to clear out; but the stones falling into the narrow corridor made it dangerous to continue. The roof was so tottering that I could not discover to what this opening led. It was about large enough to admit the figure of a man in a standing position, to look out from the top. The walls of both corridors were plastered and ornamented with paintings, and both were covered with the triangular arch. The plan of the building was new, but, instead of unfolding secrets, it drew closer the curtain that already shrouded, with almost impenetrable folds, these mysterious structures.

At the distance of four hundred and twenty feet northwest from the Caracol stands the building represented in Figure 11. It is called by the Indians Chichanchob, meaning in Spanish, Casa Colorada, and in English, Red House. The terrace is sixty-two feet long and fifty-five wide, and is still in good preservation; the staircase is twenty feet wide, and as we approached it on our first visit, a cow was coming quietly down the steps.

Fig. 11

The building measures forty-three feet front and twenty-three feet deep, and is still strong and substantial. Above the cornice it was richly ornamented, but the ornaments are now much decayed. It has three doorways, which open into a corridor running the whole width of the building; and along the top of the back wall was a stone tablet, with a row of hieroglyphics extending all along the wall. Many of them were defaced, and, from their height, in an awkward position to copy; but we had a scaffold erected, and obtained copies of the whole. Plate XXXIII represents these hieroglyphics, so far as they could be made out. When not distinct, to avoid misleading they are not given at all. Under the hieroglyphics, in the plate, is given a plan of the building, with its terrace and staircase. It has a back corridor, consisting of three chambers, all of which retain the marks of painting; and, from the convenience of its arrangements, with the platform of the terrace for a promenade, and the view of a fine open country in front, but for the greater convenience of being near the hacienda we should have been tempted to take up our abode in it.

At the short distance of two hundred feet is the building represented in Figure 12. The platform of the terrace was sixty-

Plate XXXIII

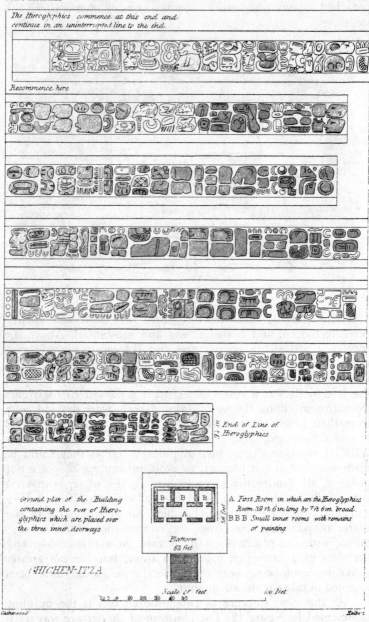

The Hieroglyphics commence at this end and continue in an uninterrupted line to the end.

Recommence here

End of Line of Hieroglyphics

Ground plan of the Building containing the row of Hieroglyphics which are placed over the three inner doorways

A. First Room in which are the Hieroglyphics Room 39 ft. 6 in long by 7 ft 6 in broad.

BBB Small inner rooms with remains of painting.

Platform 62 feet

CHICHEN-ITZA

Scale of feet

100 feet

Catherwood

Halbe:

218

four feet square, the building had three rooms, but both terrace and building are ruined, and the view is presented only because it was so picturesque that Mr. Catherwood could not resist the temptation to draw it.

Fig. 12

All these buildings are within three hundred yards of the staircase of the Monjas; from any intermediate point all are in full sight; the field is open, and intersected by cattle-paths; the buildings, staircases, and terraces were overgrown, but Indians being at hand in sufficient force, they were easily cleared, and the whole was finished with a despatch that had never before attended our progress.

These are the only buildings on the west side of the camino real which are still standing; but great vestiges exist of mounds with remains of buildings upon them, and colossal stones and fragments of sculpture at their feet, which it would be impossible to present in detail.

Passing among these vestiges, we come out upon the camino real, and, crossing it, again enter an open field, containing the extraordinary edifice represented in Plate XXXIV, which, on

Plate XXXIV

GYMNASIUM, CHICHEN ITZA

F. Catherwood.

Gumbreda.

first reaching the field of ruins, we rode in on horseback to examine. It consists of two immense parallel walls, each two hundred and seventy-four feet long, thirty feet thick, and one hundred and twenty feet apart. One hundred feet from the northern extremity, facing the open space between the walls, stands on an elevation a building thirty-five feet long, containing a single chamber, with the front fallen, and, rising among the rubbish, the remains of two columns, elaborately ornamented with sculpture; the whole interior wall being exposed to view, covered from the floor to the peak of the arch with sculptured figures in bas-relief, much worn and faded. The engraving represents the two walls, with this building in the distance. And at the other end, setting back, too, one hundred feet, and commanding the space between the walls, is another building eighty-one feet long, also ruined, but exhibiting the remains of two columns richly ornamented with sculptured figures in bas-relief. The position in which these walls and buildings stand to each other is laid down on the general plan.

In the centre of the great stone walls, exactly opposite each other, and at the height of twenty feet from the ground, are two massive stone rings, four feet in diameter, and one foot one inch thick; the diameter of the hole is one foot seven inches. On the rim and border were two sculptured entwined serpents, one of which is represented in Figure 13.

These walls, at the first glance, we considered identical in their uses and purposes with the parallel structures supporting the rings at Uxmal, of which I have already expressed the opinion that they were intended for the celebration of some public games. I have in all cases adopted the names of buildings which I found assigned to them on the spot, where any existed, and where there were none I have not attempted to give any. At Chichen all the principal buildings have names; this is called an Eglesia, or Church, of the antiguos, which was begun, but not finished, and the great open walls present not a bad idea of one of their gigantic churches before the roof is put on; but as we have already one Eglesia, and there is historical authority which, in my opinion, shows clearly the object and uses of this extraordinary structure, I shall call it, as occasion requires, the Gymnasium or Tennis-court.

In the account of the diversions of Montezuma, given by Herrera, we have the following:

"The King took much Delight in seeing Sport at Ball, which the Spaniards have since prohibited, because of the Mis-

FIG. 13

chief that often hapned at it; and was by them call'd *Tlachtli*, being like our Tennis. The Ball was made of the Gum of a Tree that grows in hot Countries, which, having Holes made in it, distils great white Drops, that soon harden, and, being work'd and moulded together, turn as black as Pitch.* The Balls made thereof, tho' hard and heavy to the Hand, did bound and fly as well as our Foot-balls, there being no need to blow them; nor did they use Chaces, but vy'd to drive the adverse Party that is to hit the Wall, the others were to make good, or strike it over. They struck it with any Part of their Body, as it hapned, or they could most conveniently; and sometimes he lost that touched it with any other Part but his Hip, which was look'd upon among them as the greatest Dexterity; and to this Effect, that the Ball might rebound the better, they fastned a Piece of stiff Leather on their Hips. They might strike it every time it rebounded, which it would do several Times one after another, in so much that it look'd as if it had been alive. They play'd in Parties, so many on a Side, for a Load of Mantles, or what the Gamesters could afford, at so many Scores. They also play'd for Gold, and Feather-work, and sometimes play'd themselves away, as has been

*Undoubtedly caoutchouc, or India-rubber.

said before. The Place where they play'd was a ground Room, long, narrow, and high, but wider above than below, and higher on the Sides than at the Ends, and they kept it very well plaster'd and smooth, both the Walls and the Floor. *On the side Walls they fix'd certain Stones, like those of a Mill, with a Hole quite through the Middle,* just as big as the Ball, and he that could strike it through there won the Game; and in Token of its being an extraordinary Success, which rarely hapned, he had a Right to the Cloaks of all the Lookers-on, by antient Custom, and Law amongst Gamesters; and it was very pleasant to see, that as soon as ever the Ball was in the Hole, the Standers-by took to their Heels, running away with all their Might to save their Cloaks, laughing and rejoicing, others scouring after them to secure their Cloaks for the Winner, who was oblig'd to offer some Sacrifice to the Idol of the Tennis-court, and the Stone through whose Hole the Ball had pass'd. Every Tennis-court was a Temple, having two Idols, the one of Gaming, and the other of the Ball. On a lucky Day, at Midnight, they perform'd certain Ceremonies and Enchantments on the two lower Walls and on the Midst of the Floor, singing certain Songs, or Ballads; after which a Priest of the great Temple went with some of their Religious Men to bless it; he uttered some Words, threw the Ball about the Tennis-court four Times, and then it was consecrated, and might be play'd in, but not before. The Owner of the Tennis-court, who was always a Lord, never play'd without making some Offering and performing certain Ceremonies to the Idol of Gaming, which shows how superstitious they were, since they had such Regard to their Idols, even in their Diversions. Montezuma carry'd the Spaniards to this Sport, and was well pleas'd to see them play at it, as also at Cards and Dice."

With some slight variation in details, the general features are so identical as to leave no doubt on my mind that this structure was erected for precisely the same object as the Tennis-court in the city of Mexico described by Herrera. The temples are at hand in which sacrifices were offered, and we discover in this something more important than the mere determining of the character of a building; for in the similarity of diversions we see a resemblance in manners and institutions, and trace an affinity between the people who erected the ruined cities of Yucatan and those who inhabited Mexico at the time of the conquest. In the account of Herrera, moreover, we see incidentally the drawing of a funeral pall over the institutions of the natives, for we learn that the sport which "Montezuma took

Plate XXXV

S.H.Gimber.

CHICHEN

F. Catherwood.

much delight in seeing," and which, beyond doubt, was a favourite diversion of the people, "the Spaniards have since prohibited."

At the southern extremity of the eastern wall, and on the outer side, stands the building represented in Plate XXXV, consisting of two ranges, one even with the ground, and the other about twenty-five feet above it, the latter being in a good state of preservation, simple, tasteful in its arrangement of ornaments, and having conspicuous a procession of tigers or lynxes, which appear on a small scale in the engraving. From its lofty position, with trees growing around it and on the roof, the effect is beautifully picturesque; but it has, besides, a far higher interest, and on some considerations may perhaps be regarded as the most important structure that we met with in our whole exploration of ruins.

The lower building, standing on the ground, is in a ruinous condition: the front has fallen, and shows only the remains of two columns covered with sculptured figures; the fall of the front has laid bare the entire wall of the chamber, covered from one end to the other with elaborately-sculptured figures in bas-relief.

Plate XXXVI represents a portion of these figures. Exposed for ages to a long succession of winds and rains, the characters were faded and worn; under the glare of a tropical sun the lines were confused and indistinct, and the reflection of the heat was so intense that it was impossible to work before it except for an hour or two in the afternoon, when the building was in the shade. The head-dress of the figures is, as usual, a plume of feathers, and in the upper row each figure carries a bundle of spears or a quiver of arrows. All these figures were painted, and the reader may imagine what the effect must have been when all was entire. The Indians call this chamber Stohl, and say that it represents a dance of the antiguos; and these bas-reliefs, too, have a distinct and independent value. In the large work of Nebel, entitled "Voyage Pittoresque et Archéologique dans le Mexique," lately published at Paris, is a drawing of the stone of sacrifice in the Museum of Mexico, and now for the first time published. It is nine feet in diameter and three feet thick, and contains a procession of figures in bas-relief, which, though differing in detail, are of the same general character with those sculptured on the wall of this building. The stone was dug up in the plaza of Mexico, near the spot on which stood, in the time of Montezuma, the great teocalis of that city. The resem-

Plate XXXVI

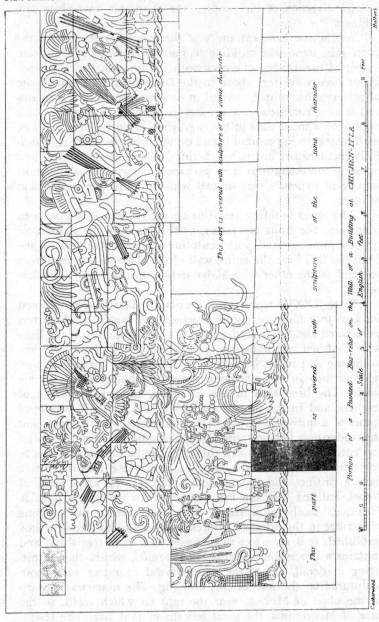

Portion of a Painted Bas-relief on the Wall of a Building at CHICHEN-ITZA.

This part is covered with sculpture of the same character

This part is covered with sculpture of the same character

Scale of English feet.

Catherwood

Halbert

226

blance stands upon a different footing from any which may exist in Mitla, or Xocichalco, or other places, the history of which is unknown, and forms another connecting link with the very people who occupied the city of Mexico at the time of the conquest. And the proofs go on accumulating. In the upper building, the back of which appears in the engraving, is presented a casket containing, though broken and disfigured, perhaps the greatest gem of aboriginal art which on the whole Continent of America now survives.

The steps or other means of access to this building are gone, and we reached it by clambering over fallen stones. The door opens upon the platform of the wall, overlooking the Tennis-court. The front corridor was supported by massive pillars, portions of which still remain, covered with elaborate sculptured ornaments. The lintel of the inner doorway is a beam of sapote richly carved. The jambs are partly buried, and above the rubbish appear sculptured figures with rich head-dresses, which anywhere else we should have considered it necessary to bring to light and copy; but between these jambs we enter an inner chamber, the walls and ceiling of which are covered, from the floor to the peak of the arch, with designs in painting, representing, in bright and vivid colours, human figures, battles, houses, trees, and scenes of domestic life, and conspicuous on one of the walls is a large canoe; but the first feeling of gratified surprise was followed by heavy disappointment, for the whole was mutilated and disfigured. In some places the plaster was broken off; in every part deep and malignant scratches appeared in the walls, and while individual figures were entire, the connexion of the subjects could not be made out. For a long time we had been tantalized with fragments of painting, giving us the strong impression that in this more perishable art these aboriginal builders had made higher attainments than in that of sculpture, and we now had proofs that our impression did them justice. Plate XXXVII represents detached portions of these paintings. The colours are green, yellow, red, blue, and a reddish brown, the last being invariably the colour given to human flesh. Wanting the various tints, the engraving, of course, gives only an imperfect idea of them, though, even in outline, they exhibit a freedom of touch which could only be the result of discipline and training under masters. But they have a higher interest than any that attaches to them as mere specimens of art; for among them are seen designs and figures which call forcibly to mind the well-known picture writings of the Mexicans; and if these

Plate XXXVII

Nº 1.

Nº 2.

Nº 3.

Nº 4.

Outlines from paintings on the walls of a Room at CHICHEN-ITZA. The colors are vivid and well preserved, and consist of Green, Yellow, Red, Blue and a Reddish brown, which last color is invariably used for the color of flesh, the color of the women is somewhat lighter than that of the men. On the line marked Nº 1. the figures follow as shewn in the drawing. On line Nº 2 the figures are all on the same line, but some figures near between the first two and last two which are omitted from being much defaced. Line Nº 3 represents figures taken from various groups. Nº 4 the same. Figures 9½ high.

Catherwood   Halbot analogies are sustained, this building attached to the walls of the Tennis-court stands an unimpeachable witness that the people who inhabited Mexico at the time of the conquest belonged to the same great race which furnished the builders of the ruined cities in Yucatan.

But to continue. At the distance of five hundred feet southeast from this rises the Castillo, represented in Plate XXXVIII, the first building which we saw, and from every point of view

FIG. 14

the grandest and most conspicuous object that towers above the plain. Every Sunday the ruins are resorted to as a promenade by the villagers of Pisté, and nothing can surpass the picturesque appearance of this lofty building while women, dressed in white, with red shawls, are moving on the platform, and passing in and out at the doors. The mound measures at the base on the north and south sides one hundred and ninety-six feet ten inches, and on the east and west sides two hundred and two feet. It does not face the cardinal points exactly, though probably so intended; and in all the buildings, from some cause not easily accounted for, while one varies ten degrees one way, that immediately adjoining varies twelve or thirteen degrees in another. It is built up apparently solid from the plain to the height of seventy-five feet. On the west side is a staircase thirty-seven feet wide; on the north, being that presented in the engraving, the staircase is forty-four feet wide, and contains ninety steps. On the ground at the foot of the staircase, forming a bold, striking, and well-conceived commencement to this lofty range, are two colossal serpents' heads, ten feet in length, with mouths wide open and tongues protruding, as represented in Figure 14. No doubt they were emblematic of some religious belief, and in the minds of an imaginative people, passing between them to ascend the steps, must have excited feelings of solemn awe.

The platform on the top of the mound measures sixty-one feet from north to south, and sixty-four from east to west; and the building measures in the same directions forty-three feet and forty-nine. Single doorways face the east, south, and west, having massive lintels of sapote wood covered with elaborate carvings, and the jambs are ornamented with sculptured figures, one of which is represented in Plate XXXIX. The sculpture is much worn, but the head-dress, ornamented with a plume of feathers, and portions of the rich attire still remain. The face is well preserved, and has a dignified appearance. It has, too, earrings, and the nose bored, which, according to the historical accounts, was so prevalent a custom in Yucatan, that long after the conquest the Spaniards passed laws for its prohibition.

All the other jambs are decorated with sculpture of the same general character, and all open into a corridor six feet wide, extending round three sides of the building.

The doorway facing the north, represented in the engraving, presents a grander appearance, being twenty feet wide, and having two short massive columns, eight feet eight inches high, with two large projections at the base, entirely covered with elab-

Plate XXXVIII

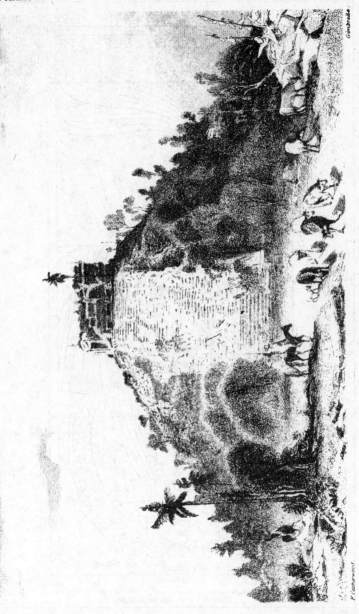

Gombrão.

CASTILLO. CHICHEN ITZA

F. Catherwood.

Plate XXXIX

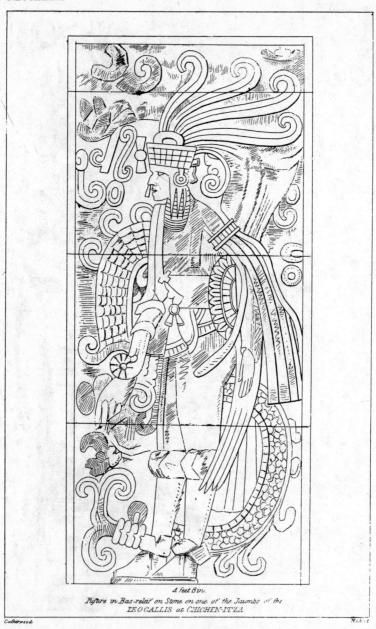

4 feet 8 in.

Figure in Bas-relief on Stone on one of the Jambs of the
TEOCALLIS at CHICHEN-ITZA.

Catherwood

orate sculpture. This doorway gives access to a corridor forty feet long by six feet four inches wide and seventeen feet high. In the back wall of this corridor is a single doorway, having sculptured jambs, over which is a richly-carved sapote beam, and giving entrance to an apartment represented in Plate XL, nineteen feet eight inches long, twelve feet nine inches wide, and seventeen feet high. In this apartment are two square pillars nine feet four inches high and one foot ten inches on each side, having sculptured figures on all their sides, and supporting massive sapote beams covered with the most elaborate carving of curious and intricate designs, but so defaced and timeworn that, in the obscurity of the room, lighted only from the door, it was extremely difficult to make them out. The impression produced on entering this lofty chamber, so entirely different from all we had met with before, was perhaps stronger than any we had yet experienced. We passed a whole day within it, from time to time stepping out upon the platform to look down upon the ruined buildings of the ancient city, and an immense field stretching on all sides beyond.

And from this lofty height we saw for the first time groups of small columns, which, on examination, proved to be among the most remarkable and unintelligible remains we had yet met with. They stood in rows of three, four, and five abreast, many rows continuing in the same direction, when they changed and pursued another. They were very low, many of them only three feet high, while the highest were not more than six feet, and consisted of several separate pieces, like millstones. Many of them had fallen, and in some places they lie prostrate in rows, all in the same direction, as if thrown down intentionally. I had a large number of Indians at work clearing them, and endeavouring to trace their direction to the end. In some places they extended to the bases of large mounds, on which were ruins of buildings and colossal fragments of sculpture, while in others they branched off and terminated abruptly. I counted three hundred and eighty, and there were many more; but so many were broken, and they lay so irregularly, that I gave up counting them. They were entirely too low to have supported a roof under which persons could walk. The idea at times suggested itself that they had upheld a raised walk of cement, but there were no remains visible. Plate XLI will give some idea of these columns, with the Castillo and part of the Tennis-court appearing in the background. They enclose an area nearly four hundred feet square; and, incomprehensible as they are in their uses

Plate XL

F. CATHERWOOD del.

Plate XLI

and object, add largely to the interest and wonder connected with these ruins.

I have now closed my brief description of the ruins of Chichen, having presented, with as little detail as possible, all the principal buildings of this ancient city. Ruined mounds exist, and detached portions of sculpture strew the ground, exhibiting curious devices, which often arrested us in wandering among them, but which I shall not attempt to give. They were the ruins which we had had longest in prospect, of which we had formed the largest expectations, and these expectations were not disappointed, but more than realized. And they had additional interest in our eyes from the fact that the broad light of day beams upon their history. The first settlement of the Spaniards in the interior was made at this very spot.

The reader may remember that in the early part of these pages he accompanied Don Francisco Montejo to Chichen, or Chichen Itza, as it was called, from the name of the people who occupied the country. The site of this place is identified beyond all peradventure as that now occupied by these ruins; and the reader, perhaps, will expect from Don Francisco Montejo, or the Spanish soldiers, some detailed account of these extraordinary buildings, so different from any to which the Spaniards were accustomed. But, strange as it may appear, no such account exists. The only existing notice of their journey from the coast says, that from a place called Aké they set out, directing their course for Chichen Itza, where they determined to stop and settle, as it appeared a proper place, on account of the strength of the great buildings that were there, for defence against attacks by the Indians. We do not even learn whether these buildings were inhabited or desolate; but Herrera says that the Indians in this region were so numerous, that in making the distribution which the adelantado was allowed by the terms of the royal grant, the least number which fell to the lot of a Spaniard was two thousand.

Having regard, however, to the circumstances of the occupation and abandonment of Chichen by the Spaniards, their silence is perhaps not extraordinary. I have already mentioned that at this place the adelantado made a fatal mistake, and, lured by the glitter of gold in another province, divided his forces, and sent one of his best captains, with fifty men, in search of it. From this time calamities and dangers pressed upon him; altercations and contests began with the Indians; provisions were withheld, the Spaniards were obliged to seek them with the sword, and all that they ate was procured at the price of blood. At length the Indians determined upon their utter destruction. Immense multitudes surrounded the camp of the Spaniards, hemming them in on all sides. The Spaniards, seeing themselves reduced to the necessity of perishing by hunger, determined to die bravely in the field, and went out to give battle. The most sanguinary fight they had ever been engaged in then took place. The Spaniards fought for their lives, and the Indians to remain masters of their own soil. Masses of the latter were killed, but great slaughter was made among the Spaniards, and, to save the lives of those who remained, the adelantado retreated to the fortifications. One hundred and fifty of the conquerors were dead; nearly all the rest were wounded, and if the Indians had attacked them in their retreat they would have perished to a man.

Unable to hold out any longer, they took advantage of a night when the Indians were off their guard, and making sallies in the evening so as to keep them awake, that weariness might afterward overtake them, as soon as all was still they tied a dog to the clapper of a bell-rope, putting some food before him, but out of his reach, and with great silence marched out from the camp. The dog, when he saw them going, pulled the cord in order to go with them, and afterward to get at the food. The Indians, supposing that the Spaniards were sounding the alarm, remained quiet, waiting the result, but a little before daylight, perceiving that the bell did not cease ringing, they drew near the fortification, and found it deserted. In the mean time the Spaniards escaped toward the coast, and in the meager and disconnected accounts of their dangers and escape, it is, perhaps, not surprising that we have none whatever of the buildings, arts, and sciences of the fierce inhabitants of Chichen.

I shall close with one general remark. These cities were, of course, not all built at one time, but are the remains of different epochs. Chichen, though in a better state of preservation than most of the others, has a greater appearance of antiquity; some of the buildings are no doubt older than others, and long intervals may have elapsed between the times of their construction.

The Maya manuscript places the first discovery of Chichen within the epochs corresponding with the time between A.D. 360 and A.D. 432. From the words used, it may be understood that the discovery was then made of an actual existing city, but it is a fair construction of these words to suppose that nothing more is meant than a discovery of what the words Chi-chen import, viz., the mouths of wells, having reference to the two great senotes, the discovery of wells being, among all primitive people, and particularly in the dry region of Yucatan, an event worthy to be noted in their history.

One of these senotes I have already mentioned; the other I did not visit till the afternoon preceding our departure from Chichen. Setting out from the Castillo, at some distance we ascended a wooded elevation, which seemed an artificial causeway leading to the senote. The senote was the largest and wildest we had seen; in the midst of a thick forest, an immense circular hole, with cragged, perpendicular sides, trees growing out of them and overhanging the brink, and still as if the genius of silence reigned within. A hawk was sailing around it, looking down into the water, but without once flapping its wings. The water was of a greenish hue. A mysterious influence seemed to pervade it, in unison with the historical account that the well of Chichen was a place of pilgrimage, and that human victims were thrown into it in sacrifice. In one place, on the very brink, were the remains of a stone structure, probably connected with ancient superstitious rites; perhaps the place from which the victims were thrown into the dark well beneath.

CHAPTER XVIII

Departure from Chichen. — Village of Kaua. — Cuncunul. — Arrival at Valladolid. — An Accident. — Appearance of the City. — Don Pedro Baranda's Cotton Factory. — A Countryman. — Mexican Revolution. — The Indians as Soldiers. — Adventures of a Demonio. — Character of the People. — Gamecocks. — Difficulty of obtaining Information in regard to the Route. — Departure for the Coast. — Party of Indians. — Village of Chemax. — Fate of Molas the Pirate. — Discouraging Accounts. — Plans deranged. — The Convent. — The Cura. — Population of the Village. — Its early History. — Ruins of Coba. — Indian Sepulchre. — Relics. — A Penknife found in the Sepulchre.

On Tuesday, the twenty-ninth of March, we left Chichen. It was still in the gray of the morning when we caught our last view of the great buildings, and as we turned away we felt that the few short months of our journey had been a time of interest and wonder, such as rarely occurs in life. At nine o'clock we reached the village of Kaua, six leagues distant, and at half past eleven the small village of Cuncunul, within an hour's ride of Valladolid, and there we determined to dine, and wait for the servants and carriers.

We remained till four o'clock, and then set out for Valladolid. As far as the suburbs the road was broken and stony. We entered by the great Church of Sisal, with convent and cloisters by its side, and a square in front, which, as we rode across it, sounded hollow under our horses' feet, and underneath was an immense senote. We passed up the Calle de Sisal, a long street with straggling houses on each side, and were directed to the house of Don Pedro Baranda, one of the largest and best in the place. This gentleman had received advices of our intended visit, and had engaged for us a house. As our luggage did not arrive, he furnished us with hammocks, and in an hour we were comfortable as in our house at Merida. About midnight Albino came clattering to the door, accompanied by only one horse, carrying our hammocks, and bringing the disastrous intelligence that the horse carrying the Daguerreotype apparatus had run away, and made a general crash. Hitherto the apparatus had always been carried by an Indian, but the road from Chichen was so good that we were not afraid to trust it on horseback. There was consolation, however, in the thought that we could not lose what we had already done with its assistance.

The next morning we were in no hurry. From Valladolid it was our purpose to prosecute our exploration through a region of which less was known than of any we had yet visited. In our short voyage with Captain Fensley from the Laguna to Sisal, he had told us of stone buildings on the coast, near Cape Catoche, which he called old Spanish forts. These accounts were confirmed by others, and we at length ascertained what we supposed to be the fact, that in two places on the coast called Tancar and Tuloom, what were taken for Spanish forts were aboriginal buildings. Our business at Valladolid was to make arrangements for reaching them, and at the same time for coasting round Cape Catoche, and visiting the Island of Cozumel. We had been told that at Valladolid we should be able to procure all necessary information about the ruins on the coast; but we could not even learn the way to reach them; and by the advice of Don Pedro Baranda we determined to remain a few days, until a person who was expected, and who was familiar with that region, should arrive.

In the mean time, a few days did not hang heavy on our hands in Valladolid. The city, which was founded at an early period of the conquest, contains about fifteen thousand inhabitants, and is distinguished as the residence of the vicar-general of the church of Yucatan.

It was built in a style commensurate with the lofty pretensions of the conquerors, and, like other cities of Spanish America, bears the marks of ancient grandeur, but is now going to decay. The roads leading to it and the very streets are overgrown with bushes. The parochial church still stands, the principal object in the plaza, and the churches of San Servacio, San Juan De Dios, Santa Lucia, Santa Ana, La Virgen de la Candelaria, and the Church of Sisal, the largest buildings in the city, are all more or less dilapidated.

The same melancholy tokens are visible in the private houses. In the principal street stand large buildings, roofless, without windows or doors, and with grass and bushes growing from crevices in the walls; while here and there, as if in mockery of human pride, a tottering front has blazoned upon it the coat of arms of some proud Castilian, distinguished among the daring soldiers of the conquest, whose race is now entirely unknown.

Among these time-shattered buildings stood one in striking contrast, remarkable for its neat, compact, and business-like appearance; and in that country it seemed a phenomenon. It was a cotton factory belonging to Don Pedro Baranda, the first established in the Mexican Republic, and for that reason, as emblematic of the dawn of a great manufacturing system, called the "Aurora de la Industria Yucateca;" and, what gave it a greater interest in our eyes, it was under the direction of that young countryman and fellow-citizen, Don Juan Burque, or Mr. John Burke, to whom I before referred as the first stranger who visited the ruins of Chichen. It seemed strange to meet in this unknown, half-Spanish and half-Indian town a citizen of New-York. It was seven years the day of our arrival since he came to Valladolid. He had almost lost the facility of expressing himself in his native tongue, but in dress, manner, appearance, and feelings he was unchanged, and different from all around him; and it was gratifying to us to know that throughout that neighbourhood it was no small recommendation to be the countryman of "the engineer."

Don Pedro Baranda, the proprietor of the factory, began life in the Spanish navy; at fifteen he was a midshipman on board the flag-ship of the Spanish admiral at the memorable battle of Trafalgar, and, though not unwounded, was one of the few who escaped the terrible slaughter of that day. At the commencement of the war of Mexican independence he was still in the Spanish navy, but, a Mexican by birth, joined the cause of his countrymen, and became admiral of the fleet, which he commanded at the taking of the Castle of San Juan de Ulloa, the closing act of the successful revolution. After this, he resigned and went to Campeachy, his native place, but, being in delicate health, removed to Valladolid, which, in the absence of all other recommendations, was celebrated for the salubrity of its climate. He had held the highest offices of honour and trust in the state, and, although his party was now down and his political influence lost, he had fallen with the respect of all, and, what was a rare thing among the political animosities of that country, the actual government, his successful opponents, gave us letters of introduction to him.

Retired from office, and unable to endure idleness, the spontaneous growth of cotton around Valladolid induced him to undertake the establishment of a cotton factory. He had great difficulties to contend with, and these began with the erection of the building. He had no architect to consult, and planned and constructed it himself. Twice the arches gave way, and the whole building came down. The machinery was imported from the United States, accompanied by four engineers, two of whom died in the country. In 1835, when Mr. Burke arrived, the factory had yielded but seventy pieces of cotton, and eighteen yards had cost eight thousand dollars. At this time the office of acting governor of the state devolved upon him, but by a political revolution he was deposed; and while his workmen were celebrating the grito de Dolores, which announced the outbreak of the Mexican revolution, they were arrested and thrown in prison, and the factory was stopped for six months. It was afterward stopped twice by a failure of the cotton crop, and once by famine; and all the time he had to struggle against the introduction of smuggled goods from Belize; but, in spite of all impediments, it had gone on, and was then in successful operation.

In walking about the yard, Don Pedro led us to the woodpile, and showed us that the logs were all split into four pieces. This wood is brought by the Indians in back-loads at a medio per load, and Don Pedro told us that at first he had requested the Indians not to split the logs, as he would rather have them entire, but they had been used to doing so, and could not alter their habits; yet these same Indians, by discipline and instruction, had become adequate to all the business of the factory.

The city of Valladolid had some notoriety, as being the place at which the first blow was struck in the revolution now in progress against the dominion of Mexico, and also as being the residence of General Iman, under whom that blow was struck. The immediate consequence was the expulsion of the Mexican garrison; but there was another, more remote and of more enduring importance. There, for the first time, the Indians were brought out in arms. Utterly ignorant of the political relations between Mexico and Yucatan, they came in from their ranchos and milpas under a promise by General Iman that their capitation tax should be remitted. After the success of the first outbreak the government endeavoured to avoid the fulfilment of this promise, but was compelled to compromise by remitting the tax upon women, and the Indians still look forward to emancipation from the whole. What the consequences may be of finding themselves, after ages of servitude, once more in the possession of arms, and in increasing knowledge of their physical strength, is a question of momentous import to the people of that country, the solution of which no man can foretell.

And Valladolid had been the theatre of stranger scenes in anicent times. According to historical accounts, it was once haunted by a demonio of the worst kind, called a demonio parlero, a loquacious or talking devil, who held discourse with all that wished at night, speaking like a parrot, answering all questions put to him, touching a guitar, playing the castanets, dancing and laughing, but without suffering himself to be seen.

Afterward he took to throwing stones in garrets, and eggs at the women and girls, and, says the pious doctor Don Sanchez de Aguilar, "an aunt of mine, vexed with him, once said to him, 'Go away from this house, devil,' and gave him a blow in the face which left the nose redder than cochineal." He became so troublesome that the cura went to one of the houses which he frequented to exorcise him, but in the mean time El Demonio went to the cura's house and played him a trick, after which he went to the house where the cura was waiting, and when the latter went away, told the trick he had been playing. After this he began slandering people, and got the whole town at swords' points to such an extent that it reached the ears of the bishop at Merida, who forbade speaking to him under pain of heavy spiritual punishments, in consequence of which the vecinos abstained from any communication with him; at first the demonio fell to weeping and complaining, then made more noise than ever, and finally took to burning houses. The vecinos sought Divine assistance, and the cura, after a severe tussle, drove him out of the town.

Thirty or forty years afterward, "when I," says the doctor Don Sanchez de Aguilar, "was cura of the said city, this demonio returned to infest some of my annexed villages, and in particular one village, Yalcoba, coming at midnight, or at one in the afternoon, with a great whirlwind, dust, and noise, as of a hurricane; stones swept over the whole pueblo; and though the Indians promptly put out the fires of their kitchens, it did not avail them, for from the flames with which this demonio is tormented proceeded flashes like nightly comets or wandering stars, which set fire to two or three houses at once, and spread till there were not people enough to put out the fire, when I, being sent for to come and drive it away, conjured this demon, and, with the faith and zeal that God gave me, commanded him not to enter that village; upon which the fires and the whirlwinds ceased, to the glory and honour of the Divine Majesty, which gave such power to the priests." Driven out here, this demonio returned to infest the village of Valladolid with new burnings; but by putting crosses in all the hills this evil ceased.

For generations this demonio has not been heard of, but it is known that he can take any shape he pleases; and I fear me much that he has at last entered the padres, and, taking advantage of that so-called amiable weakness which I before hinted at in confidence to the reader, is leading them along seeming paths of roses, in which they do not yet feel the thorns.

I have none but kind feelings toward the padres, but, either as a cause or in consequence of the ascendency of this demonio, the people of Valladolid seemed the worst we had met with, being, in general, lazy, gambling, and good for nothing. It is a common expression, "Hay mucho vago en Valladolid," "There are many idlers in Valladolid;" and we saw more gamecocks tied by the leg along the walls of the houses than we had seen in any other place we visited. Part of our business was to repair our wardrobe and procure a pair of shoes, but neither of these undertakings could we accomplish. There were no shoes ready made, and no artist would promise to make a pair in less than a week, which we learned might be interpreted as meaning at least two.

In the mean time we were making inquiries and arrangements for our journey to the coast. It is almost impossible to conceive what difficulty we had in learning anything definite concerning the road we ought to take. Don Pedro Baranda had a manuscript map, made by himself, which, however, he did not represent as very correct; and the place on the coast which we wished to visit was not laid down on it at all. There were but two persons in the town who could give us any information, and what they gave was most unsatisfactory. Our first plan was to go to the Bay of Ascension, where we were advised we could hire a canoa for our coast voyage, but fortunately, by the advice of Don Pedro Baranda, we were saved from this calamitous step, which would have subjected us to a long and bootless journey, and the necessity of returning to Valladolid without accomplishing anything, which might have disheartened us from attempting to reach the coast in another direction. Upon the information we received, we determined on going to the village of Chemax, from which, we were advised, there was a direct road to Tancah, where a boat was on the stocks, and probably then finished, which we could procure for a voyage down the coast.

Before our departure Doctor Cabot performed an operation for strabismus, under circumstances peculiarly gratifying to us, and, with the satisfaction arising from its complete success, on

Saturday, after an early dinner, we mounted for our journey to the coast, going first to the house of Don Pedro Baranda, and to the factory to bid farewell to Mr. Burke. The road was broad, and had been lately opened for carretas and calesas. On the way we met a large straggling party of Indians, returning from a hunting expedition in the forests along the seacoast. Naked, armed with long guns, and with deer and wild boars slung on their backs, their aspect was the most truculent of any people we had seen. They were some of the Indians who had risen at the call of General Iman, and they seemed ready at any moment for battle.

It was some time after dark when we reached the village. The outline of the church was visible through the darkness, and beside it was the convent, with a light streaming from the door. The cura was sitting at a table surrounded by the officials of the village, who started at the clatter of our horses; and when we appeared in the doorway, if a firebrand had been thrown among them they could not have been more astounded. The village was the Ultima Thule of population, the last between Valladolid and Tancah, and the surprise caused by our appearance did not subside when we told them that we were on our way to the latter. They all told us that it was impossible. Tancah was a mere rancho, seventy miles distant, and the whole intermediate country was a dense forest. There was no road to it, and no communication except by an overgrown footpath. It was utterly impossible to get through without sending Indians before to open a road all the way; and, to crown all, we would be obliged to sleep in the woods, exposed to moschetoes, garrapatas, and rain, which last, in our uncertain state, we regarded with real apprehension.

The rancho was established by one Molas, a smuggler and pirate, who, while under sentence of death in Merida, escaped from prison, and established himself at this lonely point, out of the reach of justice. Soldiers had been sent from Merida to arrest him, who, after advancing as far as Chemax, turned back. In consequence of new political excitements, change of government, and lapse of time, the persecution, as it is called, against poor Molas had ceased; and, having an attack of sickness, he ventured up from the coast, and made his appearance in the village, to procure such medical aid as it afforded. No one molested him; and after remaining a while he set out to return on foot with a single Indian, but, worn down by the fatigues of the journey, while yet eight leagues from the rancho he died upon the road.

These accounts came upon us most unexpectedly, and deranged all our plans. And there was nothing that more strikingly exhibited the ignorance prevailing in that country in regard to the roads, than the fact that, after diligent and careful inquiries at Valladolid, we had set out upon positive information that we could ride directly through to Tancah, and had made all our arrangements for doing so, whereas at six leagues' distance we found ourselves brought to a dead stand.

But turning back formed no part of our deliberations. The only question was whether we should undertake the journey on foot. The mere walking none of us regarded; in fact, it would have been a pleasant change, for there was no satisfaction in stumbling on horseback along those stony roads; but our servants foresaw a great accumulation of their labours, and the risk of exposure to rain was a serious consideration; moreover, I had one little difficulty, which, however, was really a serious one, and could not be remedied except by a delay of several days, in the want of shoes, those on my feet being quite incapable of holding out for such a walk. Our alternative was to go to the port of Yalahao, which, the reader will see by the map, is almost at right angles from Tancah, and thence take a canoa. This would subject us to the necessity of two voyages along the coast, going and returning, and would require, perhaps, a fortnight to reach Tancah, which we had expected to arrive at in three days; but there were villages and ranchos on the road, and the chance of a canoa was so much greater that, under the circumstances, we were glad of such an alternative.

In the midst of the vexation attending this derangement of our plan, we were cheered by the comfortable appearance of the convent, and the warm reception given us by the cura Garcia. The sala was furnished with pictures and engravings from Scott's novels, made for the Spanish market, with Spanish lettering; looking-glasses, with gilt frames, from El Norte, and a large hand organ, horribly out of tune, which, in compliment to us, the cura set to grinding out "God save the King!" And, besides all this, the smiling faces of women were peeping at us through the doors, who at length, unable to repress their curiosity, crowded each other into the room. The cura sat with us till a late hour, and when we retired followed us to our room, and stood by us till we got into our hammocks. His curacy extended to the coast. The ruins which we proposed visiting were within it, but he had never visited that part, and now talked seriously of going with us.

The next day Dr. Cabot was taken with a fever, which the cura said he was almost thankful for, and we were glad of an excuse for passing the day with him. It was Sunday, and, dressed in his black gown, I never saw a priest of more respectable appearance. And he was a politician as well as priest. He had been a member of the convention that formed the constitution of the state, had taken a prominent part in the discussions, and distinguished himself by his strong and manly eloquence. The constitution which he had assisted in forming debarred priests from holding civil offices, but through the loophole of his retreat he looked out upon the politics of the world. The relations between Mexico and Texas were at that time most interesting to him; he had received a Merida paper, containing a translation in full of President Houston's inaugural address; and often repeated, "not a dollar in the treasury, and ten to fifteen millions of debt." He predicted the downfall of that republic, and said that the conquering army in Texas would proclaim Santa Ana emperor, march back upon the capital, and place the diadem upon his head!

Amid the distraction and civil war that devastated his own country, he had looked to ours as the model of a republic, and gave us many though not very accurate details; and it seemed strange in this little interior Indian town to hear an account of late proceedings in our own capital, and to find one taking so deep an interest in them.

But the cura had more accurate knowledge in regard to matters nearer home. The village of Chemax contains nearly ten thousand inhabitants, and was in existence at the time of the conquest. Four years after the foundation of Merida the Indians in the neighbourhood of Valladolid formed a conspiracy to destroy the Spaniards, and the first blow was struck at Chemax, where they caught two brothers, whom they put upon crosses, and shot at from a distance till they were covered with arrows. At sunset they took down the bodies, dismembered them, and sent the heads and limbs to different places, to show that vengeance was begun.

The curacy of Chemax comprehended within its jurisdiction all between it and the sea. The cura had drawn up a report, by order of the government, of the condition and character of the region under his charge, and its objects of curiosity and interest, from which I copied the following notice in regard to ruins known by the name of Coba.

"In the eastern part of this village, at eight leagues' distance, and fourteen from the head of the district, near one of the three lagunas, is a building that the indigenes call Monjas. It consists of various ranges of two stories, all covered with arches, closed with masonry of rude stone, and each piece is of six square yards. Its interior pavement is preserved entire, and on the walls of one, in the second story, are some painted figures in different attitudes, showing, without doubt, according to the supposition of the natives, that these are the remains of that detestable worship so commonly found. From this edifice there is a calzada, or paved road, of ten or twelve yards in width, running to the southeast to a limit that has not been discovered with certainty, but some aver that it goes in the direction of Chichen Itza."

The most interesting part of this, in our eyes, was the calzada, or paved road, but the information from others in the village did not increase our interest. The cura himself had never visited these ruins; they were all buried in forest; there was no rancho or other habitation near; and as our time was necessarily to be much prolonged by the change we were obliged to make, we concluded that it would not be advisable to go and see them.

But the cura had much more interesting information. On his own hacienda of Kantunile, sixteen leagues nearer the coast, were several mounds, in one of which, while excavating for stone to be used in building, the Indians had di overed a sepulchre containing three skeletons, which, according to the cura, were those of a man, a woman, and a child, but all, unfortunately, so much decayed that in attempting to remove them they fell to pieces.

At the head of the skeletons were two large vases of terra cotta, with covers of the same material. In one of these was a large collection of Indian ornaments, beads, stones, and two carved shells, which are represented in Figure 15. The carving on the shells is in bas-relief, and very perfect; the subject is the same in both, and the reader will observe that, though differing in detail, it is of the same type with the figure on the Ticul vase, and those sculptured on the wall at Chichen. The other vase was filled nearly to the top with arrow-heads, not of flint, but of obsidian; and as there are no volcanoes in Yucatan from which obsidian can be procured, the discovery of these proves intercourse with the volcanic regions of Mexico. But, besides these,

FIG. 15

and more interesting and important than all, on the top of these arrow-heads lay a *penknife with a horn handle*. All these the cura had in his possession, carefully preserved in a bag, which he emptied on a table for our examination; and, as may be supposed, interesting as the other memorials were, the penknife attracted our particular attention. The horn handle was much decayed, and the iron or steel was worn and rusted. This penknife was never made in the country. How came it in an Indian sepulchre? I answer, when the fabrics of Europe and this country came together, the white man and the red had met. The figures carved on the shells, those little perishable memorials, accidentally disinterred, identify the crumbling bones in that sepulchre with the builders of Chichen, of those mysterious cities that now lie shrouded in the forest; and those bones were laid in their grave after a penknife had found its way into the country. Speculation and ingenuity may assign other causes, but, in my opinion, the inference is reasonable, if not irresistible, that at the time of the conquest, and afterward, the Indians were actually living in and occupying those very cities on whose great ruins we now gaze with wonder. A penknife—one of the petty presents distributed by the Spaniards—reached the hands of a cacique, who, far removed from the capital, died in his native town, and was buried with the rites and ceremonies transmitted by his fathers. A penknife is at this day an object of curiosity and admiration among the Indians, and, perhaps, in the whole of Yucatan there is not one in the hands of a native. At the time of the conquest it was doubtless considered precious, worthy of being buried with the heirlooms of its owner, and of accompanying him to the world of spirits. I was extremely anxious to procure these memorials. The cura said, with Spanish courtesy, that they were mine; but he evidently attached great value to them, and, much as I desired it, I could not, with any propriety, take them.

CHAPTER XIX

On Monday, the fourth of April, we took leave of the warm-hearted cura, and set out for our new point of destination, the port of Yalahao.

I am obliged to hurry over our journey to the coast. The road was lonely and rugged, mostly a complete crust of stone, broken and sharp pointed, which severely tried and almost wore out our horses. It was desperately hot; we had no view except the narrow path before us, and we stumbled along, wondering that such a stony surface could support such a teeming vegetation.

In the afternoon of the third day we were approaching the port. When within about a league of it, we came out upon a low, swampy plain, with a grove of cocoanut trees at a long distance before us, the only objects rising above the level surface, indicating, and, at the same time, hiding, the port of Yalahao. The road lay over a causeway, then wet and slippery, with numerous holes, and sometimes completely overflowed. On each side was a sort of creek, and in the plain were large pools of water. With a satisfaction perhaps greater than we had experienced in our whole journey, we reached the port, and, after a long absence, came down once more upon the shore of the sea.

The village was a long, straggling street of huts, elevated a few feet above the washing of the waves. In passing along it, for the first time in the country we came to a bridge crossing a brook, with a fine stream of running water in sight on the left. Our horses seemed as much astonished as ourselves, and we had great difficulty in getting them over the bridge. On the shore was another spring bubbling within reach of the waves.

We rode on to the house of Don Juan Bautista, to whom we had a letter from the cura of Chemax, but he had gone to his rancho. His house and one other were the only two in the place built of stone, and the materials had been obtained from the ruins of Zuza, standing on his rancho, two leagues distant on the coast.

We returned through the village to a house belonging to our friend the cura, better than any except the two stone houses, and in situation finer than these. It stood on the very edge of the bank, so near the sea that the waves had undermined part of the long piazza in front; but the interior was in good condition, and a woman tenant in possession. We were about negotiating with her for the occupation of a part; but wherever we went we seemed to be the terror of the sex, and before we had fairly made a beginning, she abandoned the house and left us in quiet possession. In an hour we were completely domesticated, and toward evening we sat in the doorway and looked out upon the sea. The waves were rolling almost to our door, and Doctor Cabot found a new field opened to him in flocks of large sea-fowl strutting along the shore and screaming over our heads.

Plate XLII represents this place as taken from the shore. Our house appears in the left corner, and at a distance down the coast is seen an ancient mound. Cut off, to a great extent, from communication with the interior, or, at least, connected with it only by a long and toilsome road, its low huts buried among the cocoanut trees, but few people moving about it, canoes in the offing, and a cannon half buried on the shore, it seemed, what it was notorious for having been, the haunt of pirates in days gone by.

In our journey to the coast we had entered a region of novel and exciting interest. On the road we had heard of quondam pirates, having small sugar ranchos, and enjoying reputations but little the worse for wear, in fact, much respected, and looked upon with a sort of compassion, as men who had been unfortunate and broken up in business. We had now reached the focus of their operations.

Plate XLII

YALAHAO.

It is not many years since the coast of Cuba and the adjacent continent were infested by bands of desperadoes, the common enemies of mankind, and doomed to be hung and shot without trial, wherever caught. Tales of piracies and murders which make the blood run cold are fresh in the remembrance of many. The sailor still repeats or listens to them with shuddering interest, and in those times of rapine and blood, this port was notorious as a rendezvous for these robbers of the sea.

It commanded a view of many leagues, and of all vessels passing between Cuba and the Spanish Main. A long, low flat extended many miles out; if the vessel was armed, and of superior force, the pirates pulled back into shoal water, and if pursued by boats, scattered and saved themselves in the interior. The plunder brought ashore was spent in gaming and revelry. Doubloons, as one of the inhabitants told us, were then as plentiful as medios are now. The prodigality of the pirates brought many people to the place, who, profiting by their ill-gotten gains, became identified with them, and pirate law prevailed.

Immediately on our arrival we had visiters, some of whom were silent and uncommunicative upon the historical associations of the place; and when they went away their good-natured neighbours spoke of them as los pobres, who had good reason to be silent. All spoke with kindness and good feeling of the leaders, and particularly of one Don Juan, the captain, a dashing, generous fellow, whose death was a great public loss. Individuals were named, then living in the place, and the principal men, who had been notoriously pirates; one had been several years in prison and under sentence of death, and a canoa was pointed out, lying in front of our door, which had been often used in pirate service.

Our house had been the headquarters of the bucaniers. It was the house of Molas, to whose unhappy end I have before referred. He had been sent by the government as commandant to put down these pirates, but, as it was said, entered into collusion with them, received their plunder, and conveyed it to the interior. At night they had revelled together in this house. It was so far from the capital that tidings of his misdoings were slow of transmission thither, and, when they were received, he persuaded the government that these reports proceeded from the malice of his enemies. At length, for his own security, he found it necessary to proceed against the pirates; he knew all their haunts, came upon them by stealth, and killed or drove away the whole band. Don Juan, the captain, was brought in wounded, and placed at night in a room partitioned off at the end of our sala. Molas feared that, if carried up to Merida, Don Juan would betray him, and in the morning the latter was found dead. It was more than whispered that he died by the hand of Molas. It is proper to add, what we heard afterward, that these stories were false, and that Molas was the victim of a malicious and iniquitous persecution. I should add, too, that the character of this place has improved. Broken up as a pirates' haunt, it became the abode of smugglers, whose business being now comparatively unprofitable, they combine with it the embarking of sugar and other products of ranchos along the coast.

We found one great deficiency at this place: there was no ramon for the horses. At night we turned them loose in the village; but the barren plain furnished them no grazing, and they returned to the house. Early in the morning we despatched Dimas to a ramon tree two leagues distant, that being the nearest point at which any could be procured; and in the mean time I set about searching for a canoa, and succeeded in engaging one, but not of the best class, and the patron and sailors could not be ready in less than two or three days.

This over, we had nothing farther to do in Yalahao. I rambled for a little while in the Castillo, a low fortress, with twelve embrazures, built for the suppression of piracy, but the garrison of which, from all accounts, connected themselves somewhat closely with the pirates. It was now garrisoned by a little Mestizo tailor, who had run away from Sisal with his wife to avoid being taken for a soldier. The meekest possible tenants of a fort, they paid no rent, and seemed perfectly happy.

The next morning, when we opened our door, we saw a sloop lying at anchor, which we soon understood was the balandra of Don Vicente Albino. Don Vicente was already on shore, and, before we had time to make many inquiries, he called upon us. We had heard of him before, but never expected to see him in person, for our accounts were that he had established a rancho on the island of Cozumel, and had been murdered by his Indians. The first part of the story was true, but Don Vicente himself assured us that the last was not, though he told us that he had had a narrow escape, and showed us a machete cut in the arm as a token.

Don Vicente was the person of all others whom we wished to see, as he was the only one who could give us any information about the island of Cozumel. While he was with us another vessel came in sight, standing in toward the shore; which, when still two leagues distant, lowered a boat, and then stood off again. Don Vicente recognized her as a Yucatecan brig of war. The commandant came ashore; we had already invited Don Vicente to dine with us, and feeling it incumbent upon us to entertain visitors of distinction, I invited the commandant to join us. This was a rather bold attempt, as we had but one spare plate, knife, and fork, but we had all been in worse straits, and were accommodating.

Amid the excitement in the port caused by the arrival of these strangers, the inhabitants were not suffered to forget us. A large sea-bird, prepared by Doctor Cabot with arsenic, and exposed to the sun to dry, had been carried off and eaten by a hog, and the report got abroad that a hog sold that day had died from eating the bird. This created somewhat of a panic, and at night all who had partaken of the suspicious meat were known throughout the port. A scientific exposition, that even if the hog had died from eating the bird, it did not follow that those would die who had eaten of the hog, was by no means satisfactory.

The next day we completed laying in our stock of provisions, to wit, chocolate, sweetened bread, beef and pork in strings, two turtles, three bushels of corn, and implements for making tortillas. We had one other important arrangement to make, which was the disposition of our horses; and, according to our previous plan, to avoid the long journey back through the interior we determined to send Dimas with them to Valladolid, and thence to the port of Silan, a journey of two hundred and fifty miles, while we should, on our return, continue down the coast with the canoa, and meet him there.

At nine o'clock we were taken off, one at a time, in a small dug-out, and put on board our canoa. We had no leave-takings. The only persons who took any interest in our movements were Dimas, who wanted to go with us, the woman whom we had dispossessed of the house, and the agent of the canoa, who had no desire to see us again.

Our canoa was known in the port of Yalahao by the name of El Sol, or the Sun. It was thirty-five feet long and six feet wide at the top, but curving toward the bottom. It carried two large sails, with the peaks held up by heavy poles secured at the masts; had a space of eight or ten feet clear in the stern, and all the rest was filled with luggage, provisions, and water-casks. We had not been on board till the moment of embarcation, and prospects seemed rather unpromising for a month's cruise. There was no wind; the sails were flapping against the mast; the sun beat down upon us, and we had no mat or awning of any kind, although the agent had promised one. Our captain was a middle-aged Mestizo, a fisherman, hired for the occasion.

Under these circumstances we set out on our voyage. It was one which we had determined upon before leaving home, and to which we had always looked forward with interest; and the precise object we had in view was, in following the track of the Spaniards along this coast, to discover vestiges or remains of the great buildings of lime and stone which, according to the historical accounts, surprised and astonished them.

At eleven o'clock the breeze set in. At twelve the patron asked if he should run ashore for us to dine, and at half past one the breeze was so strong against us that we were obliged to come to anchor under the lee of Point Moscheto. This was an island about two leagues distant from Yalahao, with a projecting point, which we had to double. We could have walked round it in an hour, but, after the experience of a few hours' navigation in El Sol, it seemed to stand out like Cape Horn. Our bark had no keel, and could do nothing against the wind. We went ashore on a barren, sandy beach, bathed, shot, and picked up shells. Toward evening the wind fell, and we crawled round the point, when we came to anchor again, for it was now dark, and El Sol could not travel at night. The patron made all secure; we had a big stone for anchor, and rode in water knee deep. In due time we turned in for sleep; and it might have been consoling to distant friends to know that, exposed as we were on this desolate coast, we made so tight a fit in the canoa that if the bottom had fallen out we could hardly have gone through.

The next morning, with the rising of her great namesake, El Sol was under way. The prevalent wind along the coast was southeast, adverse for us; but, as the captain said, on our return it would be in our favour. At one o'clock another bold point intercepted us. It was a great object to get round it, for the wind would then be fair. El Sol made a vigorous effort, but by this time the breeze had become strong, and we were fain to come to anchor under the lee of Point Frances, which was on the same island with Point Moscheto. The island itself has no name, and is a mere sand-bank covered with scrub bushes, having a passage between it and the mainland, navigable for small canoas. Our anchorage ground was in front of the rancho of a fisherman, the only habitation on the island, built like an Indian's wigwam, thatched with palm leaves close down to the ground, and having both ends open, giving free passage to a current of air, so that while without, a step from the door, the heat was burning, within there were coolness and comfort. The fisherman was swinging in his hammock, and a handsome Indian boy was making tortillas, the two presenting a fine picture of youth and vigorous old age. The former, as he told us, was sixty-five years old, tall and erect, with his face burned black, deep seams on his forehead, but without a single gray hair or other symptom of decay. He had been three months living on this desolate island, and called it amusing himself. Our skipper said he was the best fisherman from Yalahao, that he always went alone, and always made more than the rest, but in a week on shore his money was all gone. He had no milpa, and said that, with his canoa, and the sea, and the whole coast as a building spot for a rancho, he was independent of all the world. The fishing on this coast was for turtle; on one side of the hut were jars of turtle oil, and outside, rather too near when the wind was in certain quarters, were the skeletons of turtles from which he had extracted it.

Toward evening the breeze again died away, we slowly got round the point, and at half past eight came to anchor, having made six leagues on our voyage. Our captain told us that this desolate point was Cape Catoche, the memorable spot on the Continent of America at which the Spaniards first landed, and approaching which, says Bernal Dias, we saw at the distance of two leagues a large town, which, from its size, it exceeding any town in Cuba, we named Grand Cairo. The Spaniards set out for it, and passing by some thick woods, were attacked by Indians in ambuscade. Near the place of this ambuscade, he adds, were three buildings of lime and stone, wherein were idols of clay, with diabolical countenances, &c.

Navigators and geographers, however, have assigned different localities to this memorable point, and its true position is, perhaps, uncertain.

At daylight we were again under way, and soon were opposite Boca Nueva, being the entrance to a passage between the island and the main, better known to the fishermen as the Boca de Iglesia, from the ruins of a church visible at a great distance. This church was one of the objects I intended to visit; and one reason for preferring the canoa, when we had the chance of Don Vicente's sloop, was that we might do so; but our captain told us that even with our draught of water we could not approach nearer than a league; that a long muddy flat intervened; and that we could not reach the shore by wading. He said, too, what we had heard from others, and believed to be the case, that the church was certainly Spanish, and stood among the ruins of a Spanish town destroyed by the bucaniers, or, in his own words, by the English pirates. The wind was ahead, but we could make a good stretch from the coast, and, anxious to lose no advantage, we made sail for the island of Contoy. It was dark when we came to anchor, and we were already distressed for water. Our casks were impregnated with the flavour of agua ardiente, and the water was sickening. Through the darkness we saw the outline of a desolate rancho. Our men went ashore, and, moving round it with torches, made a fine piratical appearance; but they found no water.

Before daylight we were roused by the screaming of seabirds; in the gray of the morning, the island seemed covered with a moving canopy, and the air was noisy with their clamour; but, unfortunately for Doctor Cabot, we had a fine breeze, and he had no opportunity of getting at their nests. The coast was wild and rugged, indented occasionally by small picturesque bays. Below the point of the island Doctor Cabot shot two pelicans, and getting the canoa about to take them on board was like manœuvring a seventy-four gun-ship.

At eleven o'clock we reached the island of Mugeres, notorious in that region as the resort of Lafitte the pirate. Monsieur Lafitta, as our skipper called him, bore a good character in these parts; he was always good to the fishermen, and paid them well for all he took from them. At a short distance beyond the point we passed a small bay, in which he moored his little navy. The mouth was narrow, and protected by ledges of broken rocks, on which, as the patron told us, he had batteries constantly manned. On the farther point of the island we had a distant view of one of those stone buildings which were our inducement to this voyage along the coast. While looking at it from the prow of the canoa, with the patron by my side, he broke from me, seized a harpoon, and pointing with it to indicate the direction to the helmsman, we came silently upon a large turtle, apparently asleep, which must have been somewhat surprised on waking up with three or four inches of cold steel in his back. The patron and sailors looked upon him as upon a bag of dollars snatched from the deep. There are three kinds of turtles which inhabit these seas; the Cahuamo, the eggs of which serve for food, and which is useful besides only for its oil; the Tortuga, of which the meat as well as the eggs is eaten, which also produces oil, and of which the shell is worth two reales the pound; and the Karé, of which the shell is worth ten dollars a pound. It was one of this kind, being the rarest, that had crossed our path. I would not make any man unhappy, but the fishermen say that the turtle which forms the delight of the gourmand is of the commonest kind, not worth killing for the sake of the shell, and therefore sent away alive. The karé he has never tasted. It is killed for the sake of the shell, and eaten by the luxurious fishermen on the spot. I immediately negotiated with the patron for the purchase of the shell. The outer scales of the back, eight in number, are all that is valuable. Their weight he estimated at four pounds, and the price in Campeachy he said was ten dollars a pound, but he was an honest fellow, and let me have it at two pounds and a half, for eight dollars a pound; and I had the satisfaction of learning afterward that I had not paid more than twice as much as it was worth.

In the afternoon we steered for the mainland, passing the island of Kancune, a barren strip of land, with sand hills and stone buildings visible upon it. The whole of this coast is lined with reefs of rocks, having narrow passages which enable a canoa to enter and find shelter; but it is dangerous to attempt the passage at night. We had a good wind, but as the next harbour was at some distance, the patron came to anchor at about four o'clock under the lee of the point of Nesuc. Immediately we went ashore in search of water, but found only a dirty pool, in which the water was so salt that we could scarcely drink it, but still it was an agreeable change from that we had on board.

We had time for a bath, and while preparing to take it saw two large sharks moving along the shore in water four or five feet deep, and so clear that their ugly eyes were visible. We hesitated, but, from the heat and confinement of the canoa, we were in real need; and stationing Albino on the prow to keep a look out, we accomplished our purpose. Afterward we rambled along the shore to pick up shells; but toward dark we were all hurrying back, flying before the natives, swarms of moschetoes, which pursued us with the same bloodthirsty spirit that animated the Indians along this coast when they pursued the Spaniards. We heaved upon our cable, hauled up our big stone, and dropped off to some distance from the shore, with horrible apprehensions for the night, but, fortunately, we escaped.

At daylight the next morning we were again under way, and, with a strong and favourable wind, steered from the coast for the island of Cozumel. Very soon, in the comparatively open sea, we felt the discomfort and even insecurity of our little vessel. The waves broke over us, wetting our luggage and ourselves, and interfering materially with Bernaldo's cooking. At about four o'clock in the afternoon we were upon the coast of Cozumel, and here for the first time we made a discovery, at the moment sufficiently annoying, viz., that our patron was not familiar with the coast of this island; it was bound with reefs; there were only certain places where it was practicable to run in, and he was afraid to make the attempt.

Our plan was to disembark at the rancho of Don Vicente Albino, and the patron did not know where it was. It was too late to look for it, and, sailing along till he saw a passage among the reefs, he laid the old canoa into it, and then threw out the big stone, but at some distance from the shore. On the outer reef was the wreck of a brig; her naked ribs were above the water, and the fate of her mariners no one knew.

The next morning, after some hours spent in groping about, we discovered the rancho of Don Vicente, distant about three miles. Here we encountered a strong current of perhaps four miles an hour; and, taking the wind close hauled, in a little while found that El Sol was not likely to have a very brilliant career that day. At length we went close in, furled sails, and betook ourselves to poles, by means of which, after two hours' hard work, we reached the little Bay of San Miguel, on which stood the rancho of Don Vicente. The clearing around it was the only one on the island, all the rest being thick woods. This bay had a sandy beach extending some distance to a rocky point, but even here the water was discoloured by sunken reefs. In the case of a norther it was an unsafe anchorage ground; El Sol would be driven upon the rocks, and the captain wished to leave us on shore, and go in search of a better harbour; but to this we objected, and for the present directed him to run her up close; when, standing upon the bow, and leaping with our setting poles, we landed upon the desolate island of Cozumel. (Plate XLIII.)

Above the line of the shore was a fine table of land, on which were several huts, built of poles, and thatched with palm leaves. One was large and commodious, divided into apartments, and contained rude benches and tables, as if prepared for our immediate occupation. Back of the house was an enclosure for a garden, overgrown, but with any quantity of tomatoes, ripe, wasting, and begging to be put into a turtle soup then in preparation on board the canoa.

Plate XLIII

SAN MIGUEL, ISLAND OF COZUMEL.

J.N Gimbrede

F. Catherwood

This rancho was established by the pirate Molas, who, escaping from death in Merida, made his way hither. He succeeded in getting to him his wife and children and a few Indians, and for several years nothing was heard of him. In the mean time he laid the keel of a sloop, finished it with his own hands, carried it to Belize, and sold it; new subjects of excitement grew up, and, being in a measure forgotten, he again ventured to the mainland, and left the island to its solitude.

After him Don Vicente Albino undertook to establish upon it a rancho for the cultivation of cotton, which was broken up by the mutiny of his Indians and an attempt to murder him. When we met him at Yalahao he had just returned from his last visit, carrying away his property, and leaving five dogs tenants of the island. After him came a stranger occupant than either, being no other than our old friend Mr. George Fisher, that "citizen of the world" introduced to the reader in the early part of these pages, who, since our separation in Merida, had consummated the history of his wandering life by becoming the purchaser of six leagues, or eighteen miles, of the island, had visited it himself with surveyors, set up his crosses along the shore, and was about undertaking a grand enterprise, that was to make the lonely island of Cozumel known to the commercial world.

Our act of taking possession was unusually exciting. It was an immense relief to escape from the confinement of the canoa. The situation commanded a view of the sea, and, barely distinguishable, in the distance was the coast of Yucatan. On the bank were large forest trees which had been spared in the clearing, and orange and cocoanut trees planted by Molas. The place had a sort of piratical aspect. In the hut were doors and green blinds from the cabin of some unlucky vessel, and reeving blocks, tar buckets, halliards, drinking gourds, fragments of rope, fishing nets, and two old hatches were scattered on the ground. Above all, the first object we discovered, which would have given a charm to a barren sand bank, was a well of pure and abundant water, which we fell upon at the moment of landing, and were almost like the Spanish soldier in the expedition of Cordova, who drank till he swelled and died. And, besides the relief of a pressing want, this well had a higher interest, for it assured us that our visit was not bootless. We saw in it, at the first glance, the work of the same builders with whose labours on the mainland we were now so familiar, being, like the subterranean

263

chambers at Uxmal, dome shaped, but larger both at the mouth and in the interior.

This well was shaded by a large cocoanut tree. We hauled up under it one of the hatches, and, sitting around it on blocks, had served up the turtle which had been accomplishing its destiny on board the canoa. With our guns resting against the trees, long beards, and canoa costume, we were, perhaps, as piratical-seeming a trio as ever scuttled a ship at sea. In the afternoon we walked over the clearing, which was covered with a fine plantation of cotton, worth, as the patron said, several hundred dollars, with the pods open and blowing away, indicating that the rancho had been abandoned in haste, without regard to the preservation of property. Toward evening we strolled for a great distance along the shore, picking up shells, and at night we had a luxurious swing in our hammocks.

CHAPTER XX

A crippled Dog.—Island of Cozumel known to the Natives by the Name
of Cuzamil.—Discovered by Juan De Grijalva.—Extracts from the Itinerary
of his Voyage.—Towers seen by the Spaniards.—An ancient Indian Village.
—Temples.—Idols prostrated by the Spaniards.—Present State of the Island.
—Overgrown with Trees.—Terrace and Building.—Another Building.—These
Buildings probably the Towers seen by the Spaniards.—Identical with those
on the Mainland.—Ruins of a Spanish Church.—Its History unknown.—
Vanity of Human Expectations.—Opinion of the old Spanish Writers.—Their
Belief that the Cross was found among the Indians as a Symbol of Christian
Worship.—The "Cozumel Cross" at Merida.—Platform in Front of the
Church.—Square Pillars.—Once supported Crosses.—The Cozumel Cross one
of them.—The Cross never recognised by the Indians as a Symbol of Wor-
ship.—Rare Birds.—A Sudden Storm.—The Canoa in a Strait.—Fearful
Apprehensions.

The next morning, while breakfasting on the
old hatch, we saw a dog peering at us from a distance, as if wishing, but fearful to approach. The poor beast was crippled,
limped badly, and had his fore shoulder horribly mangled, the
patron said by an encounter with a wild boar. We endeavoured
to entice him to us, but, after looking at us a few moments, he
went away, and never came near us again. No doubt he was one
of the five left by Don Vicente Albino, and, abandoned once, he
had lost all confidence in man. In a few years, if these are not
eaten up by stronger beasts, a race of wild dogs may inhabit this
deserted island.

The island of Cozumel, as it is now called, was known to the
natives by the name of Cuzamil, signifying in their language the
Island of Swallows. Before setting out from home I had fixed
upon this island as one of the points of our journey. My attention was directed to it by the historical accounts of its condition
when it first became known to the Spaniards. It was discovered
accidentally in 1518 by Juan de Grijalva, who, in attempting to
follow in the track of Cordova, was driven in sight of it. The

itinerary of this voyage was kept by the chaplain-in-chief of the fleet, under the direction of Grijalva, and, with a collection of original narratives and memoirs, was published for the first time in 1838 at Paris. The itinerary opens thus:

"Saturday, the first of March of the year 1518, the commandant of the said fleet sailed from the island of Cuba. On the fourth of March we saw upon a promontory a white house. * * * * * All the coast was lined with reefs and shoals. We directed ourselves upon the opposite shore, when we distinguished the house more easily. It was in the form of a small tower, and appeared to be eight palms in length and the height of a man. The fleet came to anchor about six miles from the coast. Two little barks called canoes approached us, each manned by three Indians, which came to within a cannon shot of the vessel. We could not speak to them nor learn anything from them, except that in the morning the cacique, *i. e.*, the chief of that place, would come on board our vessel. The next morning we set sail to reconnoiter a cape which we saw at a distance, and which the pilot told us was the island of Yucatan. Between it and the point of *Cucuniel*, where we were, we found a gulf, into which we entered, and came near the shore of Cuzamil, which we coasted. Besides the tower which we had seen, we discovered fourteen others of the same form. Before leaving the first, the two canoes of Indians returned; the chief of the village was in one of them, and came on board the vessel of the admiral, and spoke to us by means of an interpreter (one of the two Indians carried off from Yucatan on the previous voyage of Cordova), and prayed the commander to come to his village, saying that it would be a great honour to him. * * * *

"We set sail, following the coast at the distance of a stone's throw, for the sea is very deep upon the borders. The country appeared very agreeable; we counted, on leaving this point, *fourteen towers* of the form indicated. At sunset we saw a large white tower, which appeared very high. We approached, and saw near it a multitude of Indians, men and women, who were looking at us, and remained until the fleet stopped within musket shot of the tower. The Indians, who are *very numerous* in this island, made a great noise with their drums.

"On Friday, the sixth of May, the commandant ordered one hundred men to arm themselves. They embarked in the boats, and landed. They were accompanied by a priest, and expected to be attacked by a great number of Indians. Being prepared for defence, they arranged themselves in good order, and

266

came to the tower, where they found no one; and in all the environs they did not see a single man. The commandant mounted upon the tower with the standard bearer, the flag unfurled. He planted this standard upon one of the façades of the tower, took possession in the name of the king, in presence of witnesses, and drew up a declaration of said taking possession.

"The ascent to this tower was by eighteen steps; the base was very massive, one hundred and eighty feet in circumference. At the top rose a small tower of *the height of two men placed* one upon the other. Within were figures, bones, and idols that they adored. From these marks we supposed that they were idolaters. While the commandant was at the top of the tower with many of our people, an Indian, followed by three others who kept the doors, put in the interior a vase with very odoriferous perfumes, which seemed of storax. This Indian was old; he burned many perfumes before the idols which were in the tower, and sang in a loud voice a song, which was always in the same tone. We supposed that he was invoking his idols. * * * * * These Indians carried our commandant with ten or twelve Spaniards, and gave them to eat in a hall constructed of stones very close together, and covered with straw. Before the hall was a large well, from which everybody drank. * * * * They then left us alone, and we entered the village, where all the houses were built of stone. Among others, we saw five very well made, and commanded by small towers. The *base* of these edifices is *very large* and *massive;* the *building is very small at the top*. They appeared to have been built a long time, but there are also *modern ones*.

"That village, or bourg, was paved with concave stones. The streets, elevated at the sides, descended, inclining toward the middle, which was paved entirely with large stones. The sides were occupied by the houses of the inhabitants. They are constructed of stone from the foundation to half the height of the walls, and covered with straw. To *judge by the edifices and houses, these Indians appear to be very ingenious;* and if we had not seen a number of recent constructions, we should have thought that these buildings were the works of the Spaniards. This island appears to me very handsome. * * * * We penetrated, to the number of ten men, three or four miles in the interior. We saw there edifices and habitations separated one from another, and very well constructed."

On the tenth of February, 1519, the armament of Cortez rendezvoused at this island. Bernal Dias was again a companion, and was an actor in a scene which he describes as follows: "There was on the island of Cozumel a temple containing some hideous idols, to which all the Indians of the neighbouring districts used to go frequently in solemn procession. One morning the courts of this temple were filled with Indians, and curiosity having also drawn many of us thither, we found them burning odoriferous resins like our incense, and shortly after an old man in a large loose mantle ascended to the top of the temple, and harangued or preached to the multitude for a considerable time. Cortez, who was present, at length called to him Melchorejo, an Indian prisoner taken on a previous voyage to Yucatan, to question him concerning the evil doctrines which the old man was delivering. He then summoned all the caciques and chief persons to come before him, and as well as he could, by signs and interpretations, explained to them that the idols which they worshipped were not gods, but evil things, which would draw their souls down to hell, and that, if they wished to remain in brotherly connexion with us, they must pull them down, and place in their stead the crucifix of our Lord, by whose assistance they would obtain good harvests and the salvation of their souls, with many other good and holy reasons, which he expressed very well. The priests and chiefs replied that they worshipped these gods as their ancestors had done, because they were kind to them, and that, if we attempted to molest them, the gods would convince us of their power by destroying us in the sea. Cortez then ordered the idols to be prostrated, which we immediately did, rolling them down some steps. He next sent for lime, of which there was abundance in the place, and Indian masons, by whom, under our direction, a very handsome altar was constructed, whereon we placed an image of the Holy Virgin; and the carpenters having made a crucifix, which was erected in a small chapel close to the altar, mass was said by the reverend father Juan Dias, and listened to by the priests, chiefs, and the rest of the natives with great attention."

These are the accounts given by eyewitnesses of what they saw on the first visits of the Spaniards. The later historians are more explicit, and speak of Cozumel as a place containing many adoratorios and temples, as a principal sanctuary and place of pilgrimage, standing to Yucatan in the same relation as Rome to the Catholic world. Gomarra describes one temple as being "like a square tower, broad at the base, having steps on the sides, and at the top a chamber covered with straw, with four doors or windows, with their breastworks or corridors. In the hollow, which seems like a chapel, they seat or paint their gods. Such was that which stood near the seacoast."

By these accounts I had been induced to visit the island of Cozumel; and an incidental notice in the Modern Traveller, speaking of existing ruins as remains of Spanish buildings, led me to suspect that their character had been mistaken, and that they were really vestiges of the original population; but on the ground we asked ourselves where to look for them. Amid all the devastations that attended the progress of the Spaniards in America, none is more complete than that which has swept over the island of Cozumel. When I resolved to visit it I was not aware that it was uninhabited; and knowing it to be but thirty miles long, I supposed that, without much difficulty, a thorough exploration could be made; but even before landing we saw that it would be impossible to accomplish this, and idle to make the attempt. The whole island was overgrown with trees, and, except along the shore or within the clearing around the hut, it was impossible to move in any direction without cutting a path. We had only our two sailors, and if we should cut by the compass through the heart of the island, we might pass within a few feet of a building without perceiving it. Fortunately, however, on the borders of the clearing there were vestiges of ancient population, which, from the directions of Don Vicente Albino, we had no difficulty in finding. One of them, standing about two hundred feet distant from the sea, and even now visible above the tops of the trees to vessels sailing by, is represented in Figure 16. It stands on a terrace, and has steps on all four of its sides. The building measures sixteen feet square; it had four doors facing the cardinal points, and, as will be seen by the figure of a man sitting on the steps, it is very low. The exterior is of plain stone, but was formerly stuccoed and painted, traces of which are still visible. The doorways open into a narrow corridor only twenty inches wide, which encompasses a small room eight feet six inches long and five feet wide, having a doorway opening to the centre.

South-southeast from this, near an opposite angle of the clearing, and five or six hundred feet from the sea, stands another building raised upon a terrace, consisting of a single apartment, twenty feet front and six feet ten inches deep, having two doorways and a back wall seven feet thick. The height is ten feet, the arch is triangular, and on the walls are the remains of paintings.

These were the only buildings in the clearing, and though,

269

FIG. 16

doubtless, many more lie buried in the woods, we saw no other on the island; but to us these were pregnant with instruction. The building presented in the engraving, standing close to the sea, answers, in all its general features, the description of the "towers" seen by Grijalva and his companions as they sailed along the coast. The *ascent is by steps,* the *base is very massive,* the *building is small at the top,* it is *about the height of two men placed one above the other,* and at this day we may say, as the Spaniards did, that, *to judge by their edifices, these Indians appear to be very ingenious.* It is an interesting fact, moreover, that not only our patron and sailors called this building a "tower," but in a late article published in the proceedings of the Royal Geographical Society at London, entitled "Sketch of the Eastern Coast of Central America, compiled from Notes of Captain Richard Owen and the Officers of her Majesty's Ship Thunder and Schooner Lark," this building, with others of the same general character, is indicated by the name of a "tower." So far as the route of Grijalva can be traced with certainty, there is strong reason to believe that the Spaniards landed for the first time in the bay on the shore of which this building stands, and there is no violence in the supposition that the building presented is the very tower in which the Spaniards saw the performance of idolatrous rites; perhaps it is the same temple from which Bernal Dias and his companions rolled the idols down the steps. And more than this, establishing the great result for which we had visited this island, these buildings were identically the same with those on the mainland; if we had seen hundreds, we could not have been more firmly convinced that they were all erected and occupied by the same people; and if not a single corroborating circumstance existed besides, they afford in themselves abundant and conclusive proof that the ruined cities on the continent, the building of which has been ascribed to races lost, perished, and unknown, were inhabited by the very same Indians who occupied the country at the time of the conquest.

At the rear of the last building, buried in the woods, so that we should never have found it but for our patron, is another memorial, perhaps equal in interest to any now existing on the island of Cozumel. It is the ruins of a Spanish church, sixty or seventy feet front and two hundred deep. The front wall has almost wholly fallen, but the side walls are standing to the height of about twenty feet. The plastering remains, and along the base is a line of painted ornaments. The interior is encumbered with the ruins of the fallen roof, overgrown with bushes; a tree is growing out of the great altar, and the whole is a scene of irrecoverable destruction. The history of this church is as obscure as that of the ruined temples whose worship it supplanted. When it was built or why it was abandoned, and, indeed, its very existence, are utterly unknown to the inhabitants of New Spain. There is no record or tradition in regard to it, and, doubtless, any attempt at this day to investigate its history would be fruitless. In the obscurity that now envelops it we read a lesson upon the vanity of human expectations, showing the ignorance of the conquerors in regard to the value of the newly-discovered countries in America. Benito Perez, a priest who accompanied the expedition of Grijalva, solicited from the king the bishopric of this island. At the same time, a more distinguished ecclesiastic was asking for that of the island of Cuba. The king advanced the latter to the higher honour of the bishopric of Cozumel, and put off Benito Perez with what was considered the comparatively insignificant see of Culhua. Cozumel is now a desert, and Culhua, or Mexico, is the richest bishopric in New Spain.

But I have a particular reason for presenting to the reader this ruined church. It is a notion, or, rather, a principle, pervading all the old Spanish writers, that at some early day Christianity had been preached to the Indians, and connected with this is the belief that the cross was found by the first conquerors in the province of Yucatan as a symbol of Christian worship. Prophecies are recorded supposed to show a traditionary knowledge of its former existence, and foretelling that from the rising of the sun should come a bearded people and white, who should carry aloft the sign of the cross, which their gods could not reach, and from which they should fly away. The same vague idea exists to this day, and, in general, when the padres pay any attention to the antiquities of the country, they are always quick in discovering some real or imaginary resemblance to the cross. A strong support of this belief is advanced in the "Cozumel Cross" at Merida, found on the island of Cozumel, and in the time of Cogolludo, as at this day, supposed to have been an object of reverence among the Indians before their conversion to Christianity.

Until the destruction of that edifice it stood on a pedestal in the patio of the Franciscan convent, and, as we were told, from the time when it was placed there, no lightning had ever struck the building, as had often happened before. It is now in the Church of the Mejorada, and in looking for it at that place, Mr. Catherwood and myself were invited into the cell of an octogenarian monk then lying in his hammock, for many years unable to cross the threshold of his door, but in the full exercise of his mental powers, who told us, in a tone which seemed to indicate that he had done what would procure him a remission from many sins, that he had himself dug it up from among the ruins, and had it set up where it is now seen. It is fixed in the wall of the first altar on the left, and is almost the first object that arrests the eye of one entering the church. It is of stone, has a venerable appearance of antiquity, and has extended on it in half relief an image of the Saviour, made of plaster, with the hands and feet nailed. At the first glance we were satisfied that, whatever might be the truth in regard to its early history, it was, at least, wrought into its present shape under the direction of the monks. And though, at that time, we did not expect ever

272

to know anything more about it, the ruins of this church cleared up in our minds all possible mystery connected with its existence.

In front of the building is a cemented platform, broken and uprooted by trees, but still preserving its form; and on this stand two square pillars, which, as we supposed on the spot, had once supported crosses, and we were immediately impressed with the belief that one of these missing symbols was that now known as the "Cozumel Cross," and that it had probably been carried away by some pious monk at or about the time when the church became a ruin and the island depopulated. For myself, I have no doubt of the fact; and I regard it as important, for, even though crosses may have been found in Yucatan, the connecting of the "Cozumel Cross" with the ruined church on the island completely invalidates the strongest proof offered at this day that the cross was ever recognised by the Indians as a symbol of worship.

At noon we had finished all our work, but there was a charm about our absolute proprietorship of this desolate island which made us regret that there was not more to give us occupation. Doctor Cabot found in it a rich field for his ornithological pursuits, but he was rather unfortunate. Two specimens of rare birds, which he had dissected and put away to dry, were destroyed by ants. In the clearing was a dead tree, holding on its topmost branches the nest of a hawk of a rare species, the eggs of which were unknown to naturalists. The nest seemed to have been built in apprehension of our visit. The dead branches were barely able to support it, and would evidently bear no additional weight. The patron and sailors cut down the tree, and the eggs were broken, but preserved in fragments.

In the afternoon we picked up shells along the shore, and toward evening we again took a bath; while we were in the water black clouds gathered suddenly, thunder rolled, lightning flashed, and sea-birds flew screaming over our heads. Rain following quickly, we snatched up our clothing and ran for the hut. Looking back for a moment, we saw our canoa under way, with scarcely a yard of mainsail, and seeming like a great bird flying over the water. As she turned the point of the island and disappeared our fears were roused. From our experience of a little rough weather we judged it impossible for her to live through a storm so sudden and violent; and our sense of thankfulness at not being on board made us feel more sensibly the danger of those who were. The patron was not familiar with the coast, there was but one place in which he could find shelter, a narrow passage, difficult to enter even by daylight, and night was almost upon him; Mr. Catherwood had timed the precise moment when he turned the point, and we knew that the canoa would not be able to reach the cove before dark, but would have to ride through the storm, and, perhaps, be driven to sea. It was fearful to think of the danger of the poor patron and sailors; and mingled with these fears was some little uneasiness on our own account. All our luggage and provisions were on board, as we had intended to sail early the next morning. The storm had come up so suddenly that though Albino stood on the bank entreating, the patron would not wait to put a single thing on shore. We had only our box of table service, with coffee, sugar, tea, chocolate, and a few biscuit; even if no accident happened, several days might elapse before the canoa could return, and if she never returned we should be five Robinson Crusoes, all alone on a desert island. We had our guns to look to for provisions, but, unluckily, we had an unusually small quantity of ammunition on shore. As the storm raged our apprehensions ran high, and we had got so far as to calculate our chances of reaching the mainland by a raft, finding some relief in the occupation of moving our hammocks occasionally to avoid the rain as it beat through the thatched roof, and at length we fell asleep.

CHAPTER XXI

Very early in the morning we were moving. The rain had ceased, but the wind was still high, and the waves exhibited its power. Albino and Bernaldo were even more interested in the missing canoa than we, for tea and coffee were nothing to them, and our supply of biscuit being exhausted at breakfast, they had literally nothing to eat. At daylight Bernaldo set off along the shore, and soon after I followed with Albino. Passing round the point which had cut off our view of the canoa, we came upon what might well be called an iron-bound coast, being a table of rock rising but a few feet above the level of the sea, washed by every storm, until it had become porous and full of holes, and the edges stuck up like points of rusted iron. The waves were still dashing over them, forming great whirlpools in the hollow spaces, and suggesting a frightful picture of the fate of any unhappy voyagers who might have been thrown upon them; and the rocks were strewed with staves and planks from some wrecked vessel. After walking two hours I became satisfied that the canoa must have taken the brunt of the storm, and my apprehensions were seriously excited when I saw, at a long distance beyond, Bernaldo, whom I at first thought I had overtaken, but discovered that he had a small pyramid on his head, consisting of cooking vessel and provisions. He had met one of the sailors coming to our relief, from whom he had taken his burden, and was then returning. We went on, and after three hours' painful walking reached the cove. It was a wild, abrupt, and narrow opening between the rocks, about fifty feet wide, with perpendicular sides, and leading into a sheltered basin, which, while the sea outside was raging, was calm and quiet as a pond. At the head of this lay the canoe, which came down and took me on board.

From the simple and unaffected account of the patron, his entry into the cove must have been sublime. Night had overtaken him, and he supposed that he had run by, when a flash of lightning disclosed the narrow passage, and he turned the old canoe short into the very middle of it. In passing through he struck upon a sunken rock, lost one man overboard, caught him by the light of another flash, and in a moment was in still water. The cove was imbosomed among noble trees. The water was twenty feet deep, and so clear that the bottom was distinctly visible; and from one end ran a creek, which the patron said was navigable for canoes into the centre of the island, where it expanded into a lake. Sails, luggage, Doctor Cabot's birds, and my copy of Cogolludo, were spread out to dry, and, after dining upon turtles' eggs laid a few minutes on the coals, I set out on my return, gathering on the way an unusual harvest of shells. Ever since we came upon the coast our idle moments had been employed in this pleasant occupation, but nowhere with the same success as on this island. Regularly, after stripping the shore, we returned in a few hours, and found others thrown up, pure and fresh from the sea. I was seldom more fatigued than when I reached the hut.

On the third day, at twelve o'clock, the canoe again hove in sight, working her way round the point, and in a short time was at her old anchorage ground. The wind was still so high that the patron was afraid to remain; we filled our water casks, in an hour were on board, and left, solitary as we found it, the once populous island of Cozumel. A hawk mourning over its mate, which we carried away, was the only living thing that looked upon our departure; but there was no place in our whole journey that we left with more regret.

From the point at which we left the island, the opposite coast of Yucatan was dimly visible, and I would remark, that, from our own observation and from information given to us by others, it is the only point from which the opposite coast can be seen at all, whence it is a conclusion almost unquestionable that it was from this same point Grijalva steered for Yucatan. The wind was high, the sea rough, and a strong current was sweeping us down toward the point of Cape Catoche. About an hour before dark we got across the current, and stood up along the coast, passing three low, square buildings, apparently in a good state of preservation, but the sea was so rough that we could not land to examine them. The account of the expedition of Grijalva says, "After leaving the island of Cozumel we saw three large villages, separated two miles from each other. They contained a great number of stone houses, with high towers, and covered with straw." This *must* have been the very part of the coast where these villages were seen. The whole is now covered with forest, but it is not unreasonable to suppose that the stone buildings visible on the shore are tokens of the buried towns in the interior. We ran on till after dark, and came to anchor under a projecting point, behind a reef of rocks. In the edge of the water was a square enclosure for turtle, and on the shore a deserted fisherman's hut.

At daylight we were again under way. We passed three more square buildings; but as the coast was rocky we could not land without endangering the safety of our precious canoa; and far off, on a high cliff, stood the Castillo of Tuloom, the extreme point at which we were aiming. At twelve o'clock we turned a point, and came upon a long, sandy beach, forming a bay, at the head of which was a small collection of huts, composing the rancho of Tancar. The entrance was difficult, being hemmed in by sunken reefs and rocks. Two women were standing in the doorway of one of the huts, except the old fisherman the only persons we had seen along this desolate coast.

It was this point which we expected to reach by land direct from Chemax. The reader will see the circuit it has cost us to make it, but the first glance satisfied us of our good fortune in not going to it direct, for we saw the frame of the sloop we had heard of still on the stocks, which probably is not yet finished. We should not have been able to get a canoa, and should have been obliged to return by the same road. The moment the stone was thrown out we were in the water, wading ashore. The sun was intensely hot, and the sand burning. In front of the principal hut, beside the sloop, was a thatched arbour to protect the carpenter who occasionally worked upon it. Near by was a ruined hut, which we had cleared out, and for the third time

277

took up our abode in a habitation erected by Molas. On leaving the island of Cozumel it was only to this desolate point on the coast that he dared venture. It was a situation that again suited his proscribed life, and having no fear of pursuit from the interior, his energy and industry did not desert him. He again cultivated his milpa, and again laid the keel of a sloop, being the same which we then saw unfinished. But, finding himself growing old, in a measure forgotten and afflicted by illness, he ventured to appear in the village of Chemax, on returning from which, as before mentioned, with a single Indian, while yet eight leagues from Tancar he died in the road; as our informant expressed it, he died like a dog, without aid either human or divine. We had heard so much of Molas, of his long succession of calamities, and of the heavy retribution that had been poured upon his aged head, and we had seen so much of his unbroken energy, that, in spite of the violence and crimes imputed to him, our sympathies were excited; and having heard afterward from other sources the opinion expressed strongly, that during these long years of proscription he was the victim of an iniquitous and unrelenting persecution, I draw a veil over his history. It was but a year since he died, and his two sons were in possession of the rancho, both young men, who paid us a visit soon after our arrival. When the old man died the Indian left the body in the road, and came on to the rancho, whence these young men went up and buried it on the spot. Afterward they went again, dug it up, put it in a box, brought it to the rancho, and embarked with it in a canoe for San Fernando, where some of their kinsmen lived. On the way they were overtaken by a storm, threw the body overboard, and, said our informant, that was the last of poor old Molas. The elder son was said to have been implicated with his father, and the curse seemed entailed upon him. He had lost entirely the use of one eye, and the other rolled feebly and lustreless in a watery orbit. Probably by this time he is perfectly blind.

Our first inquiries were upon the subject of ruins. A short path through the woods leads to a milpa, in which are numerous remains of ancient buildings standing on terraces, but all small and dilapidated. These buildings once stood erect in full view from the sea, but now the stranger sails along the coast unconscious that among the trees lie shrouded the ruins of an aboriginal town.

In the afternoon we set out for the ruins of Tuloom, a league distant on the coast, and with the Castillo on a high cliff in full sight. Our road lay for a mile and a half along the shore. The beach was sandy, and in some places so yielding that we sank above the ankles, and found it a relief to take off our shoes and stockings, and wade in the edge of the water. At the end of the beach was a high rocky promontory, standing out into the sea, and cutting off all progress along the shore. This we ascended, and continued along the cliff, which sloped toward the sea, in some places forming a perpendicular wall, and on our right rose great masses of rock, cutting off entirely the view of the Castillo. In half an hour we came unexpectedly upon a low building, apparently an adoratorio, or altar, climbing to the top of which, we again saw the Castillo. Beyond the cliff became more rugged and barren, reminding us of the witches' gathering-place in the Hartz Mountains, as described in the Faust of Goëthe; and, amid all its barrenness, from the crevices of the rocks sprang a thick growth of scrubby wild palm called tshike, covering the whole surface of the cliff. Toiling through this, we reached another low building, from the top of which we again saw El Castillo, but with a great chasm between, apparently cutting off all hope of access. By this time it was late, and, afraid of being overtaken by darkness on this wild range, we turned back. Night was upon us when we again reached the shore. The sandy beach was now a welcome relief, and at a late hour we again reached the hut, having come to a rapid conclusion that a frequent repetition of this walk would be neither pleasant nor profitable, and that, in order to get through our work with the celerity we aimed at, it would be necessary again to take up our abode among the ruins.

The next morning we set out for that purpose, escorted by the younger Molas, a fine lad of about twenty, who considered our arrival the greatest incident that had ever occurred at Tancar, and before we reached the end of the beach he wanted to go travelling with us. Ascending the cliff, and passing beyond the two buildings we had seen the day before, we descended from the rear of the last to the head of the chasm which had seemed to cut us off from the principal object of our visit; ascending again at the other end of the ravine, we entered a gloomy forest, and, passing a building on the left, with "old walls" visible in different places indistinctly through the trees, reached the grand staircase of the Castillo. The steps, the platform of the building, and the whole area in front were overgrown with trees, large and principally ramon, which, with their deep green foliage and the mysterious buildings around, presented an image of a grove sacred to Druidical worship.

Our boatmen and Molas cut a path up the steps, and, carrying up their loads, in an hour we were domesticated in the Castillo. We had undertaken our long journey to this place in utter uncertainty as to what we should meet with; impediments and difficulties had accumulated upon us, but already we felt indemnified for all our labour. We were amid the wildest scenery we had yet found in Yucatan; and, besides the deep and exciting interest of the ruins themselves, we had around us what we wanted at all the other places, the magnificence of nature. Clearing away the platform in front, we looked over an immense forest; walking around the moulding of the wall, we looked out upon the boundless ocean, and deep in the clear water at the foot of the cliff we saw gliding quietly by a great fish eight or ten feet long.

Plate XLIV represents the front of the Castillo. A few of the trees which grew around it appear in the engraving, and one is left growing on the top of the lower range, with its gnarled roots binding the front wall and obstructing the doorway, but no words and no drawing could convey a true idea of the solemnity of its living shroud, or of the impression made upon us when the ring of the axe first broke the stillness that had so long prevailed around. The building, including the wings, measures at its base one hundred feet in length. The grand staircase is thirty feet wide, with twenty-four steps, and a substantial balustrade on each side, still in good preservation, gives it an unusually imposing character. In the doorway are two columns, making three entrances, with square recesses above them, all of which once contained ornaments, and in the centre one fragments of a statue still remain. The interior is divided into two corridors, each twenty-six feet long; the one in front is six feet six inches wide, and had at each end a stone bench, or divan; and again on the walls we found the mysterious prints of the red hand.*

A single doorway leads to the back corridor, which is nine feet wide, and has a stone bench extending along the foot of the

* While these pages were passing through the press the author had an opportunity of conferring with Mr. Schoolcraft, a gentleman well known for his researches into the character and habits of our North American Indians, and was favoured by him with an interesting communication on the subject of the print of the red hand, which will be found in the Appendix, and for which the author here takes occasion to offer his acknowledgments.

Plate XLIV

T U L O O M.
Front of the Castillo

P. Catherwood.

S. H. Gimber.

wall. On each side of the doorway are stone rings, intended for the support of the door, and in the back wall are oblong openings, which admit breezes from the sea. Both apartments have the triangular-arched ceiling, and both had a convenience and pleasantness of arrangement that suited us well as tenants.

The wings are much lower than the principal building. Each consists of two ranges, the lower standing on a low platform, from which are steps leading to the upper. The latter consists of two chambers, of which the one in front is twenty-four feet wide and twenty deep, having two columns in the doorway, and two in the middle of the chamber corresponding with those in the doorway. The centre columns were ornamented with devices in stucco, one of which seemed a masked face, and the other the head of a rabbit. The walls were entire, but the roof had fallen; the rubbish on the floor was less massive than that formed in other places by the remains of the triangular-arched roof, and of different materials, and there were holes along the top of the wall, as if beams had been laid in them, all which induced us to believe that the roofs had been flat, and supported by wooden beams resting upon the two columns in the centre. From this apartment a doorway three feet wide, close to the wall of the principal building, leads to a chamber twenty-four feet wide and nine feet deep, also roofless, and having the same indications that the roof had been flat and supported by wooden beams.

Plate XLV represents the back or sea wall of the Castillo. It rises on the brink of a high, broken, precipitous cliff, commanding a magnificent ocean view, and a picturesque line of coast, being itself visible from a great distance at sea. The wall is solid, and has no doorways or entrances of any kind, nor even a platform around it. At evening, when the work of the day was ended and our men returned to the hut, we sat down on the moulding of the wall, and regretted that the doorways of our lofty habitation had not opened upon the sea. Night, however, wrought a great change in our feelings. An easterly storm came on, and the rain beat heavily against the sea wall. We were obliged to stop up the oblong openings, and congratulated ourselves upon the wisdom of the ancient builders. The darkness, the howling of the winds, the cracking of branches in the forest, and the dashing of angry waves against the cliff, gave a romantic interest, almost a sublimity to our occupation of this desolate building, but we were rather too

Plate XLV

Catherwood.

Graham.

TULOOM

hackneyed travellers to enjoy it, and were much annoyed by moschetoes.

Our first day did not suffice to finish the clearing of the area in front of the Castillo. Within this area were several small ruined buildings, which seemed intended for altars. Opposite the foot of the steps was a square terrace, with steps on all four of its sides, but the platform had no structure of any kind upon it, and was overgrown with trees, under the shade of which Mr. Catherwood set up his camera to make his drawing; and, looking down upon him from the door of the Castillo, nothing could be finer than his position, the picturesque effect being greatly heightened by his manner of keeping one hand in his pocket, to save it from the attacks of moschetoes, and by his expedient of tying his pantaloons around his legs to keep ants and other insects from running up.

Adjoining the lower room of the south wing were extensive remains, one of which contained a chamber forty feet wide and nineteen deep, with four columns that had probably supported a flat roof. In another, lying on the ground, were the fragments of two tablets, of the same character with those at Labphak.

On the north side, at the distance of about forty feet from the Castillo, stands a small isolated building, a side view of which is represented in Plate XLVI. It stands on a terrace, and has a staircase eight feet wide, with ten or twelve broken steps. The platform is twenty-four feet front and eighteen deep. The building contains a single room, having, like the Castillo, a triangular-arched roof. Over the doorway is the same curious figure we saw at Sayi, with the head down and the legs and arms spread out; and along the cornice were other curious and peculiar ornaments. The doorway is very low. Throughout the country at times we had heard the building of these cities ascribed to corcubados, or hunchbacks, and the unusual lowness of all the doorways, with the strangeness and desolation of all around, almost gave colour to the most fanciful belief.

The interior of this building consisted of a single chamber, twelve feet by seven, having the triangular-arched ceiling, and at each end a raised step or divan. The wall and ceiling were stuccoed and covered with paintings, the subjects of which were almost entirely effaced.

The day ended without our making any advances beyond this immediate neighbourhood, but the next was made memorable by the unexpected discovery that this forest-buried city was encompassed by a wall, which had resisted all the elements of

Plate XLVI

Graham

Catherwood

TULOOM

destruction at work upon it, and was still erect and in good preservation. Since the beginning of our exploration we had heard of city walls, but all vestiges of them elsewhere had been uncertain, and our attempts to trace them unsatisfactory. Young Molas had told us of these, and was on the ground early to guide us to them. We set out without much expectation of any decided result, and, following him through the woods, all at once found ourselves confronted by a massive stone structure running at right angles to the sea; and, following its direction, we soon came to a gateway and watch-tower. We passed through the gateway, and followed the wall outside, keeping as close to it as the trees and bushes would permit, down to the sea. The character of this structure could not be mistaken. It was, in the strictest sense, a city wall, the first we had seen that could be identified as such beyond all question, and gave colour to the many stories we had heard of walls, inducing us to believe that many of the vestiges we had seen were parts of continuous lines of enclosure. We immediately set about a thorough exploration, and without once breaking off, measured it from one end to the other.

Figure 17 represents the plan of this wall, as taken from

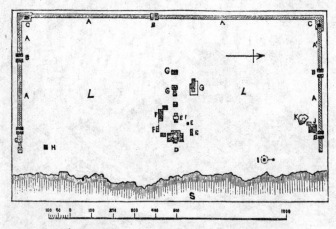

A.A.	Walls.	G.G.	Buildings last discovered.
B.B.	Gateways.	H.	Building with wooden roof.
C.C.	Watch-towers.	I.	Altar.
D.	Castillo.	J.	Guard house.
E.E.	Small adoratorios.	K.	Senote of brackish water.
F.F.	Casas.	L.L.	Thick woods.

Fig. 17

286

the sea. It forms a parallelogram abutting on the sea, the high, precipitous cliff forming a sea wall 1500 feet in length. We began our survey on the cliff at the southeast angle, where the abutment is much fallen. We attempted to measure along the base, but the close growth of trees and underbrush made it difficult to carry the line, and we mounted to the top. Even then it was no easy matter. Trees growing beside the wall threw their branches across it, thorns, bushes, and vines of every description grew out of it, and at every step we were obliged to cut down the Agave Americana, which pierced us with its long, sharp points; the sun beat upon us, moschetoes, flies, and other insects pestered us, but, under all annoyances, the day employed on the summit of this wall was one of the most interesting we passed among ruins.

The wall is of rude construction, and composed of rough, flat stones, laid upon each other without mortar or cement of any kind, and it varies from eight to thirteen feet in thickness. The south side has two gateways, each about five feet wide. At the distance of six hundred and fifty feet the wall turns at right angles, and runs parallel to the sea. At the angle, elevated so as to give a commanding view, and reached by ascending a few steps, is the watch-tower represented in Figure 18. It is twelve feet square, and has two doorways. The interior is plain, and against the back wall is a small altar, at which the guard might offer up prayers for the preservation of the city. But no guard sits in the watch-tower now; trees are growing around it; within the walls the city is desolate and overgrown, and without is an unbroken forest. The battlements, on which the proud Indian strode with his bow and arrow, and plumes of feathers, are surmounted by immense thorn bushes and overrun by poisonous vines. The city no longer keeps watch; the fiat of destruction has gone out against it, and in solitude it rests, the abode of silence and desolation.

The west line, parallel with the sea, has a single gateway; at the angle is another watch-tower, like that before presented, and the wall then runs straight to the sea. The whole circuit is twenty-eight hundred feet, and the reader may form some idea of its state of preservation from the fact that, except toward the abutments on the sea, we measured the whole length along the top of the wall. The plan is symmetrical, encloses a rectangular area, and, as appears in the engraving, the Castillo occupies the principal and central position. This, however, on account of the

FIG. 18

overgrown state of the area, we were not aware of until the plan was drawn out.

On the north side of the wall, near the east gateway, is a building thirty-six feet in front and thirty-four deep, divided into two principal and two smaller rooms, the ceilings of which had entirely fallen. At one corner is a senote, with the remains of steps leading down to it, and containing brackish water. Near this was a hollow rock, which furnished us with our supply.

Toward the southeast corner of the wall, on the brow of the cliff, stands a building fifteen feet front and ten deep. The interior is about seven feet high, and the ceiling is flat, and discloses an entirely new principle of construction. It has four principal beams of wood, about six inches in diameter, laid on the top of the wall from end to end of the chamber, with smaller beams, about three inches in diameter, laid across the larger so closely as to touch; and on these crossbeams is a thick mass of mortar and large pebbles, which was laid on moist, and now forms a solid crust, being the same materials which we had seen in ruins on the floors of other rooms. Against the back wall was an altar, with a rude triangular stone upon it, which seemed to bear marks of not very distant use. On each side of the doorway were large sea-shells fixed in the wall for the support of the doors.

These were all the buildings to which young Molas conducted us, and he said there were no others within the area of the walls, but there were many vestiges without; and it was our belief that the walls enclosed only the principal, perhaps the sacred buildings, and that ruins existed to a great distance beyond; but, with only young Molas and one boatman, being all that the patron could spare at a time, we did not consider it worth while to attempt any exploration; in fact, our occupation of this walled city was too much disturbed to allow us to think of remaining long. A legion of fierce usurpers, already in possession, were determined to drive us out, and after hard work by day, we had no rest at night;

> "There was never yet philosopher
> That could endure the toothache patiently;"

and I will venture to say that a philosopher would find the moschetoes of Tuloom worse than the toothache. We held our ground against them for two nights, but on the third, one after the other, we crawled out of our hammocks to the platform before the door. The moon was shining magnificently, lighting up the darkness of the forest, and drawing a long silvery line upon the sea. For a time we felt ourselves exalted above the necessity of sleep, but by degrees drowsiness overcame us, and at last we were all stretched at full length on the ground. The onslaught was again terrible; we returned to our hammocks, but found no peace, and emerging again, kindled a large fire, and sat down to smoke till daylight. It was aggravating to look the moon in the face, its expression was so calm and composed. A savage notice to quit was continually buzzing in our ears, and all that we cared for was to get away.

CHAPTER XXII

The next morning we finished what remained
to be done, and, after an early dinner, prepared to leave the
ruins. While the men were arranging their loads I gave Doctor
Cabot a direction to a point in the wall, where, in measuring
around it, Mr. Catherwood and I had started two ocellated turkeys. He set out to cut his way in a straight line with his hunting
knife, and very soon, while sitting on the steps of the Castillo, I
heard him calling to me that he had come upon another building which we had not seen. Having occasion to economize shoe
leather for the walk back over the cliff, I at first hesitated about
going to it, but he insisted. He was so near that we communicated without any particular effort of voice, but I could see
nothing of him or of the building. Following his path, I found
him standing before it; and while working our way around it
we discovered two others near by, almost invisible, so dense was
the foliage of the trees, but the largest, except the Castillo, and
most important of any we had seen. Our plans were all deranged,
for we could not go away without drawings of these buildings.
We returned to the steps of the Castillo, and summoned all
hands to council. The men had their back-loads ready, Bernaldo
reported two tortillas as the stock of provisions on hand, and

Plate XLVII

TULOOM

291

the idea of another night in the Castillo struck us with dismay. We had been so long accustomed to sleep that it had become part of our nature; a night's rest was indispensable, and we determined to break up and return the next day.

Before daylight the next morning Albino set off with Molas and the sailors, and by the time Mr. Catherwood arrived on the ground the clearing of the first building was made.

Plate XLVII represents the front of this building. It faces the west, measures twenty-seven feet in length and nineteen in depth, and consists of two stories. The exterior had been richly decorated, and above the cornice were fragments of rich ornaments in stucco. The lower story has four columns, making five doorways opening into a narrow corridor, which runs round and encloses on three sides a chamber in the centre. The walls of the corridor on both sides were covered with paintings, but green and mildewed from the rankness of vegetation in which the building is smothered. A small doorway in front opens into the chamber, which measures eleven feet by seven; of this, too, the walls were covered with paintings, decayed and effaced, and against the back wall was an altar for burning copal.

The building on the top stands directly over the lower chamber, and corresponds with it in dimensions, this being the only instance we met with in which one room was placed directly over another. There was no staircase or other visible means of communication between the lower and upper stories.

At the rear of this building were others attached to it, or connected with it, but uprooted and thrown down by trees, and among the ruins were two stone tablets with rounded surfaces, six feet six inches high, two feet four inches wide, and eight inches thick, having upon them worn and indistinct traces of sculpture.

At the short distance of fifty-three feet is the building represented in Plate XLVIII. It stands on a terrace six feet high, with a staircase in the centre, measures forty-five feet by twenty-six, has two pillars in the doorway, and over the centre is the head of a mutilated figure. The interior is divided into two principal and parallel apartments, and at the north extremity of the inner one is a smaller apartment, containing an enclosed altar five feet long, and three feet six inches deep, for burning copal. The roof had fallen, and trees were growing out of the floor.

Near this is another building, larger than the last, constructed on the same plan, but more ruined. These buildings were all within about two hundred feet of the steps of the Cas-

Plate XLVIII

TULOOM

tillo. We were in the very act of leaving before we discovered them, and but for the accidental attempt of Doctor Cabot to cut through in search of birds, or if he had happened to cut a few yards to the right hand or the left, we should have gone away ignorant of their existence.

It will be borne in mind that when this city was inhabited and clear of trees, the buildings were all visible from the sea; the Spaniards are known to have sailed along this coast, and the reader will ask if they have given us no accounts of its existence. The narrative of the expedition of Grijalva, taken up at the point at which we left it, after crossing from Cozumel, continues: "We ran along day and night, and the next day toward sunset we saw a bourg, or village, so large that Seville would not have appeared larger or better. We saw there a very high tower. There was upon the bank a crowd of Indians, who carried two standards, which they raised and lowered as signs to us to come and join them. The same day we arrived at a bay, near which was a tower, the highest we had seen. We remarked a very considerable village; the country was watered by many rivers. We discovered a bay *where a fleet would have been able to enter*." This account is certainly not so accurate as a coast survey would be at this day, but it is more minute than most accounts of the early voyages of the Spaniards, and, in my opinion, it is all sufficient to identify this now desolate city. After crossing over from Cozumel, twenty-four hours' sailing would bring them to this part of the coast; and the next circumstance mentioned, viz., the discovery of a bay where a fleet would have been able to enter, is still stronger, for at the distance of about eight leagues below Tuloom is the Bay of Ascension, always spoken of by the Spanish writers as a harbour in which the whole Spanish navy might lie at anchor. It is the only bay along the coast from Cape Catoche into which large vessels can enter, and constrains me to the belief that the desolate place now known as Tuloom was that "bourg, or village, so large that Seville would not appear larger or better," and that the Castillo, from which we were driven by the moschetoes, was that "highest tower which the Spaniards had seen."

Farther, it is my firm belief that this city continued to be occupied by its aboriginal inhabitants long after the conquest, for Grijalva turned back from the Bay of Ascension, again passed without landing, and after the disastrous expedition of Don Francisco Montejo, the Spaniards made no attempt upon this part of the coast, so that the aborigines must have remained for a long time in this place unmolested. And the strong impression of a comparatively very recent occupation is derived from the appearance of the buildings themselves, which, though not less ruined, owing to the ranker growth of trees, had in some instances an appearance of freshness and good keeping that, amid the desolation and solitude around, was almost startling.

Outside of the walls are several small buildings, no doubt intended for adoratorios, or altars, one of which is represented in Figure 19. It stands on a terrace, having a circular platform,

Fig. 19

on the brow of the cliff, overlooking the sea, and measures fifteen feet front by twelve deep. The doorway faces the north. The interior consists of a single chamber, and against the back wall is an altar in such a state of preservation as to be fit for its original uses. Near the foot of the steps, overgrown by the scrubby wild palm which covers the whole cliff, is a small altar,

295

with ornaments in stucco, one of which seems intended to represent a pineapple. These wanted entirely the massive character of the buildings, and are so slight that they could almost be pushed over with the foot. They stand in the open air, exposed to strong easterly winds, and almost to the spray of the sea. It was impossible to believe that the altar had been abandoned three hundred years; within that time some guardian eye had watched over it, some pious hand had repaired it, and long since the arrival of the Spaniards the Indian had performed before it his idolatrous rites.

Under the circumstances attending our visit to it, we found this one of the most interesting places we had seen in our whole exploration of ruins; but I am compelled to omit many details deserving of description and comment, and shall close with one remark. The reader knows the difficulty we had in reaching this place from the interior. The whole triangular region from Valladolid to the Bay of Ascension on one side, and the port of Yalahao on the other, is not traversed by a single road, and the rancho of Molas is the only settlement along the coast. It is a region entirely unknown; no white man ever enters it. Ruined cities no doubt exist, and young Molas told us of a large building many leagues in the interior, known to an old Indian, covered with paintings in bright and vivid colours, and the subjects of which were still perfect. With difficulty we contrived to see this Indian, but he was extremely uncommunicative; said it was many years since he saw the building; that he had come upon it in the dry season while hunting, and should not be able to find it again. It is my belief that within this region cities like those we have seen in ruins were kept up and occupied for a long time, perhaps one or two centuries, after the conquest, and that, down to a comparatively late period, Indians were living in them, the same as before the discovery of America. In fact, I conceive it to be not impossible that within this secluded region may exist at this day, unknown to white men, a living aboriginal city, occupied by relics of the ancient race, who still worship in the temples of their fathers.

The reader will, perhaps, think that I have gone far enough. We had now finished our voyage along the coast, and the end which we had in view was fully accomplished. We had seen, abandoned and in ruins, the same buildings which the Spaniards saw entire and inhabited by Indians, and we had identified them beyond question as the works of the same people who created the great ruined cities over which, when we began our journey, hung a veil of seemingly impenetrable mystery. At that time, we believed the discovery and comparison of these remains to be the surest, if not the only means, of removing this veil; and though other proofs had accumulated upon us, these were not on that account the less interesting.

Our journey in this direction is now ended, and our course is homeward. We were detained one day at Tancar by a storm, and on Tuesday morning the patron came to us in a hurry with a summons on board; the wind had veered so that he could get out of the harbour; and, bidding good-by to the carpenter and Molas, we were soon under way. The wind was still high, and the sea so rough, and kept the little canoa in such commotion, that in half an hour nearly all our party were sea-sick. The servants were completely disabled, and there was no chance for a dinner. We had a strong wind and fair, passed several small square stone buildings, like those of which representations have been given, but, on account of the rough sea and rocky shore we could not land, and late in the afternoon put in at Nesuc, where we had stopped before, distinguished by its solitary palm tree.

Early in the morning we were again under way, and coasted to the point of Kancune, where we landed in front of a rancho then occupied by a party of fishermen. Near by was another great pile of the skeletons of turtles. The fishermen were busy within the hut mending their nets, and seemed to be leading a hardy, independent, and social life, entirely different from anything seen in the interior. A short walk brought us to the point, on which stood two dilapidated buildings, one entirely fallen, and the other having dimensions like the smallest of those seen at Tuloom. It was so intensely hot, and we were so annoyed by millions of sand-flies, that we did not think it worth while to stay, but returned to the hut, embarked, and, crossing over, in two hours reached the island of Mugeres. Near the shore were immense flocks of sea-birds, sitting on the piles of a turtle enclosure; over our heads was a cloud of white ibises, and, somewhat to the surprise of the fishermen, our coming to anchor was signalized by a discharge of heavy bird artillery, and a splashing into the water to pick up the dead and wounded. In wading ashore we stuck in a mud-bank, and had time to contemplate the picturesque beauty of the scene before us. It was a small sandy beach, with a rocky coast on each side, and trees growing down to the water, broken only by a small clearing opposite the beach, in which were two palm leaf huts, and an arbour covered with palm leaves. Under the arbour hung three small hammocks, and a hardy, sun-dried fisherman sat repairing a net, with two Indian boys engaged in weaving a new one. The old fisherman, without desisting from his work, invited us to the hammocks, and, to satisfy our invariable first want on this coast, sent a boy for water, which, though not good, was better than that on board.

Along the shore, at no great distance, was a funeral pile of the carcasses of turtles, half burned, and covered with countless millions of flies, actually heaving and moving as if alive; and near this hideous pile, as if to contrast beauty and deformity, was a tree, covered to its topmost boughs with the white ibis, its green foliage appearing like an ornamental frame-work to their snowy plumage. We ordered our dinner to be brought to the arbour, and as we were sitting down a canoe came ashore; the fishermen dragged across the beach two large turtles, and leaving the carcasses to swell the funeral pile, brought down to the arbour strings of eggs, and the parts that served for food or oil, and hung them quivering in the sun along the fence, their sudden blackness from swarms of flies disturbing somewhat the satisfaction with which we had first hailed this arbour. We had again stopped to visit ruins, but in the afternoon it rained, and we could not go to them. The arbour was no protection, and we were obliged to go inside the hut, which was snug and comfortable, the oil jars being arranged under the eaves, with turtle-shells tied up carefully in bundles, and on the rafters hung strings of eggs, while nets, old sails, blocks, and other characteristic furniture of a fisherman's hut filled up the corners. It was no hardship to be obliged to pass the afternoon among these fishermen, for their hardy, independent occupation gave manliness to their character, and freedom to their speech and manners.

The island was famed among the fishermen as the rendezvous of Lafitte the pirate, and the patron told us that our host had been his prisoner two years. This man was about fifty-five, tall and thin, and his face was so darkened by the sun that it was hard to say whether he was white or of mixed blood. We remarked that he was not fond of talking of his captivity; he said he did not know how long he was a prisoner nor where he was taken; and as the business of piracy was rather complicated in these parts, we conceived a suspicion that he had not been a prisoner entirely against his will. His fellow-fishermen had no narrow feelings on the subject, and perhaps gave a preference to piracy as a larger business, and one that brought more ounces, than catching turtles. They seemed, however, to have an idea that los Ingleses entertained different views, and the prisoner, el pobre, as our patron called him, said those things were all over, and it was best not to disturb them. He could not, however, help dropping a few words in behalf of Lafitte, or Monsieur Lafitta; he did not know whether it was true what people said of him, but he never hurt the poor fishermen; and, led on by degrees he told us that Lafitte died in his arms, and that his widow, a señora del Norte from Mobile, was then living in great distress at Silan, the port at which we intended to disembark.

Besides piratical associations, this island had been the scene of a strange incident within the last two years. A sailor lay on his death-bed in Cadiz, penniless and friendless, and, to requite the kindness of his host for allowing him to die in his house, he told the latter that, some years before, he had belonged to a band of pirates, and upon one occasion, after taking a rich prize and murdering all on board, he had gone ashore with his companions at the island of Mugeres, and buried a large sum of money in gold. When the piratical hordes were broken up he escaped, and dared not return to regions where he might be recognised. He said his companions were all hanged except one Portuguese, who lived in the island of Antigua, and, as the only means of requiting his host's kindness, he advised him to seek out the Portuguese and recover the money. The host at first thought the story was told only to secure a continuance of good treatment, and paid no attention to it, but the sailor died protesting its truth. The Spaniard made a voyage to the island of Antigua, and found out the Portuguese, who at first denied all knowledge of the transaction, but at length confessed it, and said that he was only waiting for an opportunity to go and dig up the gold. Some arrangement was made between them, and the Spaniard procured a small vessel, and set sail with the Portuguese on board. The vessel became short of provisions and water, and off Yalahao encountered the patron of our canoa, who, as he said, on receiving twenty-five dollars in advance, piloted her into that place for supplies. While there the story of the treasure leaked out; the Portuguese tried to escape, but the Spaniard set sail, carrying him off. The fishermen followed in canoas. The Portuguese, under the influence of threats, indicated a place for the landing, and was carried on shore bound. He protested that in that condition he could not find the spot; he had never been there except at the time of burying the gold, and required time and freedom of movement; but the Spaniard, furious at the notoriety given to the thing, and at the uninvited company of the fishermen, refused to trust him, and set his men to digging, the fishermen joining on their own account. The digging continued two days, during which time the Portuguese was treated with great cruelty, and the sympathy of the fishermen was excited, and increased by the consideration that this island was within their fishing limits, and if they got the Portuguese into their own possession, they could come back at any time and dig up the money quietly, without any wrangle with strangers. In the mean time, our old friend Don Vicente Albino, then living at Cozumel, hearing of treasure on an island belonging to nobody, and so near his own, ran down with his sloop and put in for the Portuguese. The Spanish proprietor was obliged to give him up. Don Vicente could not get hold of him, and the fishermen carried him off to Yalahao, where, finding himself out of the actual grasp of any of them, he set up for himself, and by the first opportunity slipped off in a canoa for Campeachy, since which he had never been heard of.

Early in the morning, under the guidance of two of the fisherman, we set out to visit the ruins. The island of Mugeres is between four and five miles long, half a mile wide, and four miles distant from the mainland. The ruins were at the north end. For a short distance we kept along the shore, and then struck into a path cut straight across the island. About half way across we came to a santa cruz, or holy cross, set up by the fishermen, at which place we heard distinctly the sound of the breakers on the opposite shore. To the right a faint track was perceptible, which soon disappeared altogether; but our guides knew the direction, and, cutting a way with the machete, we came out upon a high, rocky, perpendicular cliff, which commanded an immense expanse of ocean, and against which the waves, roused by the storm of the night before, were dashing grandly. We followed along the brink of the cliff and around the edges of great perpendicular chasms, the ground being bare of trees and covered with a scrubby plant, called the uba, with gnarled roots spreading like the branches of a grape-vine. At the point terminating the island, standing boldly upon the sea, was the lonely edifice represented in Plate XLIX. Below, rocking on the waves, was a small canoa, with our host then in the act of getting on board a turtle. It was the wildest and grandest scene we had looked upon in our whole journey.

The steps which led to the building are in good preservation, and at the foot is a platform, with the ruins of an altar.

Plate XLIX

R. Catherwood.

J.N. Gambrede.

ANCIENT BUILDING, ISLAND OF MUGERES.

The front, on one side of the doorway, has fallen. When entire it measured twenty-eight feet, and it is fifteen feet deep. On the top is a cross, probably erected by the fishermen. The interior is divided into two corridors, and in the wall of that in front are three small doorways leading to the inner corridor. The ceiling had the triangular arch, and throughout the hand of the builders on the mainland could not be mistaken, but on the walls were writings which seemed strangely familiar in an aboriginal building. These inscriptions were,

D. Doyle, 1842.   A. C. Goodall, 1842.

H. M. Ship Blossom.

11th October, 1811. Corsaire Françes (Chebek) le Vengeur,

Capt. Pierre Liovet;

and wafered on the wall on separate cards were the names of the officers of the Texan schooners of war San Bernard and San Antonio.

At the distance of a few hundred feet was another building about fourteen feet square, having four doorways, with steps on three sides, dilapidated, and almost inaccessible on account of the thickets of cactus and thorn bushes growing around it.

In the account given by Bernal Dias of the expedition of Cortez, he says that, after leaving the island of Cozumel, the fleet was separated by a gale of wind, but the next day all the ships joined company except one, which, according to the surmise of the pilot, was found in a certain bay on the coast wind bound. "Here," says Bernal Dias, "several of our companions went on shore, and found in the town hard by, four temples, the idols in which represented human female figures of large size, for which reason we named this place *Punta* de las Mugeres," or the Point of the Women. Gomarra speaks of a *Cape* Mugeres, and says, "At this place there were towers covered with wood and straw, in which, in the best order, were put many idols, that appeared to be representations of women." No mention is made by any of the old historians of the *island* of Mugeres, but there is no point or cape on the mainland; and, considering the ignorance of the coast which must have existed in the early voyages, it is not impossible to believe that the Spaniards gave to the prom- ontory on which these buildings stand the name of point or cape, in which case the building presented in the engraving may be one of the temples or towers referred to by Bernal Dias and Gomarra.

Departure from the Island

We returned to the hut ready to embark, and at twelve o'clock we took leave of the fishermen, and were again on board our canoa.

The wind was fair and strong, and very soon we reached the point of the island. Toward dark we doubled Catoche, and, for the first time coasting all night, day broke upon us in the harbour of Yalahao. After the desolate regions we had been visiting, the old pirates' haunt seemed a metropolis. We anchored on a mud-bank leg deep, and now discovered that our patron, hired only for the occasion, intended to leave us, and substitute another. Afraid of the men following, and subjecting us to detention, we forwarded a threatening message to the agent, and remained on board.

At seven o'clock we were again under way, with the wind directly astern, and as much as we could carry, the canoa rolling so that we were compelled to take in the mainsail. The coast was low, barren, and monotonous. At three o'clock we passed an ancient mound, towering above the huts that constituted the port of El Cuyo, a landmark for sailors, visible at sea three leagues distant; but our patron told us that there were no buildings or vestiges of ruins.

At four o'clock we saw an old acquaintance in misfortune. It was the brig which had arrived at Sisal a few hours after we did, lying a wreck on the beach, with foremast and bowsprit broken, sails stripped, but the hull still entire; probably long before this the shore is strewed with her fragments.

CHAPTER XXIII

At daylight the next morning we crawled out from the bottom of the canoa, and found her anchored off the port of Silan, which consisted of a few huts built around a sandy square on a low, barren coast. We gave portions of our tattered garments to the waves, and waded ashore. It was three weeks since we had embarked; our coast voyage had been more interesting than we expected, but there was no part of it so agreeable as the end; we were but too happy to get rid of the discomfort and confinement to the canoa. The patron went to find lodgings for us, and I followed with one of the boatmen, carrying a load. A man just opening the door of a sort of warehouse called to me, and offered it for our accommodation, which, on looking within, I did not hesitate to accept. This man had never heard of us nor we of him, and, probably, neither will ever hear of the other again. It was another instance of the universally kind treatment we met with in all parts of the country.

Silan is the port of Izamal, which is eleven leagues distant. According to our arrangement, Dimas was to meet us here with the horses, but he had not arrived or been heard of. We learned, however, that there was no green food to be procured at this place, which Dimas had probably learned at the village, three leagues distant, and had therefore remained at that place; yet we had some uneasiness, as he had to make a journey of two hundred and fifty miles, and our first business was to despatch Albino for information. Next we had a great enterprise in procuring breakfast, and after this in providing for dinner, which we determined should be the best the country afforded, to consist of fish and fowl, each of which had to be bought separately, and, with separate portions of lard, sent to different houses to be cooked.

During the interval of preparation I took a walk along the shore. Toward the end of a sandy beach was a projecting point, on a line with which I noticed on the water what seemed to be a red cloud of singular brilliancy, and, at the same time, delicacy of colour, which, on drawing nearer, I found to be a flat covered with flamingoes. On my return I reported the discovery to Doctor Cabot, when our host gave us such a glowing account of flamingoes, scarlet ibises, and roseate spoonbills at Punta Arenas, about two leagues distant, that my imagination was excited by the idea of such clouds of beautiful plumage. Doctor Cabot was anxious for closer acquaintance with the birds, and we determined, in case our horses arrived, to go thither that same afternoon, and, after a few hours' shooting, overtake Mr. Catherwood the next day at Izamal. In good time our horses arrived with Dimas, in fine order; and as he had had some days' rest, we took him and an Indian procured by our host, and at about four o'clock set out. For the first league our road lay directly along the shore, but farther on there were projecting points, to cut off which a footpath led among mangrove trees, with shoots growing from the branches into the ground, forming what seemed a naked and impenetrable canebrake, surmounted by thick green foliage. In many places it was difficult to advance on horseback; from time to time we came out upon a broken, stony shore, and, considering that we had set out merely for a short ride, we found ourselves travelling on one of the wildest roads we had met with in the country. At dusk we reached a hut in a beautifully picturesque position, imbosomed in a small bay, with a frail bridge, about two feet wide, running out some distance from the shore, and a canoa floating at the end. The hut consisted of two parts, connected by a thatched arbour, empty, and apparently begging for a tenant. A string of fish hung on one of the beams, and on the ground were a few smothered coals. We swung our hammocks, kindled a fire, and when the occupant arrived had a cup of chocolate ready for him, and endeavoured to make him feel himself at home; but this was no easy matter. He was a lad of about sixteen, the son of the proprietor, who had gone away that day, the fishing season being nearly over. He certainly was not expecting us, and was taken somewhat by surprise; he had never seen a foreigner in his life, and was by no means reassured when we told him that we had come to shoot flamingoes and spoonbills. Our Indian gave him some indistinct notion of our object, of which, however, he must have had a very imperfect notion himself; and seeming to intimate that we were beyond his comprehension, or, at all events, entirely too many for him, the boy withdrew to the other division of the hut, and left us in full possession. Instead of a rough night we were well provided for, but, unfortunately, there was no ramon or water for the horses. We made an affecting appeal to our young host, and he spared us part of a small stock of maize, which he had on hand for the making of his own tortillas, but they had to go without water, as none could be procured at night.

In the gray of the morning we heard a loud quacking of ducks, which almost lifted us out of our hammocks, and carried us out of doors. Beyond the point of the little dock was a long sand-bank, covered with immense flocks of these birds. Our host could not go with us till he had examined his fishing nets, and Dimas had to take the horses to water, but we pushed off with our Indian to set the canoe. Very soon we found that he was not familiar with the place, or with the management of a canoe, and, what was worse, we could not understand a word he said. Below us the shore formed a large bay, with the Punta de Arenas, or Point of Sand, projecting toward us, bordered down to the water's edge with trees, and all over the bay were sand-banks, barely appearing above water, and covered with wild fowl of every description known, in numbers almost exceeding the powers of conception. In recurring to them afterward, Doctor Cabot enumerated of ducks, the mallard, pin-tail, blooming teal, widgeon, and gadwall; of bitterns, the American bittern, least bittern, great and lesser egret, blue crane, great blue heron, Louisiana heron, night heron, two kinds of rail, one clapper rail, white ibis, willets, snipes, red-breasted snipe, least snipe, semi-palmated sandpiper, black-breasted plover, marble godwit, long-billed curlew, osprey or fish-hawk, black hawk, and other smaller birds, of which we took no note, and all together, with their brilliant plumage and varied notes, forming, as we passed among them, an animated and exciting scene, but it was no field for sporting. It would have been slaughter to shoot among them. In an hour we could have loaded our canoe with birds, of which one or two brace would be considered a fair morning's work. But we did not know what to do with them, and, besides, these were not what we were looking for. A single flock of flamingoes flew by us, but out of reach, and at the moment we were stuck in the mud. Our Indian made horrible work in setting us, and continued to hit every flat till we reached the head of the bay, and entered a branch like a creek. Unable to hold discourse with him, and supposing that he was setting right, we continued to move slowly up the stream, until we found that we were getting beyond the region of birds; but the scene was so quiet and peaceful that we were loth to return; and still on each bank the snowy plumage of the white ibis appeared among the green of the trees, and the heron stood like a statue in the water, turning his long neck almost imperceptibly, and looking at us. But we had no time for quiet enjoyment, and turned back. Near the mouth of the creek a flock of roseate spoonbills flew over our heads, also out of reach, but we saw where they alighted, and setting toward them till we were stopped by a mud-bank, we took to the water, or rather to the mud, in which we found our lower members moving suddenly downward to parts unknown, and in some danger of descending till our sombreros only remained as monuments of our muddy grave. Extricating ourselves, moving in another direction, and again sinking and drawing back, for two hours we toiled, struggled, floundered, and fired, a laughing stock to the beautiful spoonbills in the free element above. At length Dr. Cabot brought one down, and we parted. In following our separate fortunes along the shore I shot one, which fell at the other side of a stream. As I rushed in, the water rose above all my mud stains, and I fell back, and hastily disencumbered myself of clothing. A high wind was sweeping over the bay; having no stone at hand with which to secure them, my hat and light garments were blown into the water, and at the same moment the roseate bird stood up, opened its large wings, and fluttered along the beach. Distracted between the bird and the fugitive clothing, I let the latter go, and gave chase to the bird, after securing which, and holding it kicking under my arm, I pursued my habiliments, now some distance apart, into the water, and at length got back to dry land with my miscellaneous load, and stood on the beach a picture of an antiquary in distress, doubtless illustrating the proverb to the Indian, who now came to my relief, if he had ever met with it in the course of his reading, that no man can be a hero to his valet de chambre. In honor of the event I determined to make an essay in dissection, and to carry the bird home with me as a memorial of this place.

By this time Doctor Cabot joined me, and it was necessary to return. We had procured but one bird each, and had been disappointed of the grand spectacle of clouds of beautiful plumage, but the account of our host was no doubt true to the letter, for the season was late, and the brilliant birds we were seeking had wended their way north; but even of these, with the knowledge we had acquired of localities, two canoes, and good setters, in another day we could have procured any number we wanted. For mere sporting, such a ground is not often seen, and the idea of a shooting lodge, or rather hut, on the shores of Punta de Arenas for a few months in the season, with a party large enough to consume the game, presented itself almost as attractively as that of exploring ruined cities. On our return, each of us made a single shot, from which we picked up between thirty and forty birds, leaving others crippled and hopping on the beach. We got back to the hut, and tumbled them all into a dry pot (the feathers being, of course, taken off), and sat down ourselves to the business of dissection. With a finishing touch from Doctor Cabot, I prepared a miserable specimen of a beautiful bird, looking upon it, nevertheless, with great satisfaction as the memorial of a remarkable place and an interesting adventure. In the mean time, the birds on the fire were getting on swimmingly, in a literal sense, giving decided evidence touching the richness of their feeding-grounds. We had only tortillas as an accompaniment, but neither we nor the birds had any reason to complain.

At four o'clock we took leave of our young host, and at dark reached the port, and rode across the sandy plaza. The door which had opened to us with so much alacrity was now shut, but not by the hand of inhospitality. Mr. Catherwood and the owner had left for the village, and the house was locked up. Some of the villagers, however, came to us, and conducted us to the quartel, which was garrisoned by two women, who surrendered at discretion, provided us with chocolate, and, although the hut was abundantly large for all of us, unexpectedly bade us good-night, and withdrew to a neighbour's to sleep. If they had remained, not being worn down by fatigue as we were, and, consequently, more wakeful, a sad catastrophe might have been prevented. We laid our birds carefully on a table to dry; during the night a cat entered, and we were awaked to see the fruits of our hard day's labour dragged along the floor, and the cat bounding from them, and escaping through a hole in the side of the hut. It was no consolation to us, but if she had nine lives, the arsenic used for preserving the birds had probably taken them all.

Before daylight the next morning we were again in the saddle. For some distance back from the port the ground had been washed or overflowed by the sea, and was a sandy, barren mangrove brake. Beyond commenced the same broken, stony surface, and before we had proceeded far we discovered that Doctor Cabot's horse was lame. Not to lose time, I rode on to procure another, and at eight o'clock reached the village of Silan. In the suburbs I discovered unexpectedly the towering memorial of another ruined city, and riding into the plaza, saw at one angle, near the wall of the church, the gigantic mound represented in Plate L, the grandest we had seen in the country. Much as we had seen of ruins, the unexpected sight of this added immensely to the interest of our long journeying among the remains of aboriginal grandeur. Leaving my horse at the casa real, and directing the alcalde to see about getting one for Doctor Cabot, I walked over to the mound. At the base, and inside of the wall of the church, were five large orange trees, loaded with fruit. A group of Indians were engaged in getting stone out of the mound to repair the wall, and a young man was superintending them, whom I immediately recognised as the padre. He accompanied me to the top of the mound; it was one of the largest we had seen, being about fifty feet high and four hundred feet long. There was no building or structure of any kind visible; whatever had been upon it had fallen or been pulled down. The church, the wall of the yard, and the few stone houses in the village, had been built of materials taken from it.

In walking along the top we reached a hole, at the bottom of which I discovered the broken arch of a ceiling, and looked through it into an apartment below. This explained the character of the structure. A building had extended the whole length of the mound, the upper part of which had fallen, and the ruins had made the whole a long, confused, and undistinguishable mass. The top commanded an extensive view of a great wooded plain, and near by, rising above the trees, was another mound, which, within a few years, had been crowned with an edifice, called, as at Chichen and Tuloom, El Castillo. The padre, a young man, but little over thirty, remembered when this Castillo stood with its doorways open, pillars in them, and corridors

Plate L

M. Osborne.

F. Catherwood.

ANCIENT MOUND. VILLAGE OF SILAN.

around. The sight of these ruins was entirely unexpected; if they had been all we had met with in the country, we should have gazed upon them with perplexity and wonder; and they possessed unusual interest from the fact that they existed in a place, the name of which was known and familiar to us as that of an existing aboriginal town at the time of the conquest.

In tracing the disorderly flight of the Spaniards from Chichen Itza, we find them first at Silan, which is described by Herrera as being "Then a fine Town, the Lord whereof was a Youth of the Race of the Cheles, then a Christian, and great Friend to Captain Francis de Montejo, who received and entertained them. Tirrok was near Silan; that and the other Towns along the Coast were subject to the Cheles, who, having been no way disobliged by the Spaniards, did not disturb them, and so they continued some Months, when, seeing no Possibility of being supplied with Men and other Things they wanted, they resolved quite to abandon that Country. In order to it, they were to march to Campeachy, forty Leagues from Silan, which was looked upon as very dangerous, because the Country was very populous; but the Lord of Silan and others bearing them Company, they arrived in Safety, and the Cheles returned to their own Homes." Cogolludo, too, traces the routed Spaniards to Silan, but thence, with more probability, he carries them by sea to Campeachy; for, as he well suggests, the lords of Silan would not have been able to give them safe escort through forty leagues of territory inhabited by different tribes, all hostile to the Spaniards, and some of them hostile to the Cheles themselves. This difference, however, is unimportant; both accounts prove that there was a large town of aboriginal inhabitants in this vicinity, and, as at Ticul and Nohcacab, we must either suppose that these great mounds are the remains of the aboriginal town, or we must believe that another town of the same name existed in this immediate neighbourhood, of which no trace whatever now remains.

The reader may remember that we left the port before daylight. As I stood on the top of the mound, all that I needed to fill up the measure of my satisfaction was the certainty of a breakfast. The padre seemed to divine my thoughts; he relieved me from all uneasiness, and enabled me to contemplate with a tranquil mind the sublimity of these remains of a fallen people. When Doctor Cabot arrived he found a table that surprised him.

Silan was known to us as the scene of a modern and minor

event. Our ambiguous friend on the island of Mugeres had told us that at this place Lafitte died and was buried, and I inquired for his grave. The padre was not in the village at the time, and did not know whether he was buried in the campo santo or the church, but supposed that, as Lafitte was a distinguished man, it was in the latter. We went thither, and examined the graves in the floor, and the padre drew out from amid some rubbish a cross, with a name on it, which he supposed to that of Lafitte, but it was not. The sexton who officiated at the burial was dead; the padre sent for several of the inhabitants, but a cloud hung over the memory of the pirate: all knew of his death and burial, but none knew or cared to tell where he was laid. We had heard, also, that his widow was living in the place, but this was not true. There was, however, a negress who had been a servant to the latter, and who, we were told, spoke English; the cura sent for her, but she was so intoxicated that she could not make her appearance.

The last of the padre's good offices was procuring a horse for Doctor Cabot, which the alcalde had not been able to do. It was the last time we were thrown upon the hospitality of a padre, and in taking leave of him, I do repent me that in my confidential intercourse with the reader I have at times let fall what I might better have kept to myself.

At ten o'clock we set out, and at half past twelve reached Temax, two and a half leagues distant. It had a fine plaza, with a great church and convent, and a stone casa real, with a broad corridor in front, under which the guarda were swinging in hammocks.

We were but six leagues from Izamal, at which place, we learned, a fiesta was then going on, and there was to be a ball in the evening; but we could neither push our horses through, nor procure a calesa, though the road was good for wheel carriages.

Early in the evening we took to our hammocks, but had hardly lain down, when one of the guarda came to inform us that a caricoche had just arrived from Izamal, and wanted a return freight. We had it brought down to the casa real, and at two o'clock, by a bright moonlight, we started, leaving Dimas to follow with the horses. The caricoche was drawn by three mules, and had in it a bed, on which we reclined at full length.

At nine o'clock we entered the suburbs of Izamal, but fifteen leagues from Merida. The streets had lamps, and were designated by visible objects, as at Merida. Peeping through the curtain, we rode into the plaza, which was alive with people.

dressed in clean clothes for the fiesta. There was an unusual proportion of gentlemen with black hats and canes, and some with military coats, bright and flashing to such a degree that we congratulated ourselves upon not having made our entry on horseback. We had on our shooting-clothes, with the mud stains from Punta Arenas, and by computation our beards were of twenty-eight days' growth. In the centre of the plaza our driver stopped for instructions. We directed him to the casa real, and as we were moving on, our English saddles, strapped on behind, caught the eye of Albino, who conducted us to the house in which Mr. Catherwood was already domiciled. This house was a short distance from the plaza, built of stone, and about sixty feet front, divided into two large salas, with rooms adjoining, a broad corridor behind, and a large yard for horses, for all which the rent was three reales per day, being, as we were advised, but two more than anybody else would have been obliged to pay. In a few moments we had done all that our scanty wardrobe would allow, and were again in the street.

It was the last day of the fiesta of Santa Cruz. By the grace of a beneficent government, the village of Izamal had been erected into a city, and the jubilee on account of this accession of political dignity was added to the festival of the holy cross. The bull-fights were over, but the bull-ring, fancifully ornamented, still remained in the centre of the plaza, and two bulls stood under one of the corridors, pierced with wounds and streaming with blood, as memorials of the fight. Amid a crowd of Indians were parties of vecinos, or white people, gay and well dressed in the style and costume of the capital, and under the corridor of a corner house, with an arbour projecting into the plaza, music was sounding to summon the people to a ball. From desolation and solitude we had come into the midst of gayeties, festivities, and rejoicings. But amid this gay scene the eye turned involuntarily to immense mounds rising grandly above the tops of the houses, from which the whole city had been built, without seeming to diminish their colossal proportions, proclaiming the power of those who reared them, and destined, apparently, to stand, when the feebler structures of their more civilized conquerors shall have crumbled into dust.

One of these great mounds, having at that time benches upon it, commanding a view of the bull-fight in the plaza, blocked up the yard of the house we occupied, and extended into the adjoining yard of the Señora Mendez, who was the owner of both. It is, perhaps, two hundred feet long and thirty high. The part in our yard was entirely ruined, but in that of the señora it appeared that its vast sides had been covered from one end to the other with colossal ornaments in stucco, most of which had fallen, but among the fragments is the gigantic head represented in Plate LI. It is seven feet eight inches in height and seven feet in width. The ground-work is of projecting stones, which are covered with stucco. A stone one foot six inches long protrudes from the chin, intended, perhaps, for burning copal on, as a sort of altar. It was the first time we had seen an ornament of this kind upon the exterior of any of these structures. In sternness and harshness of expression it reminded us of the idols at Copan, and its colossal proportions, with the corresponding dimensions of the mound, gave an unusual impression of grandeur.

Two or three streets distant from the plaza, but visible in all its huge proportions, was the most stupendous mound we had seen in the country, being, perhaps, six or seven hundred feet long and sixty feet high, which, we ascertained beyond all doubt, had interior chambers.

Turning from these memorials of former power to the degraded race that now lingers round them, the stranger might run wild with speculation and conjecture, but on the north side of the plaza is a monument that recalls his roving thoughts, and holds up to his gaze a leaf in history. It is the great church and convent of Franciscan monks, standing on an elevation, and giving a character to the plaza that no other in Yucatan possesses. Two flights of stone steps lead up to it, and the area upon which they open is probably two hundred feet square; on three sides is a colonnade, forming a noble promenade, overlooking the city and the surrounding country to a great distance. This great elevation was evidently artificial, and not the work of the Spaniards.

At the earliest period of the conquest we have accounts of the large aboriginal town of Izamal, and, fortunately, in the pious care of the early monks to record the erection of their church and convent, the only memorials which, to the exclusive and absorbing spirit of the times, seemed worth preserving, we have authentic records which incidentally dispel all uncertainty respecting the origin of these ancient mounds.

According to the account of the padre Lizana, in the year 1553, at the second chapter held in the province, the padre Fr. Diego de Landa was elected guardian of the convent of Izamal, and charged to erect the building, the monks having lived

Plate LI

IZAMAL

Gigantic Head

315

until that time in houses of straw. He selected as the place for the foundation one of the cerros, or mounds, which then existed, "made by hand," and called by the natives Phapphol-chac, which, says the padre Lizana, "signifies the habitation or residence of the priests of the gods; this place was selected in order that the devil might be driven away by the divine presence of Christ sacrificed, and that the place in which the priests of the idol lived, and which had been the place of abomination and idolatry, might become that of sanctification, where the ministers of the true God should offer sacrifices and adoration due to his Divine Majesty."

This is clear and unmistakeable testimony as to the original use and occupation of the mound on which the church and convent of Izamal now stand; and the same account goes on farther, and says: "At another mound, on which was the idol called Kinick Kakmo, he founded a village or settlement, calling it San Ildefonzo, and to the other cerro, called Humpictok, where falls the village of Izamal, he gave for patron San Antonio de Padua, demolishing the temple which was there; and where was the idol called Haboc he founded a village called Santa Maria, by which means he sought to sweep away the memory of so great idolatry."

It is unnecessary to comment upon these accounts. Testimony, never intended for that purpose, proves, beyond the shadow of a doubt, that these great mounds had upon them temples and idols, and the habitations of priests, in the actual use of the Indians who were found occupying the country at the time of the conquest; and, in my opinion, if it stood alone, unsupported by any other, it is sufficient to dispel every cloud of mystery that hangs over the ruins of Yucatan.

At the present day Izamal is distinguished throughout Yucatan for its fair, but it has a stronger hold upon the feelings of the Indians in the sanctity of its Virgin. From the history of the proceedings of the monks, it appears that the Indians continued to worship El Demonio, and the venerable padre Landa, after severe wrestling with the great enemy, proposed to procure an image of the holy Virgin, offering to go for it himself to Guatimala, in which city there was a skilful sculptor. At the same time, another was wanted for the convent at Merida. The two images were brought in a box, and though there was much rain on the way, it never fell on the box, or on the Indians who carried it, or within some steps of them. At Merida the monks selected for their convent the one which had the most beautiful countenance and seemed most devout; the other, though brought by the Indians of Izamal, and intended for that place, the Spaniards of Valladolid claimed, and said that it ought not to remain in a village of Indians. The Indians of Izamal resisted, the Spaniards attempted to carry their purpose into execution, and when in the suburbs of the village, the image became so heavy that the bearers could not carry it. Divine Majesty interposed on behalf of the Indians of Izamal, and there was not sufficient human force to remove the statue. The devotion of the faithful increased at the sight of these marvels, and in all parts, by land and sea, by means of invocation to this Virgin, innumerable miracles have been wrought, of which, says Cogolludo, a volume might have been written, if proper care had been taken.

But, alas! though this Virgin could save others, herself she could not save. On the left of the door of the church is a square stone set in the wall, with an inscription, which tells the mournful tale, that in the great burning of the church the Santa Virgen was entirely consumed; but the hearts of the faithful are cheered by the assurance that one as good as she has been put in her place.

After our visit to the church we returned to the corridor overlooking the plaza. A young girl whom I had noticed all day sitting in one of the corridors was still there, looking down upon the gay scene in the plaza, but apparently abstracted, pensive, perhaps looking in vain for one who did not appear.

In the evening we went to the ball, which was held in, or rather out of, a house on the corner of the plaza. The sala was opened as a refreshment room. In the corridor was a row of seats for those who did not take part in the dance, and in front was an arbour projecting into the plaza, with a cemented floor for the dancers. The ball had begun at eight o'clock the evening before, and, with an intermission of a few hours toward daylight, had been continued ever since; but it was manifest that there were limits to the capabilities of human nature even in dancing. The room was already less crowded than it had been during the day. Two officers of the army (militia), who had been toiling all day with a determination that promised well for Yucatan under the threatened invasion of Mexico, had danced off their military coats, but still kept the floor in light jackets. One placed a chair for his drooping partner during the intervals of the dance. Another followed his example, and by degrees every lady had her seat of relief. At the last call only four couples appeared on the floor. Ladies, fiddlers, and lights were all wearing out together, and we went away. Before we were in our hammocks a loud burst of music, as it were a last effort of expiring nature, broke up the ball.

CHAPTER XXIV

The next morning we started for Merida, with the intention of diverging for the last time to visit the ruins of Aké. The road was one of the best in the country, made for carriages, but rough, stony, and uninteresting. At Cacalchen, five leagues distant, we stopped to dine and procure a guide to Aké.

In the afternoon we proceeded, taking with us only our hammocks, and leaving Dimas to go on direct with the luggage to Merida. Turning off immediately from the main road, we entered the woods, and following a narrow path, a little before dark we reached the hacienda of Aké, and for the last time were among the towering and colossal memorials of an aboriginal city. The hacienda was the property of the Conde Peon, and, contrary to our expectations, it was small, neglected, in a ruinous condition, and entirely destitute of all kinds of supplies. We could not procure even eggs, literally nothing but tortillas. The major domo was away, the principal building locked up, and the only shelter we could obtain was a miserable little hut, full of fleas, which no sweeping could clear out. We had considered all our rough work over, but again, and within a day's journey of Merida, we were in bad straits. By great ingenuity, and giving them the shortest possible tie, Albino contrived to swing our hammocks, and having no other resource, early in the evening we fell into them. At about ten o'clock we heard the tramp of a horse, and the major domo arrived. Surprised to find such unexpected visiters, but glad to see them, he unlocked the hacienda, and walking out in our winding sheets, we took possession; our hammocks followed, and were hung up anew. In the morning he provided us with breakfast, after which, accompanied by him and all the Indians of the hacienda, being only six, we went round to see the ruins.

Plate LII represents a great mound towering in full sight from the door of the hacienda, and called El Palacio, or the Palace. The ascent is on the south side, by an immense staircase, one hundred and thirty-seven feet wide, forming an approach of rude grandeur, perhaps equal to any that ever existed in the country. Each step is four feet five inches long, and one foot five inches in height. The platform on the top is two hundred and twenty-five feet in length, and fifty in breadth. On this great platform stand thirty-six shafts, or columns, in three parallel rows of twelve, about ten feet apart from north to south, and fifteen from east to west. They are from fourteen to sixteen feet in height, four feet on each side, and are comoposed of separate stones, from one to two feet in thickness. But few have fallen, though some have lost their upper layer of stones. There are no remains of any structure or of a roof. If there ever was one, it must have been of wood, which would seem most incongruous and inappropriate for such a solid structure of stones. The whole mound was so overgrown that we could not ascertain the juxtaposition of the pillars till the growth was cleared away, when we made out the whole, but with little or no enlargement of our knowledge as to its uses and purposes. It was a new and extraordinary feature, entirely different from any we had seen, and at the very end of our journey, when we supposed ourselves familiar with the character of American ruins, threw over them a new air of mystery.

In the same vicinity are other mounds of colossal dimensions, one of which is also called the Palace, but of a different construction and without pillars. On another, at the head of the ruined staircase, is an opening under the top of a doorway, nearly filled up, crawling through which, by means of the crotch of a tree I descended into a dark chamber fifteen feet long and ten wide, of rude construction, and of which some of the stones in the wall measured seven feet in length. This is called Akabna,

Plate LII

AKE

Ruined Structure on Mound.

casa obscura, or dark house. Near this is a senote, with the remains of steps leading down to water, which once supplied the ancient city. The ruins cover a great extent, but all were overgrown, and in a condition too ruinous to be presented in a drawing. They were ruder and more massive than all the others we had seen, bore the stamp of an older era, and more than any others, in fact, for the first time in the country, suggested the idea of Cyclopean remains; but even here we have a gleam of historic light, faint, it is true, but, in my mind, sufficient to dispel all unsettled and wavering notions.

In the account of the march of Don Francisco Montejo from the coast, presented in the early part of these pages, it is mentioned that the Spaniards reached a town called Aké, at which they found themselves confronted by a great multitude of armed Indians. A desperate battle ensued, which lasted two days, and in which the Spaniards were victorious, but gained no easy triumph.

There is no other mention of Aké, and in this there is no allusion whatever to the buildings, but from its geographical position, and the direction of the line of march of the Spanish army from the coast, I have little doubt that their Aké was the place now known by the same name, and occupied by the ruins last presented. It is, indeed, strange that no mention is made of the buildings, but regard must be had to the circumstances of danger and death which surrounded the Spaniards, and which were doubtless always uppermost in the minds of the soldiers who formed that disastrous expedition. At all events, it is not more strange than the want of any description of the great buildings of Chichen, and we have the strongest possible proof that no correct inference is to be drawn from the silence of the Spaniards, for in the comparatively minute account of the conquest of Mexico, we find that the Spanish army marched under the very shadow of the great pyramids of Otumba, and yet not the slightest mention whatever is made of their existence.

I have now finished my journey among ruined cities. I know that it is impossible by any narrative to convey to the reader a true idea of the powerful and exciting interest of wandering among them, and I have avoided as much as possible all detailed descriptions, but I trust that these pages will serve to give some general idea of the appearance which this country once presented. In our long, irregular, and devious route we have discovered the crumbling remains of forty-four ancient cities, most of them but a short distance apart, though, from the great change that has taken place in the country, and the breaking up of the old roads, having no direct communication with each other; with but few exceptions, all were lost, buried, and unknown, never before visited by a stranger, and some of them, perhaps, never looked upon by the eyes of a white man. Involuntarily we turn for a moment to the frightful scenes of which this now desolate region must have been the theatre; the scenes of blood, agony, and wo which preceded the desolation or abandonment of these cities. But, leaving the boundless space in which imagination might rove, I confine myself to the consideration of facts. If I may be permitted to say so, in the whole history of discoveries there is nothing to be compared with those here presented. They give an entirely new aspect to the great Continent on which we live, and bring up with more force than ever the question which I once, with some hesitation, undertook to consider: Who were the builders of these American cities?

My opinion on this question has been fully and freely expressed, "that they are not the works of people who have passed away, and whose history is lost, but of the same races who inhabited the country at the time of the Spanish conquest, or of some not very distant progenitors." Some were probably in ruins, but in general I believe that they were occupied by the Indians at the time of the Spanish invasion. The grounds of this belief are interspersed throughout these pages; they are interwoven with so many facts and circumstances that I do not recapitulate them; and in conclusion I shall only refer briefly to those arguments which I consider the strongest that are urged against this belief.

The first is the entire absence of all traditions. But I would ask, may not this be accounted for by the unparalleled circumstances which attended the conquest and subjugation of Spanish America? Every captain or discoverer, on first planting the royal standard on the shores of a new country, made proclamation according to a form drawn up by the most eminent divines and lawyers in Spain, the most extraordinary that ever appeared in the history of mankind; entreating and requiring the inhabitants to acknowledge and obey the church as the superior and guide of the universe, the holy father called the pope, and his majesty as king and sovereign lord of these islands, and of the terra firma; and concluding, "But if you will not comply, or maliciously delay to obey my injunction, then, with the help of God, I will enter your country by force; I will carry on war against you with the utmost violence; I will subject you to the yoke of obedience, to the church and king; I will take your wives and children, and make them slaves, and sell or dispose of them according to his majesty's pleasure. I will seize your goods, and do you all the mischief in my power, as rebellious subjects, who will not acknowledge or submit to their lawful sovereign; and I protest that all the bloodshed and calamities which shall follow are to be imputed to you, and not to his majesty, or to me, or the gentlemen who serve under me."

The conquest and subjugation of the country were carried out in the unscrupulous spirit of this proclamation. The pages of the historians are dyed with blood; and sailing on the crimson stream, with a master pilot at the helm, appears the leading, stern, and steady policy of the Spaniards, surer and more fatal than the sword, to subvert all the institutions of the natives, and to break up and utterly destroy all the rites, customs, and associations that might keep alive the memory of their fathers and their ancient condition. One sad instance shows the effects of this policy. Before the destruction of Mayapan, the capital of the kingdom of Maya, all the nobles of the country had houses in that city, and were exempted from tribute; according to the account from which Cogolludo derives his authority, in the year 1582, forty years after the conquest, all who held themselves for lords and nobles still claimed their solares (sites for mansions) as tokens of their rank; but now, he says, "from the change of government and the little estimation in which they are held, it does not appear that they care to preserve nobility for their posterity, for at this day the descendants of Tutul Xiu, who was the king and natural lord by right of the land of Maya, if they do not work with their own hands in manual offices, have nothing to eat." And if at that early date nobles no longer cared for their titles, and the descendants of the royal house had nothing to eat but what they earned with their own hands, it is not strange that the present inhabitants, nine generations removed, without any written language, borne down by three centuries of servitude, and toiling daily for a scanty subsistence, are alike ignorant and indifferent concerning the history of their ancestors, and the great cities lying in ruins under their eyes. And strange or not, no argument can be drawn from it, for this ignorance is not confined to ruined cities or to events before the conquest. It is my belief, that among the whole mass of what are called Christianized Indians, there is not at this day one solitary tradition which can shed a ray of light upon any event in their history that occurred one hundred and fifty years from the present time; in fact, I believe it would be almost impossible to procure any information of any kind whatever beyond the memory of the oldest living Indian.

Besides, the want of traditionary knowledge is not peculiar to these American ruins. Two thousand years ago the Pyramids towered on the borders of the African Desert without any certain tradition of the time when they were founded; and so long back as the first century of the Christian era, Pliny cites various older authors who disagreed concerning the persons who built them, and even concerning the use and object for which they were erected. No traditions hang round the ruins of Greece and Rome; the temples of Pæstum, lost until within the last half century, have no traditions to identify their builders; the "holy city" has only weak inventions of modern monks. But for written records, Egyptian, Grecian, and Roman remains would be as mysterious as the ruins of America; and to come down to later times and countries comparatively familiar, tradition sheds no light upon the round towers of Ireland, and the ruins of Stonehenge stand on Salisbury plain without a tradition to carry us back to the age or nation of their builders.

The second argument I shall notice is, that a people possessing the power, art, and skill to erect such cities, never could have fallen so low as the miserable Indians who now linger about their ruins. To this, too, it might be sufficient to answer that their present condition is the natural and inevitable consequence of the same ruthless policy which laid the axe at the root of all ancient recollections, and cut off forever all traditionary knowledge. But waiving this ground, the pages of written history are burdened with changes in national character quite equal to that here exhibited. And again, leaving entirely out of the question all the analogous examples which might be drawn from those pages, we have close at hand, and under our very eyes, an illustration in point. The Indians who inhabit that country now are not more changed than their Spanish masters. Whether debased, and but little above the grade of brutes, as it was the policy of the Spaniards to represent them, or not, we know that at the time of the conquest they were at least proud, fierce, and warlike, and poured out their blood like water to save their inheritance from the grasp of strangers. Crushed, humbled, and bowed down as they are now by generations of bitter servitude, even yet they are not more changed than the descendants of those terrible Spaniards who invaded and conquered their country. In both, all traces of the daring and warlike character of their ancestors are entirely gone. The change is radical, in feelings and instincts, inborn and transmitted, in a measure, with the blood; and in contemplating this change in the Indian, the loss of mere mechanical skill and art seems comparatively nothing; in fact, these perish of themselves, when, as in the case of the Indians, the school for their exercise is entirely broken up. Degraded as the Indians are now, they are not lower in the scale of intellect than the serfs of Russia, while it is a well-known fact that the greatest architect in that country, the builder of the Cazan Church at St. Petersburgh, was taken from that abject class, and by education became what he is. In my opinion, teaching might again lift up the Indian, might impart to him the skill to sculpture stone and carve wood; and if restored to freedom, and the unshackled exercise of his powers of mind, there might again appear a capacity to originate and construct, equal to that exhibited in the ruined monuments of his ancestors.

The last argument, and that upon which most stress has been laid, against the hypothesis that the cities were constructed by the ancestors of the present Indians, is the alleged absence of historical accounts in regard to the discovery or knowledge of such cities by the conquerors. But it is manifest that even if this allegation were true, the argument would be unsound, for it goes to deny that such cities ever existed at all. Now there can be no doubt as to the fact of their existence; and as it is never pretended that they were erected since the conquest, they must be allowed to have been standing at that time. Whether erected by the Indians or by races perished and unknown, whether desolate or inhabited, beyond all question the great buildings were there; if not entire, they must at least have been far more so than they are now; if desolate, perhaps more calculated to excite wonder than if inhabited; and in either case the alleged silence of the historian would be equally inexplicable.

But the allegation is untrue. The old historians are not silent. On the contrary, we have the glowing accounts of Cortez and his companions, of soldiers, priests, and civilians, all concurring in representations of existing cities, then in the actual use and occupation of the Indians, with buildings and temples, in style and character like those presented in these pages. Indeed, these accounts are so glowing that modern historians, at the head of whom stands Robertson, have for that reason thrown discredit over them, and ascribed them to a heated imagination. To my mind, they bear on the face of them the stamp of truth, and it seems strange that they have been deemed worthy of so little reliance. But Robertson wrote upon the authority of correspondents in New Spain, one of whom, long resident in that country, and professing to have visited every part of it, says that "at this day there does not remain the smallest vestige of any Indian building, public or private, either in Mexico or any province of New Spain." Robertson's informants were probably foreign merchants resident in the city of Mexico, whose travels had been confined to the beaten road, and to places occupied by the Spaniards; and at that time the white inhabitants were in utter ignorance of the great cities, desolate and in ruins, that lay buried in the forests. But at this day better information exists; vast remains have been brought to light, and the discoveries prove incontestably that those histories which make no mention of these great buildings are imperfect, those which deny their existence are untrue. The graves cry out for the old historians, and the mouldering skeletons of cities confirm Herrera's account of Yucatan, that "there were so many and such stately Stone Buildings that it was Amazing; and the greatest Wonder was that, having no Use of any Metal, they were able to raise such Structures, which seem to have been Temples, for their Houses were all of Timber, and thatched." And again, he says, that "for the Space of twenty Years there was such Plenty throughout the Country, and the People multiplied so much that Men said the whole Province looked like one Town."

These arguments then—the want of tradition, the degeneracy of the people, and the alleged absence of historical accounts—are not sufficient to disturb my belief, that the great cities now lying in ruins were the works of the same races who inhabited the country at the time of the conquest.

Who these people were, whence they came, and who were their progenitors, are questions that involve too many considerations to be entered upon at the conclusion of these pages; but all the light that history sheds upon them is dim and faint, and may be summed up in a few words.

According to traditions, picture writings, and Mexican manuscripts written after the conquest, the Toltecs, or Toltecans, were the first inhabitants of the land of Anahuac, now known as New Spain or Mexico, and they are the oldest nations on the continent of America of which we have any knowledge. Banished, according to their own history, from their native country, which was situated to the northwest of Mexico, in the year 596 of our era, they proceeded southward under the directions of their chiefs, and, after sojourning at various places on the way for the space of one hundred and twenty-four years, arrived at the banks of a river in the vale of Mexico, where they built the city of Tula, the capital of the Toltecan kingdom, near the site of the present city of Mexico.

Their monarchy lasted nearly four centuries, during which they multiplied, extended their population, and built numerous and large cities; but direful calamities hung over them. For several years Heaven denied them rain; the earth refused them food; the air, infected with mortal contagion, filled the graves with dead; a great part of the nation perished of famine or sickness; the last king was among the number, and in the year 1052 the monarchy ended. The wretched remains of the nation took refuge, some in Yucatan and other in Guatimala, while some lingered around the graves of their kindred in the great vale where Mexico was afterward founded. For a century the land of Anahuac lay waste and depopulated. The Chechemecas, following in the track of their ruined cities, reoccupied it, and after them the Acolhuans, the Tlastaltecs, and the Aztecs, which last were the subjects of Montezuma at the time of the invasion by the Spaniards.

The history of all these tribes or nations is misty, confused, and indistinct. The Toltecans, represented to have been the most ancient, are said to have been also the most polished. Probably they were the originators of that peculiar style of architecture found in Guatimala and Yucatan, which was adopted by all the subsequent inhabitants; and as, according to their own annals, they did not set out on their emigration to those countries from the vale of Mexico until the year 1052 of our era, the oldest cities erected by them in those countries could have been in existence but from four to five hundred years at the time of the Spanish conquest. This gives them a very modern date compared with the Pyramids and temples of Egypt, and the other ruined monuments of the Old World; it gives them a much less antiquity than that claimed by the Maya manuscript, and, in fact, much less than I should ascribe to them myself. In identifying them as the works of the ancestors of the present Indians, the cloud which hung over their origin is not removed; the time when and the circumstances under which they were built, the rise, progress, and full development of the power, art, and skill required for their construction, are all mysteries which will not easily be unravelled. They rise like skeletons from the grave, wrapped in their burial shrouds; claiming no affinity with the works of any known people, but a distinct, independent, and separate existence. They stand alone, absolutely and entirely anomalous, perhaps the most interesting subject which at this day presents itself to the inquiring mind. I leave them with all their mystery around them; and in the feeble hope that these imperfect pages may in some way throw a glimmer of light upon the great and long vainly mooted question, who were the peoplers of America? I will now bid farewell to ruins.

CHAPTER XXV

At two o'clock we mounted for Merida, nine leagues distant. We did not expect to reach it till night, and, from the unfortunate condition of our travelling costume, did not care to enter the capital by daylight; but, pushing on, and miscalculating the pace of our horses, we found ourselves in the suburbs at that unlucky hour when, the excessive heat being over, the inhabitants, in full dress, were sitting in the doorways or along the side-walks, talking over the news of the day, and particularly alive to the appearance of such a spectacle as our party presented. We rode the whole length of the principal street, running the gauntlet between long rows of eyes, and conscious that we were not looked upon as making a very triumphal entry. Approaching the plaza, an old aquaintance greeted us, and accompanied us to the Casa de las Diligencias, a new establishment, opened since our departure, opposite the convent, one of the largest and finest in the city, and equal to a good hotel in Italy. Very soon we had the best apartments, and were sitting down to *thé du China*, in English, tea, and *pan Françes*, or bread without sweetening. After our hard journey among Indian ranchos and unwholesome haciendas, at times all prostrated by illness, we had returned to Merida, successful beyond our utmost hopes. Our rough work was all over, and our satisfaction cannot easily be described.

While lingering over the table, we heard the loud ringing of the porter's bell, followed by landlord and servants running and tumbling along the corridor, all crying out "La Diligencia," and presently we heard the tramp of horses and the rattling of the post-coach from Campeachy, into the court-yard. The passengers came up, and among them we greeted with lively satisfaction our old friend Mr. Fisher, that citizen of the world, the last traces of whom we had seen on the desolate island of Cozumel. Another passenger, whose voice we had heard rising in English from the court-yard above the jargon of Spanish and Indian, as if entirely on private account, and indifferent whether it was understood or not, immediately accosted me as an acquaintance; said that I had been the cause of his coming to that place, and if he did not succeed, should come upon me for damages; but I soon learned that I had nothing to fear. Mr. Clayton had already created, perhaps, a greater sensation than any stranger who ever visited that country; he had obtained a hold upon the feelings of the people that no explorers could ever win, and will be remembered long after we are forgotten. He had brought from the United States an entire circus company, with spotted horses, a portable theatre, containing seats for a thousand persons, riders, clowns, and monkeys, all complete. No such thing had ever been seen before; it threw far into the shade Daguerreotype and curing biscos. He had turned Campeachy upside down, and leaving his company there to soothe the excitement and pick up the pesos, he had come up to make arrangements for opening in Merida. And this was by no means Mr. Clayton's first enterprise. He had brought the first giraffes into the United States from the Cape of Good Hope, and his accounts of penetrating fifteen hundred miles into the interior of Africa, of his adventures among the Caffres, of shooting lions, and his high excitement when, on a fleet horse, he ran down and shot his first giraffe, made the exploration of ruins seem a rather tame business. He reached the Cape with four giraffes, but two died after their arrival, and with the others he embarked for New-York, where he expected to deliver them over to the parties interested; but from the great care required in their treatment, it became indispensable for him to travel with them while they were exhibited. In one of the Western states he encountered a travelling circus company, which undertook to run an opposition on the same line of travel. The giraffes were rather too strong for the horses, and a proposition was made to him to unite the two and become director of both, which he accepted. He afterward bought the latter out, and so became the manager of a strolling circus company. With it he travelled all over the United States, but in

Canada his last giraffe died, and left him with a stock of horses and a company on hand. He returned to New-York, chartered a brig, and after touching and exhibiting at several West India Islands, sailed for Campeachy, where he was received with such enthusiasm, that among the benefits conferred upon mankind by authors, I rank high that of having been the means of introducing a circus company into Yucatan, in the belief that it may prove the first step toward breaking up the popular taste for bull-fights.

The next morning we advertised for sale our horses and equipments, and sallied out to visit our friends. Great changes had taken place since our departure. Abroad the political horizon was stormy. News had been received of increased difficulties, complicated and uncertain negotiations, and apprehensions of war between our own country and England; also of the failure of the Santa Fé expedition, the capture and imprisonment of American citizens, and that Texas and the whole valley of the Mississippi were in arms to carry the war into Mexico. And black clouds were lowering, also, over Yucatan. The governor had lost his popularity. The great question opened by the revolution two years before was not yet decided. Independence was not declared; on the contrary, during our absence a commissioner had arrived from Mexico, and had negotiated a treaty for the return of Yucatan to the Mexican confederacy, subject to the approval or disapproval of the Mexican government. In the mean while, electors were called to nominate deputies to the Mexican Congress, as if the treaty was approved, and at the same time the Legislature was summoned in extraordinary session, to provide for the protection of the state against invasion, in case the treaty should be rejected. Both bodies were then sitting. Three days after our return, a vessel arrived at Sisal, having on board a special envoy, bearing Santa Ana's ultimatum. He was detained one day at the port, while the government considered the expediency of permitting him to visit the capital. Apartments were prepared for him at our hotel, but he was taken to the house of the secretary of war, ostensibly to save him from insult and violence by the populace, who were represented as highly excited against Mexico, but in reality to prevent him from holding communication with the partisans in favour of reunion. Great dissensions had grown up. The revolution had been almost unanimous, but two years of quasi independence had produced a great change of feeling. The rich complained of profligate expenditures, merchants of the breaking up of trade by the closing of the Mexican ports, and while many asked what they had gained by a separation, a strong "independent" party was more clamorous than ever for breaking the last link that bound them to Mexico. I was in the Senate Chamber when the ultimatum of Santa Ana was read. A smile of derision flitted over the faces of senators, and it was manifest that the terms would not be accepted, yet no man rose to offer a declaration of independence. In the lobby, however, an open threat was made to proclaim it *viva voce* in the plaza on the coming Sunday, and at the mouth of the cannon. The condition of the state was pitiable in the extreme. It was a melancholy comment upon republican government, and the most melancholy feature was that this condition did not proceed from the ignorant and uneducated masses. The Indians were all quiet, and, though doomed to fight the battles, knew nothing of the questions involved. It is my firm conviction that the constant and unceasing convulsions of the southern republics more than from any other cause grow out of the non-recognition or the violation of that great saving principle known among us as state rights. The general government aims constantly at dominion over the states. Far removed by position, ignorant of the wants of the people, and regardless of their feelings, it sends from the capital its military commandant, places him above the local authorities, cripples the strength of the state, and drains its coffers to support a strong, consolidated power. Such were the circumstances which had placed Yucatan in arms against the general government, and such, ere this, might have been the condition of our own republic, but for the triumphant assertion of the great republican principal that the states are sovereign, and their rights sacred.

While the clouds were becoming darker and more portentous, we were preparing for our departure from the country. A vessel was then at Sisal ready to sail. It was one which we had hoped never to be on board of again, being the old Alexandre, in which we made our former unlucky voyage, but we had now no alternative, being advised that if we lost that opportunity, it was entirely uncertain when another would present itself. At the request of the governor, we delayed our departure a few days, that he might communicate with a relative in Campeachy, who wished a surgical operation performed by Doctor Cabot, and had passed two months in Merida awaiting our return. In the mean time the governor procured the detention of the vessel.

On Sunday, the sixteenth of May, early in the morning, we sent off our luggage for the port, and in the afternoon we joined for the last time in a paseo. All day we had received intimations that an outbreak was apprehended; a volcano was burning and heaving with inward fires, but there was the same cheerfulness, gayety, and prettiness as before, producing on our minds the same pleasing impression, making us hope that these scenes might be long continued, and, above all, that they might not be transformed into scenes of blood. Alas! before these pages were concluded, that country which we had looked upon as a picture of peace, and in which we had met with so much kindness, was torn and distracted by internal dissensions, the blast of civil war was sounding through its borders, and an exasperated, hostile army had landed upon its shores.

In the evening we rode to the house of Doña Joaquina Peon, said farewell to our first, last, and best friends in Merida, and at ten o'clock started for the port.

On Tuesday, the eighteenth, we embarked for Havana. The old Alexandre had been altered and improved in her sailing, but not in her accommodations. In fact, having on board eleven passengers, among whom were three women and two children, these could not well have been worse, and at one time our voyage threatened to be as long as the other of unfortunate memory, but the captain, a surviver of the battle of Trafalgar, was the same excellent fellow as before. On the second of June we anchored under the walls of the Moro Castle. Before obtaining passports to land, a barque entered, which we immediately recognised as an American, and on landing, learned that she was the Ann Louisa, Captain Clifford, one of a line of packets from Vera Cruz, had put in short of water, and was to sail the next day for New-York. The yellow fever had already broken out; there was no other vessel in port, and we determined, if possible, to get on board, but we were met with a difficulty, which at first threatened to be insuperable. By the regulations of the port, it was necessary for all luggage to be carried to the custom-house for inspection, and a list furnished beforehand of every article. The last was utterly impossible, as we had on board the whole miscellaneous collection made on our journey, with no such thing as a memorandum of the items. But by the active kindness of our late consul, Mr. Calhoun, and the courtesy of his excellency the governor, a special order was procured for transferring the whole without inspection from one vessel to the other. The next day was occupied in the details of this business, and in the afternoon we joined in a paseo, the style and show of which, for the moment, made us think slightingly of the simple exhibition at Merida; and after dark, by the light of a single candle, with heads uncovered, we stood before the marble slab enclosing the bones of Columbus.

On the fourth we embarked on board the Ann Louisa. She was full of passengers, principally Spaniards escaping from the convulsions of Mexico, but Captain Clifford contrived to give us accommodations much better than we were used to, and we found on board the comforts and conveniences of Atlantic packets. On the seventeenth we reached New-York. The reader and I must again part, and trusting that he will find nothing in these pages to disturb the friendship that has hitherto existed between us, I again return him my thanks for his kindness, and bid him farewell.

APPENDIX

A MANUSCRIPT WRITTEN IN THE MAYA LANGUAGE, TREATING OF THE PRINCI-
PAL EPOCHS OF THE HISTORY OF THE PENINSULA OF YUCATAN BEFORE THE
CONQUEST. WITH COMMENTS BY DON PIO PEREZ.

Principal Epochs of the Ancient History of Yucatan.

Maya.	*Translation.*

LAI u tzolan Katun lukci ti cab ti yotoch Nonoual cánte anílo Tutul Xiu ti chikin Zuina; u luumil u talelob Tulapan chiconahthan. Cante bin ti Katun lic u ximbalob ca uliob uaye yetel Holon Chantepeuh yetel u cuchulob: ca hokiob ti petene uaxac Ahau bin yan cuchi, uac Ahau, can Ahau cabil Ajau, cankal haab catac hunppel haab; tumen hun piztun oxlahun Ahau cuchie ca uliob uay ti petene cankal haab catac hunppel haab tu pakteil yete cu xinbalob lukci tu luumilob ca talob uay ti petene Chacnouitan lae.

THIS is the series of "Katunes," or epochs, that elapsed from the time of their departure from the land and house of Nonoual, in which were the four Tutul Xiu, lying to the west of Zuina, going out of the country of Tulapan. Four epochs were spent in travelling before they arrived here, with Tolonchantepeuj and his followers. When they began their journey toward this island, it was the 8th Ajau, and the 6th, 4th, and 2d were spent in travelling; because in the first year of the 13th Ajau they arrived at this island, making together eighty-one years they were travelling, between their departure from their country and their arrival at this island of Chacnouitan.

Vaxac Ahau, uac Ahau, cabil Ajau kuchci Chacnouitan Ahmekat Tutul Xiu hunppel haab minan ti hokal haab cuchi yanob Chacnouitan lae.

In the 8th Ajau arrived Ajmekat Tutul Xiu, and ninety-nine years they remained in Chacnouitan.

Laitun uchci u chicpahal Tzucubte Ziyan-caan lae Bakhalal, can Ahau, cabil Ahau, oxlahun Ahau oxkal haab cu tepalob Ziyan-caan ca emob uay lae: lai u haabil cu tepalob Bakhalal chuulte laitun chicpahi Chichen Itza lae.

Then took place the discovery of the province of Ziyan-caan, or Bacalar; the 4th Ajau, the 2d, and the 13th, or sixty years, they ruled in Ziyan-caan, when they came here. During these years of their government of the province of Bacalar occurred the discovery of Chichen Itza.

Buluc Ahau, bolon Ajau, uuc Ahau, ho Ahau, ox Ahau, hun Ahau uac kal haab cu tepalob Chichen Itza ca paxi Chichen Itza, ca binob cahtal Chanputun ti yanhi u yotochob ah Ytzoab kuyen uincob lae.

Vac Ahau, chucuc u luumil Chanputun, can Ahau, cabil Ahau, oxlahun Ahau, buluc Ahau, bolon Ahau, uuc Ahau, ho Ahau, ox Ahau, hun Ahau, lahca Ahau, lahun Ajau; uaxac Ahau paxci Chanputun, oxlahun kaal haab cu tepalob Chanputun tumenel Ytza uincob ca talob u tzaclé u yotochob tu caten, laix tun u katunil binciob ah Ytzaob yalan che yalan aban yalan ak ti numyaob lae.

Vac Ahau, can Ahau, ca kal haab catalob u heɔob yotoch tu caten ca tu zatahob Chakanputun.

Lai u katunil cabil Ahau, u heɔci cab Ahcuitok Tutul Xiu Vxmal. Cabil Ahau, oxlahun Ahau, buluc Ahau, bolon Ahau, uuc Ahau, ho Ahau, ox Ahau, hun Ahau, lahca Ahau, lahun Ahau, lahun kal haab cu tepalob yetel u halach uinicil Chichen,Itza yetel Mayalpan.

Lai u katunil buluc Ajau, bolon Ahau, uac Ahau, uaxac Ahau, paxci u halach uinicil Chichen Itza tumenel u kebanthan Hunac-eel, ca uch ti Chacxib-chac Chichen Itza tu kebanthan Hunac-eel u halach uinicil Mayalpan ichpac. Cankal haab catac lahun piz haab, tu lahun tun uaxac Ahau cuchie; lai u haabil paxci tumenel Ahzinteyutchan yetel Tzunte-cum, yetel Taxcal, yetel Pantemit, Xuch-ucuet, yetel Ytzcuat, yetel Kakaltecat lay u kaba uinicilob lae nuctulob ahmayapanob lae.

The 11th Ajau, 9th, 7th, 5th, 3d, and 1st Ajau, or 120 years, they ruled in Chichen Itza, when it was abandoned, and they emigrated to Champoton, where the Ytzaes, holy men, had houses.

The 6th Ajau they took possession of the territory of Champoton; the 4th Ajau, 2d, 13th, 11th, 9th, 7th, 5th, 3d, 1st, 12th, 10th, and the 8th, Champoton was destroyed or abandoned. Two hundred and sixty years reigned the Ytzaes in Champoton, when they returned in search of their homes, and then they lived for several epochs under the uninhabited mountains.

The 6th Ajau, 4th Ajau, after 40 years, they returned to their homes once more, and Champoton was lost to them.

In this Katun of 2d Ajau, Ajcuitok Tutul Xiu established himself in Uxmal; the 2d Ajau, the 13th, 11th, 9th, 7th, 5th, 3d, 1st, the 12th and the 10th Ajau, equal to 200 years, they governed and reigned in Uxmal, with the governors of Chichen Itza and of Mayapan.

After the lapse of the Ajau Katunes of 11th, 9th, 6th Ajau, in the 8th the Governor of Chichen Itza was deposed, because he murmured disrespectfully against Tunac-eel; this happened to Chacxibchac of Chichen Itza, who had spoken against Tunac-eel, governor of the fortress of Mayalpan. Ninety years had elapsed, but the 10th of the 8th Ajau was the year in which he was overthrown by Ajzinte-yutchan, with Tzuntecum, Taxcal, Pantemit, Xuch-ucuet, Ytzcuat, and Kakaltecat; these are the names of the 7 Mayalpanes.

340

Laili u katunil uaxac Ahau, lai ca binob u p̃â ah Vlmil Ahau tumenel u uahal-uahob yetel ah Ytzmal Vlil Ahau lae Oxlahun uuɔ u katunilob ca paxob tumen Hunac-eel tumenel u ɔabal u naɔtob; uac Ahau ca ɔoci: hunkal haab catac can lahun pizí.

Vac Ahau, can Ahau, cabil Ahau, oxlahun Ahau, buluc ahau, chucuc u luumil ich pâ Mayalpan, tumenel u pach tulum, tumenel multepal ich cah Mayalpan, tumenel Ytza uinicob yetel ah Vlmil Ahau lae, can kaal haab catac oxppel haab: yocol buluc Ahau cuchie paxci Mayalpan tumenel ahuitzil ɔul, tan cah Mayalpan.

Vaxac Ahau lay paxci Mayalpan lai u katunil uac Ahau, can Ahau, cabil Ahau, lai haab ca yax mani upañoles u yaxilci caa luumi Yucatan tzucubte lae, oxkal haab pâxac ich pâ cuchie.

Oxlahun Ahau, buluc Ahau, uchci mayacimil ich pâ yetel nohkakil: oxlahun Ahau cimci Ahpulá uacppel haab u binel ma ɔococ u xocol oxlahun Ahau cuchie, ti yanil u xocol haab ti lakin cuchie, canil kan cumlahi pop, tu holhun Zip catac oxppeli, bolon Ymix u kinil lai cimi Ahpulá; laitun año cu ximbal cuchi lae ca oheltabac lay u xoc numeroil años lae 1536 años cuchie, oxkal haab paaxac ich pâ cuchi lae.

Laili ma ɔococ u xocol buluc Ahau lae lai ulci erpañoles kul uincob ti lakin u talob ca uliob uay tac hurmil lae bolon Ahau hoppci cristianoil uchci caputzihil: laili ichil u

In this same period, or Katun, of the 8th Ajau, they attacked King Ulmil, in consequence of his quarrel with Ulil, king of Yzamal; thirteen divisions of troops had he when he was routed by Tunac-eel; in the 6th Ajau the war was over, after 34 years.

In the 6th Ajau, 4th Ajau, 2d Ajau, 13th Ajau, 11th Ajau, the fortified territory of Mayalpan was invaded by the men of Ytza, under their King Ulmil, because they had walls, and governed in common the people of Mayalpan; eighty-three years elapsed after this event, and at the beginning of the 11th Ajau Mayalpan was destroyed by strangers of the Uitzes, or Highlanders, as was also Tancaj of Mayalpan.

In the 6th Ajau Mayalpan was destroyed; the epochs of 6th Ajau, 4th and 2d Ajau, elapsed, and at this period the Spaniards, for the first time, arrived, and gave the name of *Yucatan* to this province, sixty years after the destruction of the fortress.

The 13th Ajau, 11th Ajau, pestilence and smallpox were in the castles. In the 13th Ajau Ajpula died; six years were wanting to the completion of the 13th Ajau; this year was counted toward the east of the wheel, and began on the 4th "Kan." Ajpula died on the 18th day of the month Zip, in the 9th Ymix; and that it may be known in numbers, it was the year 1536, sixty years after the demolition of the fortress.

Before the termination of the 11th Ajau the Spaniards arrived; holy men from the East came with them when they reached this land. The 9th Ajau was the commencement of

katunil lae ulci yax obispo Toroba   baptism and Christianity; and in
u kaba.   this year was the arrival of Toral,
                                       the first bishop.

Thus far only from the Maya manuscript, because the other events cited are posterior to the conquest, and of little historical interest. Although this manuscript may contain some errors which should be rectified, still, as these are committed in the numeration of the epochs, or Ajaues, which do not keep a correlative numerical order, it was very easy for the author, who wrote from memory, to transpose them; preserving solely the number of periods which elapsed between the occurrence of one and the other event, without designating correctly the sign of the period. I repeat that the writer of this epitome did it from memory, because it was done long after the conquest: the histories, paintings, and hieroglyphics of the Indians had about this period been collected by order of Bishop Landa, as is related by Cogolludo in his history; and likewise because his historical narrative is so succinct, that it appears rather a list than a circumstantial detail of the events. But, notwithstanding these defects, as the manuscript is the only one which has been found treating of this matter, it is well worthy the trouble of correcting and analyzing it, on account of the ideas which it communicates respecting the ancient history and establishment of the principal peoples of that time, whose ruins are admired at the present day, such as those of Chichen and Uxmal; deducing from these, what were the others which the traveller encounters, and whose origin is unknown.

The manuscript may be abridged in the following manner: "Four epochs were expended by the Toltecos between their departure from their city under the direction of Tolonchante Peech, and their arrival at Chacnouitan.* They arrived at this province of Chacnouitan in the first year of the following epoch, and remained in the same place with their captain Ajmekat Tutul Xiu during the space of four epochs more.† They discovered Ziyancan, or Bacalar, and governed in it three epochs, until they came to Chichen Itza.‡ They remained here until their departure to colonize Champoton, a period of six epochs.§ From the discovery of Champoton, where they settled and reigned until it was destroyed, and they lost it, thirteen epochs elapsed.‖ They were wanderers among the hills during two epochs, when they established themselves for the second time at Chichen Itza.¶ In the following epoch, Ajcuitok Tutul Xiu colonized Uxmal, and reigned with the governor of Mayapan during ten epochs.** After a farther lapse of three epochs, and on the tenth year of the one following, Chacxibchac, governor of Chichen Itza, was defeated by Tunac-eel, gov-

---

* From the year 144 of the vulgar era up to 217.   † From 218 until 360.
‡ From 360 until 432.   ◊ From 432 until 576.   ‖ From 576 until 888.
¶ From 888 until 936.   ** From 936 until 1176.

ernor of Mayapan, and his seven generals.* In this same epoch of the defeat of the Governor of Chichen, they marched to attack Ulmil, king of Chichen, because he had made war against Ulil, king of Yzamal, and the object was effected by Tunac-eel in the following epoch.† After this epoch, Ulmil, king of Chichen, recovering from his defeat, invaded the territory of Mayapan in the following epoch, and, after the lapse of two more, and in the third year of the one following, Mayapan was destroyed by the strangers, inhabitants of the hills.‡ After the lapse of three more epochs, the Spaniards arrived for the first time, and gave to this province the name of Yucatan.§ In the following epoch occurred the plague, which visited even the temples and castles; and in its sixth year Ajpula died, on the 11th of September, 1493.‖ In the eleventh epoch, and the last of this record, was the arrival of the conquerors; this happened in 1527.¶ In the following epoch the conquest was finished, and the first bishop reached the province: the first occurred in January, 1541, and the other in 1560."

MEMORANDUM FOR THE ORNITHOLOGY OF YUCATAN.

THE genus Accipitres, including eagles, falcons, buzzards, &c., is very numerous, and of these three or four new varieties were obtained. One, a beautiful hawk, resembling in its markings the goshawk (Falco Atricapillus), differing, however, in its form, in the bill, colour of its eyes (dark brown), in not having the white line over the eyes, and in the bands on the tail. The first specimen was killed at Uxmal, but afterward many others were procured, and two were brought home. Another new and beautiful species is a falcon of a very noble character in the form of its bill and head, and in its habits; of which two specimens were obtained at Chichen Itza, the male being shot over the senoté during a heavy shower. No others but this pair were seen. Another is undescribed, or, if described, imperfectly so, under the name of the mingled buzzard of Latham (La Busc Mixté Noire. Voy. d'Azara, vol. iii., No. 20). It is a large black hawk, and was obtained, the female at Punta Française, and the male at the island of Cozumel, where a nest also was found, but was destroyed, together with the eggs, in consequence of Dr. Cabot's being obliged to have the tree felled. He afterward procured an egg from a nest between Silan and Las Bockas de Silan. Another very beautiful hawk is shaped much like the little corporal of Audubon, and belongs to the same division of hawks as the hobby falcon of Europe. It is a bold hawk, and is met with about

---

* From 1176 until 1258, in which was the defeat. † From 1258 until 1272.

‡ From 1272 until 1368, the date of the destruction of Mayapan. And the following, from 1368 to 1392. § From 1392 until 1488. ‖ From 1488 until 1512.

¶ From 1512 until 1536, which concluded the eleventh epoch; the following one beginning in 1536, and concluding in the year 1560.

the ruins and on the tops of the churches. It is quite abundant in Yucatan, though only one specimen was obtained, which was shot from the top of the cross over the gateway at the hacienda of the senoté (Mucuyché), as we rode up on our way to Uxmal. There does not appear to be any published description of this hawk. Still another hawk was procured, which also seems not to have been described; but, as it appears to be in immature plumage, it may be the young of some known bird. Besides these, among the specimens is the laughing falcon (Falco Cachinnans of Lin.). It is called by the natives koss, and was shot at Chichen Itza near the Castillo, and was stuffed. Another specimen of the same bird was procured on the way from Nohcacab to Uxmal, after our first attack of sickness. These birds are quite numerous throughout Yucatan.

Of the genus Strix but three varieties were seen, and of those two were preserved, both of which are believed to be undescribed. The first, a little owl, about six inches and a half long, of a tawny colour, lighter beneath, which was shot near Merida. The second is about six inches long, of a brown above and lighter beneath, called by the natives tiquim thohca. Several specimens of both these owls were seen. The third was caught in one of the ruined buildings, and kept alive for a little while, but afterward escaped. It resembled somewhat the Strix Aluco of Europe. One was afterward shot at Sabachshé, but was so much injured that it could not be stuffed.

Of the genus Corvus were procured three species, two of which are apparently not described. The first is a very beautiful jay, the head and belly black; back, wings, and tail of a beautiful blue; the bill of the male is yellow, and of the female black; the legs yellow. It was first seen and shot near Sisal, on the way up to Merida, and afterward several other specimens were obtained in different parts of the country, for they are numerous throughout Yucatan. The other was first met with at Uxmal, where a female was shot, and afterward two males. They are of a dark brown on the head, neck, back, and tail; belly white; bill of male black, and female yellow; they have a most singular formation of the trachea, there being a sort of membranous sack or bag coming off in front of the trachea at about the middle of its length, and intimately connected with the skin of the neck; this formation, together with the great muscularity of the larynx, may account for their excessively loud and disagreeable cry. The other jay is the Corvus Peruvianus, Peruvian jay. (Shaw, vol. viii., plate 27.) This most beautiful bird is found in great abundance in almost all parts of Yucatan, which is probably its native country, as it is mentioned as rare in Peru.

Of the genus Psittacus were procured four species, three of which have been described, and perhaps the fourth also; but, as the specimen is bad, it is not easy to ascertain positively whether it has or not. One, the Psittacus Albifrons (Ind. Orn., vol. i., p. 119), white-crowned parrot (Shaw, vol. viii., p. 519), is very numerous throughout Yucatan. It is a beautiful bird, coloured with green, blue, red, white, and yellow. Another, supposed to be the Psittacus Guianensis (Gen. Lil., vol. i., p. 323), the green parrot of Guiana (Gen. Syn., i., 231), is not so abundant as the last, but still quite numerous. The specimens were procured at Ticul, and some were afterward shot near Iturbide. The third species was not seen in the wild state, the only specimen procured being given to Dr. Cabot, alive, by the padre Curillo, of Ticul. It is the Psittacus Macao (Ind. Orn., vol. i., p. 82), red and blue macaw (Gen. Syn., i., 199).

Of the genus Ramphastos one specimen was procured, the yellow-breasted toucan (Gen. Syn., vol. i., p. 326), Ramphastos Tucanus (Ind. Orn., vol. i., p. 136). This specimen does not agree with the description in Latham, but is the same as the one described by Mr. Edwards from a living specimen in Lord Spencer's collection. It was procured at Uxmal on the day when Dr. Cabot went down to the hacienda to operate on an Indian's leg. Two or three different species were afterward seen at Macobà, but Dr. C. did not succeed in killing any of them.

Of the genus Momotus were obtained two species: the first, the common Brazilian or blue-headed motmot; this was quite common in Yucatan, but not so common as the other, as to which it is doubtful whether it has been described. It is about the same length as the blue-headed, but the tail is longer in proportion to the body. The markings on the plumage are very different from those of the Brazilian; there is a black stripe extending down from the chin to the middle of the breast, bordered on each side with light blue; a broad, light blue, almost white, stripe extends over the eye from the base of the bill almost to the hind head. The general colour is a sort of greenish bay; primaries and tail light green, tipped with black; the two central feathers of the tail much longer than in the Brazilian, having the shaft bare to a much greater degree, and the feather at the tip is bright pale green, tipped broadly with black.

Of the genus Crotophaga one species was procured, the lesser ani (Crotophagi Ani. Ind. Orn., vol. i., p. 448). These were very abundant in all parts of the country.

Of the genus Oriolus, including under this denomination Icterus and Cassicus, were procured five species, one of which is supposed to be new, three doubtful, and one known. The male of the new species is nine inches and a half long; head, neck, cheeks, breast, belly, rump, tertiaries, and nearly the whole length of the outer tail feathers and the lower part of the third, and occasionally a stripe on the fourth, bright chrome yellow; face, throat, primaries, secondaries, back, and four, and sometimes six tail feathers, black; legs bluish; bill black, except the base of lower mandible, which is bluish; sings finely. Female eight inches and seventh eighths long; marked like the male, but not so brilliant; irides hazel. One of the doubtful comes very near to Latham's description of the lesser Bonana bird

(Oriolus Xanthornus. Ind. Orn., vol. i., p. 181), but is an Icterus, and differs in some particulars of plumage. Another of the doubtful resembles closely the black oriole, and another the black cassican, but is smaller. The known species is the St. Domingo oriole (Oriolus Dominicensis. Ind. Orn., vol. i., p. 182). Two specimens of this bird were procured, being the only two that were seen.

Of the genus Cuculus, including Polophilus, were procured two species. One resembles somewhat the bird described by Latham as the variegated coucal (Polophilus Variegatus); the other the Cayenne cuckoo (Cuculus Cayanus. Ind. Orn., vol. i., p. 221). These were both quite abundant throughout the country.

Of the genus Picus were procured three species, two of which are perhaps new. One of these resembles the little woodpecker of Europe (Picus Minor) very closely. The other resembles Latham's description of the Brazilian woodpecker (Picus Braziliensis). The known one is the lineated woodpecker (Picus Lineatus. Ind. Orn., vol. i., p. 226).

Of the genus Certhia were obtained two species, of one of which no description has been found, though Dr. Cabot was under the impression that he had seen specimens of it in some of the cabinets of Europe. It is three inches and seven eighths long; top of head, neck, and back, dark brown, each feather having a light, buff-coloured, pear-shaped mark in the centre; chin light buff colour; breast and belly light brown, each feather having also a light buff-coloured mark down the centre; primaries, secondaries, tertiaries, and tail dun-coloured; bill one inch and three eighths along the ridge, and one inch and five eighths along the gap, bent in its whole length, and horn-coloured. They were not numerous. The other species is the yellow-bellied nectarinia (Nectarinia Flaveola. Vieill., Ois. Dor. Certh., plate 51, p. 102). They were quite numerous at Cozumel, where two specimens were procured. They were not seen in any other part of the country.

Of the genus Trochilus were procured two or three species, one of which is undescribed; another is probably the young of the same, and one is described. The undescribed, male, is four inches long; bill six eighths of an inch, yellowish, tipped with black; upper parts of head and back dull green; throat and upper part of breast bright emerald green in scales, with metallic lustre; lower part of breast, belly, and tail dun or bay colour; the feathers of the tail fringed and tipped with black; primaries dark brown, with some purplish reflections. The four middle tail feathers have greenish reflections on them. The female is rather less, and wants the bright emerald throat, the whole under parts being bay-coloured; the male has some white about the thighs. The known species is the Ourissia humming-bird (Trochilus Maugeri. Lesson.).

Of the genus Turdus were procured two species, thought to be new. One agrees very nearly with Le Merle de Paraguai, or Calandra, as described in Vieillot, but it wants the white on the wings. The other is a good deal like the Turdus Plumbeus, as described by the same author. The first is quite common throughout Yucatan, but the second is rather rare.

Of the genus Loxia were obtained four species, three of which are in immature plumage, and cannot, therefore, be placed with certainty. The other does not appear to have been described, though there are some descriptions which come near it. The male is nearly ten inches long; head and chin, extending down the sides of the neck, and in a crescent across the upper part of the breast, black; cheeks very dark steel gray; a white line extending from the bill over the eye almost to the hind head; hind head, back, secondaries, outer edge of the primaries, yellow olive; also the tail; the shafts of the feathers are black; part of the chin and throat pure white; breast, belly, and thighs cinereous; vent, and under the tail coverts, light bay; bill quite stout, nearly an inch long, and black; the female is about nine inches long, having dark cinereous brown in place of the olive; the other markings much the same as the male, but not so vivid. They are very common throughout Yucatan, and said to be very destructive in the fields and gardens: called by the Indians *tsapin.*

Of the genus Emberiza one was procured, in immature plumage; probably the painted bunting.

Of the genus Pipra one: the blue and yellow manakin, not common in Yucatan.

Of the genus Tanagra were procured two species, one of which is the red-crested tanager of Latham. But one pair was seen. The other is believed to be undescribed. The specimen was a male, six inches and a quarter long; bill inflated, and strongly toothed; at about the middle of the upper mandible, six eighths of an inch along the gap, top of the head, wings, and tail, of a deep raspberry, approaching maroon colour; back cinereous, tinged with red; chin and throat bright rose colour; breast and belly light cinereous; vent and under tail coverts light rosy red.

Of the genus Fringilla was procured one species, believed to be described in Latham as the cinereous finch (Fringilla Cinerea); they were quite common about Merida in the latter part of May.

Of the genus Lanius three species were obtained, all of which have been described. They are the Cayenne shrike (L. Cayanus. Ind. Orn., vol. i., p. 80), the rusty shrike (L. Rubiginosus), and the gray-headed shrike (Tanagra Guianensis. Ind. Orn., vol. i., p. 427), more properly the Lanius G. This bird sings quite prettily, and is rather common in Yucatan. The other two were rarer, especially the second.

Of the genus Muscicapa were obtained five species, four of which have been described. The specimen procured of the fifth was a male. It is six inches and a half long; bill one inch along the gap quite stout and broad; top of the head and nape black; back, wings, and tail very dark, slaty brown; breast, belly, cheeks, and chin light cinereous; throat and upper part of the breast bright rose colour; legs black. This was the only specimen seen in the country. The others were Muscicapa Coronata (round-crested flycatcher. Shaw, vol. v., pl. 13). This is quite common throughout Yucatan. Muscicapa Sulphuratus, not rare; M. Barbata, quite common; M. Ferox, very common.

Of the genus Sylvia one was obtained, in young plumage, and, therefore, uncertain whether new or not.

Of the genus Caprimulgus one species was obtained; the specimen so poor that nothing can be made of it.

Of the genus Columba were procured two species, one of which is in such imperfect plumage that its character cannot be made out. The other agrees very nearly with the blue pigeon (Columba Cærulea. Ind. Orn., vol. ii., p. 601). Both are common in Yucatan.

Of the genus Meleagris was procured one species (Meleagris Ocellata), the ocellated turkey, Cuv. This most magnificent bird is common throughout Yucatan.

Of the genus Penelope were procured two species; one the crested guan (P. Crestata. Ind. Orn., vol. ii., p. 619). These are called kosh by the natives; the only specimen seen was given to Dr. Cabot by the brother of the padrecito at Ticul, and was still alive in November, 1842. The other is the Penelope, or Phasianus Paragua (Ind. Orn., vol. ii., p. 632). They are common in all parts of Yucatan, where they are called chachalacha, from the noise they make, which is perfectly astounding, and also bach by the Indians. They have a most remarkable arrangement of the trachea, which passes down on the external surface of the muscles, between them and the skin, in a long loop as low as the pubis, and then passes up on the other side, and enters the thorax.

Of the genus Crax two species were obtained; the red curassow (Crax Rubra, Lin., vol. i., p. 270), and C. Globicera (globose curassow). They are found throughout the country, and are called by the natives kambool.

Of the genus Tinamus one species was obtained, the variegated tinamou (T. Variegatus). They are quite common throughout Yucatan, where they are called by the natives partridges. They are kept tame in many of the houses, being very useful in destroying scorpions, &c.

Of the genus Ortyx one species was obtained, which, as far as the plumage and size go, is undescribed, but it has the same note, habits, &c., as our quail or partridge. It is smaller; the throat of the male is jet black, and most of the markings are different, though having a general resemblance to the Ortyx or Perdix Virginianus. They are very numerous in all parts of Yucatan.

Of the genus Cancroma one specimen was procured, the cinereous boat-bill, which was killed at the senoté at Chichen.

Of the genus Jacana also one species was obtained, the variable jacana

Memorandum for the Ornithology

(Parra or Jacana Variabilis. Ind. Orn., vol. i., p. 763). It was killed at Uxmal, at one of the small aguadas, and was the only one seen in the country.

Of the genus Gallinula Dr. Cabot procured two species, the Cayenne gallinule (G. Cayanensis. Ind. Orn., vol. ii., p. 767) and the black-bellied gallinule (G. Ruficollis. Ind. Orn., vol. ii., p. 767).

Of the long-billed wren one specimen only was seen. The violet-headed trogon was more common, several having been procured in different places.

Besides the birds enumerated above, the following list comprises those which were procured in Yucatan, and which are found also in the United States, and have been well described by different naturalists.

Birds observed in Yucatan during the winter of 1841, '2, between the months of October and June, which are also found in the United States, and have been figured and described by Wilson, Audubon, Bonaparte, and Nuttall.

Cathartes Jota, all parts.
Cathartes Papa, at Labphak.
Cathartes Aura, all parts; less numerous than the C. Jota.
Aquila (?) Caracara, all parts.
Falco Pennsylvanicus.
Falco Haliætos.
Falco Cyaneus.
Falco Sparverius.
Icterus Spurius.
Quiscalus Major.
Quiscalus Versicolor.
Muscicapa Crinita.
Muscicapa Virens.
Muscicapa Atra.
Muscicapa Ruticilla.
Muscicapa Verticatis. (?)
Turdus Polyglottus.
Turdus Noveboracensis.
Turdus Lividus, Felisox.
Sylvia Virens.
Sylvia Mitrata.
Sylvia Trichas.
Sylvia Protonotarius.
Sylvia Maculosa. (?)
Sylvia Æstiva.
Sylvia Americana.
Sylvia Coronata.

Tanagra Æstiva.
Tanagra Rubra.
Fringilla Ludoviciana.
Fringilla Ciris.
Fringilla Cyanea.
Loxia Cœrulea.
Loxia Cardinalis.
Picus Carolinensis.
Trochilus Colubris.
Trochilus Mango.
Alcedo Alcyon.
Hirundo Rufa.
Hirundo Lunifrons. (?)
Hirundo Riparia.
Cypselus Pelasgius.
Caprimulgus Carolinensis.
Columba Passerina.
Columba Leucocephala.
Columba Zenaida.
Calidris Arenaria.
Himantopus Nigricollis.
Hæmatopus Ostralagus.
Charadrius Melodus.
Charadrius Wilsonius. (?)
Charadrius Semipalmatus. (?)
Charadrius Helveticus.
Strepsilus Interpres.
Ardea Herodias.

349

Ardea Rufescens.

Ardea Egretta.

Ardea Candidissima.

Ardea Ludoviciana. (?)

Ardea Nycticorax.

Ardea Cœrulea.

Ardea Lentiginosa.

Ardea Virescens.

Ardea Exilis.

Aramus Scolopaceus.

Phœnicopterus Ruber.

Platalea Ajaja.

Ibis Alba.

Numenius Longirostris.

Tringa Wilsonii.

Tringa Semipalmata.

Totanus Semipalmatus.

Totanus Vociferus.

Totanus Flavipes.

Totanus Chloropygius.

Totanus Macularius.

Totanus Bartramius.

Limosa Fedoa.

Scolopax Grisea.

Scolopax Wilsonii.

Gallinula Martinica.

Podiceps Minor.

Sterna Cayana.

Sterna Boysii.

Larus Atricilla.

Thalassidroma Wilsonii.

Anas Boschas.

Anas Strepera.

Anas Acuta.

Anas Americana.

Anas Discors.

Pelecanus Onocrotalus.

Phalacrocorax Carbo.

Phalacrocorax Graculus.

Trachypetes Aquilus.

Phæton Æthereus. (?)

COMMUNICATION FROM MR. SCHOOLCRAFT.

THE RED HAND.

The figure of the human hand is used by the North American Indians to denote supplication to the Deity or Great Spirit; and it stands in the system of picture writing as the symbol for strength, power, or mastery, thus derived. In a great number of instances which I have met with of its being employed, both in the ceremonial observances of their dances and in their pictorial records, I do not recollect a single one in which this sacred character is not assigned to it. Their priests are usually drawn with outstretched and uplifted hands. Sometimes one hand and one arm, but more commonly both are uplifted. It is not uncommon for those among them who profess the arts of medicine, magic, and prophecy (the three are sometimes united and sometimes not) to draw or depict a series of representative or symbolical figures on bark, skins of animals, or even tabular pieces of wood, which are a kind of notation, and the characters are intended to aid the memory in singing the sacred songs and choruses. When the inscriptions are found to be on wood, as they often are in the region of Lake Superior and the sources of the Mississippi, they have been sometimes called "music boards." I induced a noted meta, or priest, to part with one of these figured boards, many years ago, and afterward obtained impressions from it in this city by passing

350

it through Mr. Maverick's rolling press. It was covered with figures on both sides, one side containing forty principal figures; six embrace the symbol of the uplifted hand, four of which had also the arm, but no other part of the body, attached. Their import, which the man also imparted to me, is given in the general remark above. On the reverse of this board, consisting of thirty eight characters, nine embrace the uplifted hand, in one case from a headless trunk, but in the eight others connected with the whole frame.

The design of the hand is uniformly the same with our tribes, whether it be used disjunctively or alone, or connected with the arm alone, or with the whole body. In the latter cases it is a compound symbol, and reveals some farther particular or associated idea of the action. The former is the most mysterious use of it, precisely because there are no accessories to help out the meaning, and it is, I think, in such isolated cases, to be regarded as a general sign of devotion.

In the course of many years' residence on the frontiers, including various journeyings among the tribes, I have had frequent occasion to remark the use of the *hand alone* as a symbol, but it has generally been a symbol applied to the naked body after its preparation and decoration for sacred or festive dances. And the fact deserves farther consideration, from these preparations being generally made in the arcanum of the medicine, or secret lodge, or some other private place, and with all the skill of the priest's, the medicine man's, or the juggler's art. The mode of applying it in these cases is by smearing the hand of the operator with white or coloured clay, and impressing it on the breast, the shoulder, or other part of the body. The idea is thus conveyed, that a secret influence, a charm, a mystic power is given to the dancer, arising from his sanctity or his proficiency in the occult arts. This use of the hand is not confined to a single tribe or people. I have noticed it alike among the Dacotahs, the Winnebagoes, and other Western tribes, as among the numerous branches of the red race still located east of the Mississippi River, above the latitude of 42°, who speak dialects of the Algonquin language.

A single additional fact appears to me to be pertinent to your inquiry. In an excursion which I made in the year 1831 into the more unfrequented and interior parts of the Chippewa country, lying between the group of the Twelve Apostles' Islands in Lake Superior and the Falls of St. Anthony, I came to a curious edifice, situated in the edge of the forest, on the elevated banks of a fine lake, which was exclusively used as the village temple. It was built of stout posts, describing a circle, firmly and well sheathed with thick bark, fastened on transverse pieces. It constituted a peculiarity in this structure that there was a circular building within, or, rather, it was arranged after the manner of the whorls of a sea-shell, so that a person could, as it were, involve himself in a labyrinth. It had a single door, subject to the entrance of the priest only. As this person was the political chief of the band, and a man of more than ordinary intellect, he appeared to have adopted this mode of exhibiting his skill and securing and extending his power. He permitted me to inspect the building. Drums, rattles, and other insignia of the priest's art, were hung up on the wall. Heads of men were rudely carved or inscribed, and numerous marks of the hand, as in the case of naked dancers, were impressed on the involutions of the inner walls.

I have expressed the opinion that the human hand denotes strength, or power, or mastery arising from devotional acts. The want or absence of the hand or arm, therefore, in these symbolical figures, should imply impotence, weakness, or cowardice, arising from fright, subjugation, or other causes; and such is found to be the import of the armless figure of the human body in two of the symbols of the ancient hieroglyphic inscription on the Assonet, or Dighton Rock, as explained by the well-known American chief Chingerauk.

THE END.

Este libro se terminó de imprimir el día
13 de agosto de 1986 en los talleres de
Offset Marvi, Leiria núm. 72, 09440
México, D.F. Se tiraron 2 000 ejemplares